KUGELS & COLLARDS

STORIES OF FOOD,

FAMILY, AND TRADITION

IN JEWISH SOUTH CAROLINA

KUGELS & COLLARDS

RACHEL GORDIN BARNETT and LYSSA KLIGMAN HARVEY

with JOHN M. SHERRER III

Foreword by MARCIE COHEN FERRIS

THE UNIVERSITY OF
SOUTH CAROLINA PRESS

© 2023 Rachel Gordin Barnett and Lyssa Kligman Harvey

Foreword © 2023 Marcie Cohen Ferris

Photographs © 2023 Forrest Clonts, unless otherwise indicated

KUGELS & COLLARDS

Kugels & Collards is a registered trademark of Historic Columbia

kugelsandcollards.org

Published by the University of South Carolina Press

Columbia, South Carolina 29208

uscpress.com

Manufactured in Canada

Book design and composition: Nicole Hayward

32 31 30 29 28 27 26 25 24 23

10 9 8 7 6 5 4 3 2 1

Library of Congress Cataloging-in-Publication Data can be found at http://catalog.loc.gov/.

ISBN: 978-1-64336-421-6 (hardcover)

ISBN: 978-1-64336-422-3 (ebook)

*For the women who came before us and
for our children who will continue to tell
our southern Jewish food stories.*

CONTENTS

Foreword   The Language and Legacy of
Southern Jewish Foodways   ix

Introduction   WHY KUGELS & COLLARDS   1

Chapter 1   THE JOURNEY   5

Chapter 2   SOUTHERN ROOTS   45

Chapter 3   SOUTH CAROLINA JEWISH FOODWAYS   81

Chapter 4   AROUND THE JEWISH TABLE   123

Chapter 5   OUR MOTHERS AND GRANDMOTHERS   155

Chapter 6   THE LEGACY   197

Afterword   225

Acknowledgments   227

Glossary   229

Contributors   231

Recipe Index   233

About the Authors   235

THE LANGUAGE AND LEGACY OF SOUTHERN JEWISH FOODWAYS

MARCIE COHEN FERRIS

> Food is an archive, a keeper of secrets.
> —Michael Twitty, *The Cooking Gene*

MY FOOD LANGUAGE IS SOUTHERN AND JEWISH, and I learned to speak it in northeastern Arkansas where my Ukrainian and Belarusian Jewish ancestors settled in the early 1920s. By the late 1940s, my mother, Huddy Horowitz Cohen, a newlywed from Connecticut, and her Odessa-born mother-in-law (my paternal grandmother, Luba Tooter Cohen), were of a generation of Jewish at-home mothers and working women, native southerners and newcomers alike, who built and sustained their small synagogue, Temple Israel. These women shaped my southern Jewish experience. I witnessed deep friendships as they cooked holiday meals at home and in the synagogue kitchen and supported one another through life passages, celebrations, and loss. Jewish women's networks and the expressive power of foodways—what people eat and why—became the heart of my scholarship.

When my friend and colleague Dale Rosengarten introduced me to Rachel Gordin Barnett and Lyssa Kligman Harvey's *Kugels & Collards* project, it resonated with the moving food narratives I had collected across the South.[1] The South Carolinians Barnett and Harvey documented sounded like my people, except I soon recognized historic names, ancestors, and landmarks connected to the earliest history of the Jewish South, stretching back to the seventeenth century. Jews came to the Arkansas Delta much later, at the

ix

Miller's Delicatessen, forerunner of
Groucho's Deli, Columbia, SC, ca. 1942.
COURTESY BRUCE MILLER.

turn of the twentieth century when the booming cotton industry and railroads attracted merchants and peddlers to the region.

South Carolina Jewish history is fundamental to our understanding of the Jewish South, a fact convincingly illustrated in the groundbreaking exhibition *A Portion of the People: Three Hundred Years of Southern Jewish Life* (2002) and the accompanying publication of the same title, edited by Dale and Theodore Rosengarten.[2] Throughout the exhibit and book, I marveled at the food-related material culture of Jewish South Carolina in vintage advertisements and photographs of Jewish-owned groceries and general stores and in artifacts, such as a printed menu and wedding invitation from 1918; a shohet's knife and drainboard for kosher butchering; a noodle dough cutter; a food hamper; a satin Passover matzo cover; a Russian samovar (an urn used to boil water for tea); and precious silver items, from an English sugar bowl to a family's cake knife, kiddush cup, and rice serving spoon.

The ca.-1830 silver spoon, owned by the Lazarus family of Charleston and held by Black women who served rice to well-to-do family members and their guests, references the prosperous economy of which the Lazaruses were a part. By the 1780s, Carolina Gold rice produced great wealth for Lowcountry planters and Jewish merchants, some

of whose descendants appear in this volume. For enslaved laborers who worked the crop, many skilled in wetland rice farming in their homelands in West Africa, the pearly white grain represented indescribable toil and suffering.[3]

Throughout the era of slavery and continuing after the Civil War and well into the twentieth century, people of African descent worked as cooks, housekeepers, and caterers in Jewish homes and in synagogues. The dynamics of this labor system and its racial interactions were complex, both intimate and exploitative. Beginning with the post–World War I outmigration of thousands of largely rural Black southerners during the Great Migration and continuing at various rates through the civil rights movement into the 1970s, Black South Carolinians voted with their feet. Many chose to leave the region and its systemic racism to pursue education and work elsewhere in America.

Consider another object—a young woman's commonplace book—that, like the rice spoon, the shohet's knife, and the samovar, reveals a space where region, food, and religion converged in the Jewish South. The booklet's front cover is inscribed, "The property of Miriam G. Moses, 1828." Now preserved in the archives of the Southern Historical Collection at the University of North Carolina at Chapel Hill, the book belonged to Miriam Gratz Moses (1808–91).[4] After the death of her mother, Rachel Gratz Moses, and her infant sister, Gertrude, during the High Holiday season of 1823, teenager Miriam and her five siblings were raised in Philadelphia by her aunt, the well-known Jewish educator and philanthropist Rebecca Gratz.[5] Miriam's commonplace book was typical of the era, with its mix of recipes, recent books read, foreign language exercises, extracts of published verse and prose, and highlighted lists of historical happenings. More distinctive, though, was the particular mix of the recipes she chose to include.

In her commonplace book, Miriam wrote out, in measured and elegant script, recipes that spoke of her racial and class privilege, her observant Judaism, being a young woman on the precipice of marriage, and the possibility of that match taking her to the American South. Most of the recipes are canonical dishes of early nineteenth-century middle-class America, from tomato ketchup to rice pudding, flannel cakes (pancakes), and gingerbread, and others are evidence of a monied, Atlantic-world family who enjoyed chocolate, brandy, tropical fruits, roasted meats, poultry, and fresh fish. Miriam's list of ingredients for "Tomahawk Punch" includes two bottles of still champagne, one pint of Curaçao, the "aroma of a pound of Green tea," and last, "dash the whole with Glenlivet," the now-renowned Scotch whiskey, which had only started being produced a few years before in 1824 and would certainly have been a prized possession in America. A recipe for "N.Y. Black Cake," a dense, dark, spiced fruitcake composed of raisins, currants, citron, rose water, ten eggs, a pound of brown sugar, a gill of brandy, and "enough flour to mix the fruit with," connotes the Gratzes' economic ties to the Caribbean.[6] Southern standards are also included, such as biscuits, cornbread, sweet potato pudding, and pound cake.

The recipes reflect Miriam's family observance of kashrut, including the absence of pork and shellfish.[7] Meat and dairy are not cooked together, and for dishes eaten on the Sabbath, such as beef fricassee, she specified to "separate the meat from the sauce." She includes kosher-style recipes for veal cutlets, mutton stew, "kimmeled meat or fresh tongue" (beef stewed with root vegetables, spices, and port wine to which caraway seed and vinegar is added; kümmel, a German herbal liqueur flavored with caraway seeds and cumin connects back to the Gratzes' Prussian origins), and "fried black fish or sea bass," as well as instructions on how "to render fat." There are recipes for Jewish holidays such as "Pesach Sponge Cake," "koogle" (kugel, a central European sweet or savory egg pudding usually made with noodles or potatoes), "Haroseth," (a sweet fruit and nut paste eaten at the Passover seder), and "Passover soup dumplings" (matzo balls).

In 1836, Miriam married Solomon Cohen Jr. of Georgetown, South Carolina, and assumed the role of a wealthy planter's wife.[8] A thriving mercantile city, Georgetown served the region's rice plantations and was also the second oldest Jewish community in the state after Charleston. The presence of southern—and Jewish—recipes in her commonplace book suggests the influence of the South's much-touted cuisine in this era, as well as a young woman preparing for her responsibilities as a Jewish wife and mother in South Carolina. It is not improbable that Miriam would have encountered southern-style dishes prepared by a skilled Black cook. The federal census in 1820 and 1830 listed two free people of color in Miriam's childhood home in Philadelphia, including a woman, possibly a cook.[9] Miriam could have also copied recipes from published cookbooks, at a time when Black women's culinary influence was present but unrecognized, including Mary Randolph's *The Virginia House-wife* (1824).[10] Miriam's copied recipe for biscuits is near verbatim to Randolph's.[11]

Like other Jewish men of means in the region, Solomon Cohen Jr. was civically engaged, serving as a bank director, a founding member of the prestigious Planters Club, a state legislator, intendant (mayor), and a nullifier—a follower of John C. Calhoun's pro-slavery, states' rights party that claimed a state could veto, or nullify, federal laws.[12] Cohen held title to more than twenty enslaved people, making him one of the largest Jewish slaveowners in the region.[13] Typically, Jewish merchants enslaved one or two people who worked in the home or in the family store. In 1838, the Cohens moved to Savannah. After receiving a gift of grits by mail from Solomon, Miriam's beloved aunt Rebecca Gratz wrote her niece, asking her to thank him for his thoughtfulness. She assured them that she enjoyed her breakfast and remembered how much the Cohens's toddler son Gratz liked the quintessential South Carolina cereal.[14]

Throughout the Civil War, Miriam continued to correspond with her Aunt Rebecca, "veiling their political differences"—particularly with regard to slavery—by focusing on the changing seasons, family, domestic life, and their shared Judaism.[15] Miriam personally experienced the pain of the Lost Cause—the Confederate invention and romanticization of a noble "Old South"—as she watched her son, Gratz, stymied by a physical disability, repeatedly engage and leave Confederate forces while briefly enrolled at the University of Virginia.[16] He finally served as an aide-de-camp to a Confederate officer. In 1865, both mother and maternal great-aunt learned of Gratz's death at age twenty on a North Carolina battlefield, allegedly killed by a Confederate bullet in the chaos of battle.[17]

Kugels & Collards brings to the fore food-related stories of South Carolina Jewish women—and men—and begins to acknowledge the African American labor and creativity that infused southern Jewish cuisine. Culinary historian Michael Twitty, award-winning author of *The Cooking Gene: A Journey Through American Culinary History in the Old South* (2017), argues that "kosher/soul cookery" flourished in the coastal colonial South, where a culinary syncretism emerged between Black women cooks—enslaved, then free—and Jewish women, like Miriam Gratz Moses Cohen, at the center of elite families.[18]

In his pioneering work on the Gullah community, South Carolinian and southern historian Charles Joyner spoke of food as an expressive language of place. In this language, enslaved cooks adapted a vocabulary of local ingredients, fruits, vegetables, grains, fish, meats, and more, to their own "grammar"—ancestral taste preferences, recipes, and African methods of cooking and spicing.[19] Joyner defined culinary grammar as "the appropriate way to put those ingredients together to generate meaning."[20] Vocabulary was *encountered*; grammar was *remembered*. This incisive analysis is a compelling model to apply to the narratives and recipes of Jewish South Carolinians gathered in *Kugels & Collards*. In dishes such as chicken and rice, chopped liver, okra gumbo, hummus, salmon and grits, collards, kugel, and peach cobbler, we can easily identify a South Carolina vocabulary of core ingredients such as rice, grits, collards, and peaches, while the grammar reveals the influence of remembered recipes and cooking methods from eastern and central Europe, Africa, and even the Middle East. This is South Carolina Jewish food.

From the earliest decades of European and African settlement in Carolina, Jews were linked to one another around the Atlantic world by religion, business connections, family ties, marriage, memories, and a shared language of food. They also participated in the global forces of colonialism, empire, and capitalism, and benefitted from its outcomes in the American South. Jewish women and men worked in food-related trades; they were dry goods merchants, traders, grocers, innkeepers, and fruit peddlers. Jewish homes and synagogues were central locations for sharing food traditions. A small number of Jewish-owned specialty businesses, from delicatessens to bakeries and kosher butcher shops, provided the essential infrastructure for living a kosher life for strictly observant households and those who purchased traditional foods only for Jewish holidays and significant family occasions. These Jewish food practices represented an evolving southern Judaism across the American South.

Southern Jews revealed who they were and what they believed through the foods they ate—and did *not* eat—in a region where treyfe (nonkosher) pork, shellfish, and wild game were at the center of local cuisine. Kashrut, the body of ancient Jewish dietary laws, delineates which foods are forbidden and how foods that are kosher, which means "fit" or "proper," should be prepared and eaten. Southern Jews, including Jewish South Carolinians, invented their own regional rules of kashrut; for example, eating barbecue and shrimp only "out"—in a garage, on a screen porch, or at the beach, but not inside the home.

Some Jewish cooks—and Black cooks who worked for Jewish families—might substitute a local kosher fish like red snapper in the Lowcountry classic "shrimp and grits," adding a splash of Caribbean hot sauce. For observant Jews, obtaining kosher meats and other food products was challenging, especially after kosher businesses closed as a result of competition from new chain grocery stores in the mid-twentieth century. Kosher foods were ordered from kosher food businesses in Atlanta and Charlotte, and any trip to New York, Baltimore, or Miami included a promise to return home with bagels, lox, schnecken, and kosher salami.

The religious, cultural, and socioeconomic lives of southern Jews were shaped by complex and varied experiences of mobility, adaptation, and pragmatism. Scholar of modern Judaism and American religions Shari Rabin explains that the "eclectic material" worlds of southern Jews across the region (food and the negotiation of kashrut lie here, too) were a way of "transforming anonymity, scarcity, and uncertainty into stable identities."[21] Traditional and evolving Jewish recipes were shared from one generation to the next, indelibly tying them to first-generation immigrants from Russia, Germany, England, Holland, South America, and the West Indies.

The contemporary South Carolina food landscape is no longer bounded by the Jewish home, synagogue, or kosher butcher shops and bakeries. A new generation of Jewish chefs, restaurateurs, farmers, artisanal makers, food activists, and consumers value the region's Jewish history and food traditions but also support a thriving food movement that emphasizes local and seasonal ingredients, environmental sustainability, food equity, and social justice. Consider also the College of Charleston students who today study topics from the Jewish South to modern Israeli politics with world-class faculty while enjoying vegan and vegetarian dishes at Marty's Place, a kosher dining hall associated with the college's Yaschik/Arnold Jewish Studies Program and its visionary director emeritus, Martin Perlmutter.

I close my remarks with memories of a warm Friday evening in June 2019, when university faculty from across the country gathered at the President's House at the College of Charleston for a "Southern Shabbat" celebrating the end of a two-week institute. Titled "Privilege and Prejudice: Jewish History in the American South," the program, funded by the National Endowment for the Humanities, was codirected by Dale Rosengarten and Shari Rabin of the college's Pearlstine/Lipov Center for Southern Jewish Culture, and by Michael Cohen, chair of Jewish Studies at Tulane University. My teaching session, "The Edible—Jewish—South: The Power of Food and the Making of Jewish Southerners," explored the historical food landscapes of the South and how racial etiquette and racist institutions affected Jewish food practices. In the unsteady racial hierarchy of the region, where otherness was a dangerous liability, even the politics of eating were fraught.

The underlying ethnography of the South Carolina and Jewish landscape was symbolically expressed in the menu I created in collaboration with Kevin Mitchell of the Culinary Institute of Charleston, who deftly executed the multicourse meal with the college's chef, Trey Dunton. Chef Mitchell, who coauthored *Taste the State: South Carolina's Signature Foods, Recipes, and Their Stories* (2021) with historian David Shields, spoke that evening about the African American voice in southern Jewish cuisine.[22] Food journalist Hanna Raskin told us about Crosby's Seafood market in Charleston, which kept a file noting their Jewish customers' specific recipes for gefilte fish (an Eastern European stewed or baked stuffed fish boiled in vegetable broth). Jonathan Ray, director of institutional events at the college, baked beautiful loaves of Sabbath challah (braided egg bread). Ray has deep Sephardic roots in Charleston. His partner, archivist and author Harlan Greene, shared a story about his mother's Meissen china, which he uses today. To protect it from harm when Nazi troops occupied Warsaw, Harlan's family buried the china and silverware at a farm outside the city. These precious items were later recovered. After imprisonment in Siberia, his parents went to the American sector in Vienna, Austria, where they were sponsored to come to the United States by family members living in Charleston.

In each course served at this special South Carolina Shabbat table, we combined histories of the American South and the continent of Africa, the port of Charleston, and the countries of origin of the state's Jewish inhabitants. From a briny bite of pickled okra and syrupy Bradford watermelon to Lowcountry-style gefilte fish—(made with local shad and sheepshead because the traditional pike, whitefish, and carp are unavailable in southern waters); to beet borscht, an Eastern European sweet and sour soup, topped with benne oil and benne seed derived from Africa; to a whole grilled fish for the Sabbath, rice sourced from South Carolina's Anson Mills; and finally, a southern (and Jewish) classic—pound cake, topped with Madeira-infused fruits.

In *Kugels & Collards*, Rachel Gordin Barnett and Lyssa Kligman Harvey bring dozens of recipes and stories together in a volume that celebrates the food history and narratives of generations of Jewish South Carolinians. Woven throughout this work are the fundamentals of South Carolina Jewish foodways: the power of family and transregional kinship and religious connections, the historical influence of skilled African American cooks and food entrepreneurs, and the culinary flavors and ingredients of the changing global South. In tribute to South Carolina *and* Jewish hospitality, I raise a bourbon toast with spirits provided by Charleston's own High Wire Distillery, with gratitude to Rachel and Lyssa as well as their proud Eastern European and Sephardic ancestors. Mazel tov!

NOTES

Many thanks to Dale Rosengarten for her editorial assistance and to Jason Friedman, Mark Greenberg, Laura Arnold Leibman, and Shari Rabin for their counsel; and deep appreciation to Ken Albala and K. C. Hysmith for their expert consult on historical recipes.

1. Marcie Cohen Ferris, *Matzoh Ball Gumbo: Culinary Tales of the Jewish South* (Chapel Hill: University of North Carolina Press, 2005).

2. Dale and Theodore Rosengarten, eds., *A Portion of the People: Three Hundred Years of Southern Jewish Life* (Columbia: University of South Carolina Press, 2002).

3. William Dusinberre, *Them Dark Days: Slavery in the American Rice Swamps* (Athens: University of Georgia Press, 2000).

4. *Miriam Gratz Moses Cohen Commonplace and Recipe Book*, 1828, in the Miriam Gratz Moses Cohen Papers #2639, Southern Historical Collection, The Wilson Library, University of North Carolina at Chapel Hill.

5. Dianne Ashton, *Rebecca Gratz: Women and Judaism in Antebellum America* (Detroit: Wayne State University Press, 1997), 112; Dianne Ashton, "Shifting Veils: Religion, Politics, and Womanhood in the Civil War Writings of American Jewish Women," in *Women and American Judaism: Historical Perspectives*, eds. Pamela S. Nadell and Jonathan D. Sarna (Hanover, NH: Brandeis University Press/University Press of New England, 2001), 93; Laura Arnold Leibman, *Once We Were Slaves: The Extraordi-nary Journey of a Multiracial Jewish Family* (New York: Oxford University Press, 2021), 135.

6. Julia Moskin, "A Fruitcake Soaked in Tropical Sun," *New York Times*, December 19, 2008, https://www.nytimes.com/2007/12/19/dining/19cake.html.

7. *Miriam Gratz Moses Cookbook and Commonplace Book*, 1828; Manuscript Cookbooks Survey, 2022, https://www.manuscriptcookbookssurvey.org/.

8. Pamela S. Nadell, *America's Jewish Women: A History from Colonial Times to Today* (New York: W. W. Norton & Company, 2019), 41; "Georgetown, S.C.: Historical Overview," *Encyclopedia of Southern Jewish Communities - Georgetown, South Carolina*, Jackson, MS, Goldring/Woldenberg Institute of Southern Jewish Life, 2022, https://www.isjl.org/south-carolina-georgetown-encyclopedia.html.

9. Solomon Moses in 1820 U.S. Census; Census Place: Philadelphia Locust Ward, Philadelphia, Pennsylvania; Page: 69; NARA Roll: M33_108; Image: 80; Year: 1830; Census Place: Philadelphia Middle Ward, Philadelphia, Pennsylvania; Series: M19; Roll: 159; Page: 191; Family History Library Film: 0020633.

10. Toni Tipton-Martin, *The Jemima Code: Two Centuries of African American Cookbooks* (Austin: University of Texas Press, 2015). Tipton-Martin examines the erasure of Black women's culinary intellectual property and documents the rich heritage of Black-authored cookbooks in the American experience, as well as their essential voice in the foundations of American cuisine.

11. Recipe for "Biscuit," Commonplace and recipe book of Miriam Gratz Moses; Folder 13: V-2639/2: 1828, 40 pages: Scan 4, in the Miriam Gratz Moses Cohen Papers #2639, Southern Historical Collection, The Wilson Library, University of North Carolina at Chapel Hill; "To Make Nice Biscuit," in *Mary Randolph, The Virginia Housewife: Or, Methodical Cook* (Baltimore: Plaskitt, Fite, 1838), 137; *Feeding America*, MSU Libraries, Michigan State University, https://d.lib.msu.edu/fa.

12. Charles Joyner, "A Community of Memory: Assimilation and Identity among the Jews of Georgetown," in *Shared Traditions: Southern History and Folk Culture* (Urbana: University of Illinois Press, 1999), 180–81.

13. Ibid., 182.

14. Jason K. Friedman, "Searching for Solomon Cohen," *Moment*, Summer Issue 2021, https://momentmag.com/solomon-cohen/; Folder 5, 1847–54: scan 24, in the Miriam Gratz Moses Cohen Papers #2639, Southern Historical Collection, The Wilson Library, University of North Carolina at Chapel Hill.

15. Ashton, "Shifting Veils," 93–95, 97.

16. Friedman, "Searching for Solomon Cohen."

17. Ibid.

18. Twitty, 77.

19. Charles Joyner, "Southern Folk Culture: Unity in Diversity," in *Shared Traditions: Southern History and Folk Culture* (Urbana: University of Illinois Press, 1999), 17–18.

20. Joyner, 17–18.

21. Shari Rabin, *Jews on the Frontier: Religion and Mobility in Nineteenth-Century America* (New York: New York University Press, 2017), 79.

22. Kevin Mitchell and David S. Shields, *Taste the State: South Carolina's Signature Foods, Recipes, and Their Stories* (Columbia: University of South Carolina Press, 2021).

WHY KUGELS & COLLARDS

FROM A LITHUANIAN KUGEL RECIPE that made its way to South Carolina, to flanken soup cooked for carnival workers at the South Carolina State Fair, to the southern fried chicken that graced Shabbat meals, tales of food and family fill the pages of *Kugels & Collards*. A collection of essays and recipes from families who arrived in Charleston in 1791 to families of today, this book is a poignant—and delicious—compendium of South Carolina Jewish life, from the Lowcountry to the Upstate, revealed through the voices of its community. Food is a lens on the South Carolina Jewish experience.

We have learned that food provokes strong memories, uncovers little-known histories, and brings forth voices silenced in the past. Delicious aromas, the taste of a special spice, a treasured china pattern used for a holiday dinner—all can elicit feelings, take us back to a particular time and place, and define a moment in time. *Kugels & Collards* is not a typical cookbook; rather, it is a collection of essays and family recipes from many contributors—Jewish and non-Jewish, White and Black, women and men—whose culinary memories are firmly rooted in the Palmetto State. Sabbath dinner brisket and kugel, chopped liver variations, Thanksgiving corn pie and collards, and heirloom pound cakes made for special occasions are examples of what awaits.

We are Jewish South Carolinians. Our families' stories reflect the journeys that generations of Jewish immigrants made to America. As women pulled by the forces of both our region and our religion, we recognize the expressive power of food. Our inspiration to create *Kugels & Collards* came from our mothers and grandmothers, descendants of Eastern European and Sephardic immigrants, as well as the African American women who worked in our homes as housekeepers and cooks and shared their culinary knowledge. We are not the experts of their respective experiences. But we gratefully gather their memories and meals in their honor.

The goal of this book is exploration and recognition. Does a South Carolina Jewish culinary tradition exist? To what extent has assimilation of ingredients and preparation

Wengrow family, Columbia, SC, 1960s.
COURTESY ARNOLD WENGROW.

methods shaped our southern Jewish tables? How has the struggle to keep kosher in the land of shrimp, crab, and pork shaped our daily life or challenged our values? How did Black women and men influence the food cultures of Jewish homes, and how did Jewish foodways impact the African American community? In our journey to answer these—and other—questions, we have grown far more aware of nuances in southern Jewish foods and connections spanning cultures, races, pantries, and people. And, we have discovered the presence of boundaries—cultural, dietary, and physical—that have existed historically and, in some instances, remain today.

Like the diversity of ingredients found in our favorite meals, we seek to acknowledge the contributions of individuals underrepresented in or absent from earlier accounts. What we consider "typical southern fare" reveals the culinary legacy of Africans brought against their will to the American South centuries ago. On South Carolina Jewish tables, it is not unusual to have African American staples such as collard greens, black-eyed peas, and rice, alongside European Jewish dishes such as brisket, tzimmes, and kugel. The aromas, textures, and tastes of these meals made their way into the homes of our immigrant grandparents through generations of Black South Carolinians working in their traditional Jewish kitchens.

South Carolinians who relish their southern and Jewish food cultures contributed to this book. Some wrote their own stories, and others told their stories to us. Others contributed beloved "family" recipes, many of which were created by—and appropriated from—skilled Black cooks who worked under their family's roof. Several wrote about favorite family dishes for which the recipes are long gone. Virtual interviews provided access to people who would otherwise have been inaccessible because of pandemic-driven health concerns or geographic distance. While sharing stories, people laughed, cried, and smiled, remembering times that revolved around food. Their stories reflect the confluence of experiences that constitute a special part of South Carolina's cultural and physical landscape.

We have come to appreciate how food marks time and place, season and generation, tragedy and trauma, milestones and memory. Food can tell a story and bring us together in times of both joy and pain. This book includes narratives and iconic recipes such as chopped liver, matzo ball soup, gefilte fish, chicken and rice, peach cobbler, and okra gumbo. Some recipes were created by the contributors to this book. Others were passed down through multiple generations—conveyed verbally or jotted on scraps of paper, recorded in a journal or diary, and printed on recipe cards. Some of these unwritten or told recipes, historically formed by taste, sight, and memory, have been reconstructed for the book. We have gently adjusted a few ingredients in some recipes to better fit with contemporary tastes and health.

Food weaves a powerful, complex tale of people and community. It connects us and sometimes divides us. It reminds us by whose hands our meals were made and the difficult histories that underlie our foodways. Within these pages you may come to remember or be introduced to a South Carolina and Jewish culinary legacy that, shaped by African, Mediterranean, and European cultures, the past and the present, family, regional ingredients, and seasons, continues to evolve. This is our southern Jewish table.

KUGELS & COLLARDS IN SOUTH CAROLINA 9
Rachel Gordin Barnett and Lyssa Kligman Harvey

Ethel Glover's Collards
Grandma Ida's Lokshen Kugel

FAMILY PRIDE: RECIPES FROM A SEPHARDIC FAMILY 13
Anita Moïse Rosefield Rosenberg

Nita's White Chicken Stew
Ira's Grouper
Miniature Rum Cakes
Southern Barbeque Chicken

THE POWER OF RICE 18
Kim Cliett Long

Richard Weedman's
Savory Chicken and Rice

KUSHKIE AND KISHKA 20
Faye Goldberg Miller, as told to Lyssa Kligman Harvey

Duck, or "Kushkie"
Stuffed Derma, or Kishka

KREPLACH, MATZO BALLS, AND THE SOUP LADY 25
Lilly Stern Filler

Kreplach
Kneidlach (Matzo Balls)
Chicken Soup

YOU ARE GOING TO REMEMBER THIS 28
Minda Lieberman Miller, Rita Miller Blank, and Esther Goldberg Greenberg

Sponge Cake
Gefilte Fish

FEEDING THOUSANDS 33
Larisa Gershkorich Aginskaya, as told to Lyssa Kligman Harvey

Larisa's Mushroom Barley Soup

THE LATKE KING 35
Janis Dickman

Potato Latkes
Pickled Corned Beef or Tongue

THE JEWISH SPEAKER OF THE HOUSE AND SMOKED BEEF TONGUE 38
Michael Tonquor

A JEWISH KID FROM LONG ISLAND LANDS IN MYRTLE BEACH 41
Donald Sloan

Gloria Sloan's Schnecken, or Rugelach

By the time our grandparents made their way to South Carolina in the early 1900s, Jews had called the Palmetto State home for more than two centuries. Their story parallels those of fellow immigrant groups seeking safety and opportunity in the New World and, later, in the United States. By contrast, Africans who arrived here were brought as captives, shackled to a future with no hope of freedom. With each came a unique palate shaped by culture, stories of ancestry, love, and difficult journeys as well as ingredients and geography. Through the culinary inheritance of foods and family recipes, this chapter's contributors pay respect to the edible legacies these immigrants—White and Black—carried to South Carolina.

The earliest Jews arrived in South Carolina in the late 1600s. The majority were Sephardim, whose ancestors were exiled from Spain and Portugal during the Inquisition and sought refuge in the Protestant countries of western Europe. Anita Moïse Rosefield Rosenberg, a direct descendent of these Sephardic Jews, remembers "the historical family names included: Moïse, Moses, Lazarus, Lopez, Harbie, Harby, Rodrigues, Solomon, Solomons, Benjamin, de Torres. And the history behind those names takes us back centuries."

The long journey of some southern staple ingredients—including okra, black-eyed peas, benne seed, yams, watermelon, and rice—began in Africa. West Africans have a long history of growing and preparing these global southern foods. Kim Cliett Young writes about her first known paternal ancestor who arrived in Charleston in 1705 and the ubiquity of rice in the Lowcountry: "Among all the cultures, nationalities and nations, the most common food eaten in all is rice. Rice transcends all boundaries: social, cultural, economic, and ideological."

Ashkenazim—Jews from German-speaking areas of central and eastern Europe—were present in South Carolina from the beginning. Their numbers swelled through the eighteenth century so that by the time of the American Revolution they accounted for most of the Jewish population. A new wave of German and Yiddish

Previous: Double wedding of Bluma and Felix Goldberg and Cela and David Miller, displaced persons camp, Landsburg, Germany, 1946.
COURTESY ESTHER GOLDBERG GREENBERG.

speakers arrived in the antebellum period and, by 1854, had organized the state's first Ashkenazic synagogue, Brith Sholom, known locally as the Polish and German shul.

Between 1880 and 1924, from the flood of Eastern European immigrants who passed through New York City's harbor, a trickle flowed south, opening dry goods stores, groceries, dairies, and bakeries in cities and small towns across South Carolina. These Orthodox newcomers infused the cuisine with a dose of Old Country cooking and kashrut. Zalkin's meat market and the Mazo brothers' delis in Charleston, Charles Zaglin's market in Greenville, Caba Rivkin's grocery and deli in Columbia, and Jake Kalinsky's itinerant shochet services in the Midlands served the needs of the kosher kitchen of the immigrants' generation. In the years after World War II, this Old World influence was strengthened, tragically, by refugees and survivors of the Holocaust, who arrived in South Carolina traumatized but with a longing for foods they remembered from home. No matter how harrowing or hopeful the different circumstances and journeys to the Palmetto State were, Jewish immigrants brought their food cultures with them.

Gordin/Yelman family, St. Matthews, SC, n.d.
COURTESY GORDIN FAMILY.

KUGELS & COLLARDS IN SOUTH CAROLINA

RACHEL GORDIN BARNETT AND LYSSA KLIGMAN HARVEY

———

*Rachel Gordin Barnett and Lyssa Kligman Harvey write
about their immigrant grandparents' different yet similar
experiences in settling in South Carolina.*

———

OUR GRANDPARENTS IMMIGRATED from Eastern Europe and Russia in the early 1900s. They were among the two-and-a-half million Jews who made the voyage to the United States between 1881 and 1924, when the United States tightened restrictions on immigration on the basis of racist quotas tied to national origin. Pursuing religious freedom and prosperity in the Golden Medina, our families brought with them their religion, traditions, customs, and foodways. Fortunately for us, they found their way to South Carolina!

Small-Town Jewish Immigrants, the Gordins

RACHEL GORDIN BARNETT

After arriving in America through Ellis Island, my paternal grandfather, Morris Gordin (1885–1957), came south like so many immigrants of the early 1900s. He and his brothers, Rubin and Louis, opened dry goods stores in the small farming communities of Summerton and Pinewood, providing local farmers with everything from clothing for Sunday church to overalls for working on the farm. As cash was limited, merchants bought goods on time from wholesalers such as the Baltimore Bargain House. When the crops came in, farmers could pay their bills and, in turn, merchants paid their wholesalers. Traveling salesmen also played a role as matchmakers. More than dresses, shoes, and suit coats came from Baltimore—so did my grandmother, Sarah Levin Gordin (1892–1951). She and my grandfather were married in the 1920s. I often wonder what her first impressions were of small-town South Carolina. Like many other newcomers, she took it in stride and became a part of the community. This included working in the store often until late in the evening.

To keep the family fed and the house clean, my grandmother hired an African American housekeeper. Ethel Mae Glover (1901–98) came to work for the Gordins in the 1930s. Ethel and her husband, Willie Glover, were sharecroppers on a local farm. Sarah and Ethel were an unlikely pair, but they formed a bond that extended for nearly six decades, well beyond Sarah's death, with Ethel continuing to work for the family until 1990.

Sarah taught Ethel traditional Jewish recipes and kosher rules, and, in a reciprocal fashion, Ethel brought African American and southern

Ethel Mae Glover, Summerton, SC, 1970s.
COURTESY GORDIN FAMILY.

dishes such as fried chicken, macaroni and cheese, rice, squash casserole, okra and tomatoes, collards, and many vegetable recipes to the Gordin home. Their recipes were never written but were told and passed down for generations. Through trial and error, I have reconstructed several of Ethel Glover's recipes, including the one for collards that follows.

ETHEL GLOVER'S COLLARDS

Ethel's collards had a very straightforward but delicious recipe. There was no pork in the recipe she cooked for us, as our family was semi-kosher. She took a large bunch of collards and washed repeatedly until the sand was gone. Then, she chopped the collards and placed them in a large pot. To the clean collards, add a pinch of sugar, salt, and pepper to taste, and a pat of butter. Cook until soft. These collards truly melt in your mouth. I have adapted Ethel's recipe to include onion and tomatoes. Although fresh collards still abound, you can also purchase bagged collards chopped and ready to go.

1 tablespoon olive oil
1 small onion, diced
8 ounces water or chicken broth
Large bunch or 27-ounce bag of collards (if in a bunch, clean and chop the collards)
2 tomatoes, chopped
Salt and pepper to taste
½ teaspoon dried oregano
½ teaspoon sugar

Add olive oil in a large pot and heat. Add the diced onions and cook until translucent and soft. Add the collards, tomatoes, and water or broth to cover (~8 ounces). Add the seasonings and cook until tender, about 20 minutes. Taste and adjust the seasonings before serving.

MAKES 6 SERVINGS

A Capital City Jewish Family, the Kligmans

LYSSA KLIGMAN HARVEY

Louis Kligman (Kligerman) (1898–1973) came to America to escape military service in Russia. He was one of ten children: three sons and seven daughters. His sisters, Esther and Clara Kligerman, were already living in Estill, South Carolina, where they married two brothers, Jake and Frank Baker. Jake Baker sponsored my grandfather when he arrived in South Carolina in August 1924. He later moved from Estill to Columbia, where he married my grandmother, Ida Lomansky, in 1927. Ida's parents owned a grocery store at the intersection of Assembly and College streets. The Lomansky store was close to Clara and Frank Baker's grocery store on Park Street. This is where they learned about running a retail business in the South while honoring their Eastern European Jewish culture and religion. My grandparents eventually owned their own grocery store on Barnwell Street and an Army–Navy store and a liquor store on Assembly Street.

My grandmother was a good cook and brought many Eastern European dishes into her home. She observed religious holidays by baking and cooking traditional Jewish foods. I remember going to synagogue on Friday nights at Beth Shalom on Marion Street and then having Shabbat dinner with them, when my grandmother made chicken in a pot, brisket, and, of course a wonderful kugel!

Kligman Army-Navy Store, Columbia, SC, 1935.
COURTESY KLIGMAN FAMILY.

GRANDMA IDA'S LOKSHEN KUGEL

Lokshen is Yiddish for noodles.

8 ounces wide egg noodles

6 tablespoons butter

1 cup sour cream

3 ounces cream cheese

½ cup sugar

3 eggs

Raisins (optional)

1 cup milk

1 teaspoon salt

1 cup apricot jam

Topping

2½ cups crushed corn flakes

¼ cup sugar

1 teaspoon cinnamon

Boil the noodles and drain. Add the butter and sour cream. Cream the sugar and cream cheese together and add to the mixture. Beat the eggs and add to the mixture. Add raisins, if desired. Add the milk and apricot jam slowly. Add salt and mix all together. Put the mixture into a 9 × 13-inch buttered Pyrex pan.

To make the topping: Mix the topping ingredients together and sprinkle over the kugel. (What could be more American than topping her kugel with cornflakes [as many Jewish home cooks began to do in the early twentieth century with the widespread availability of processed, convenience foods like boxed cereals]?) Bake 45 minutes to 1 hour at 350°F. Freezes well.

MAKES 6 TO 8 SERVINGS

FAMILY PRIDE
Recipes from a Sephardic Family

ANITA MOÏSE ROSEFIELD ROSENBERG

––––––

Moïse family members from Sumter, Charleston, and along the South Carolina coast, gather on many occasions to eat delicious food, drink favorite libations, and tell stories of the family history—old and new.

––––––

Moïse family members, Sumter, SC, 1974.

© SANDLAPPER SOCIETY, INC. FOR MORE INFORMATION CONTACT THE SOUTH CAROLINA STATE LIBRARY AT: STATELIBRARY.SC.GOV.

LOOKING BACK, there's no doubt that family stories told and retold have been embellished, but at the root of each one is a well of family pride in those who came before us and those who came together in celebration. This is how I heard it.

The historical family names included: Moïse, Moses, Lazarus, Lopez, Harbie, Harby, Rodrigues, Solomon, Solomons, Benjamin, and de Torres—and the history behind those names takes us back centuries. On August 3, 1492, a day after Spain issued its Edict of

Expulsion ordering the exodus of the country's Jews, Luis de Torres sailed on the *Niña* to the New World as Christopher Columbus's cartographer and translator. The Harbie family, along with other Sephardic refugees, escaped to Fez, Morocco, where the family lived for several generations. There, Isaac Harbie served the king of Morocco as secretary and lapidary. His son Solomon Harby (the spelling of the family name changed) arrived in Charleston in 1781 and married Rebecca Moses, daughter of Myer Moses, in 1787. Their son, Isaac Harby, Jewish reformer and intellectual, was born in Charleston in 1788.

During the Spanish Inquisition, other family members went north to London, Amsterdam, and Alsace–Lorraine on the border of France and Germany, and eventually to the Caribbean. It is known that Abraham Moïse was a prosperous landowner and tradesman living in Saint-Domingue with his wife, Sarah, and four sons before they fled to Charleston in 1791, leaving behind everything they owned. Abraham and Sarah had five more children in Charleston. The family was active in Kahal Kadosh Beth Elohim. Their daughter Penina was a prolific poet, writer, and teacher, who wrote the lyrics for the congregation's hymnal—the first collection of Jewish hymns published in America.

Today, as descendants of these pioneers, we work, enjoy leisure and family time, worship, and cook using Sephardic recipes long modified and surely influenced by Lowcountry and Gullah–Geechee traditions adapted to our Carolina surroundings. Any occasion demands a family gathering. Toasts, great food, and storytelling dominate the hours. We come from near and far across the United States to celebrate each other. A family reunion demands our attendance.

In 1975, Ethel McCutchen Moïse wrote an article about the family cookbook for *Sandlapper Magazine*, which was published from 1968 until 1983. Here is an excerpt:

Family get-togethers are not unusual, and neither is recipe swapping, but recently I became involved in what turned out to be a unique recipe swapping situation. It all began when several of our Moïse clan in Sumter were having dinner together. One of the topics Moïse always seem to enjoy talking about is food and this was no exception—except that talk turned to fond remembrances of some of the great cooks we have had in the family, some of whom had gone to their reward, taking many of their treasured and unrecorded recipes with them. One suggested we put together a cookbook for the family; another said, "Ethel, you do it;" the next thing I knew, I was sending letters to all the far-flung members of the Moïse clan. Response was prompt and overwhelming with favorite family recipes coming from Pennsylvania, Indiana, Florida, Texas, California, Arizona, Hawaii, and all points in between—but all with roots in South Carolina.

All recipes are verbatim from the historic Moïse family cookbook.

NITA'S WHITE CHICKEN STEW

ANITA HARBY MOÏSE

"Nita" was Grandmother Anita Harby Moïse, who gets credit for the original recipe.

Large pot of water (to cover hen)
1 hen
1 onion
Butter

Boil the hen in a large pot of water until tender. Remove the hen from the soup. Keep the soup very hot.

Fry 1 onion, chopped fine, lightly brown in butter. Put into the hot soup.

Sauce
3 eggs, well beaten
¼ cup cornstarch
1 teaspoon dried ginger
Juice of large lemon
Pinch of celery seed

To make the sauce: Mix the sauce ingredients and add a little hot soup to mix and pour back into the hot soup.

Cut the chicken into large pieces and place in soup. Keep hot in a double boiler until ready to serve. Just before removing from heat, add thinly sliced lemon.

IRA'S GROUPER

IRA ROSENBERG

1 stick butter
1 teaspoon lemon juice
Garlic salt
Celery salt
Seafood seasoning
Grouper fillets

Judiciously choose 35 to 40 pieces of whole charcoal and ignite a grill.

To make the sauce: Melt 1 stick of butter, and add 1 teaspoon lemon juice. Sprinkle with garlic salt, celery salt, and a pinch of seafood seasoning. Stir and warm for basting.

When coals are hot, place the rack at the highest level to allow for slow and thorough cooking. Place the fish on the rack and thoroughly baste the top. Keep basting while cooking (about every 10 minutes). Cook on the first side 30 to 45 minutes, depending on thickness. Turn only once and baste, again about every 10 minutes. Cook until done (flaky). Remove from the grill and serve.

MINIATURE RUM CAKES

ANITA R. ROSENBERG

The original recipe for rum cakes came from Virginia Moses Phelps. The cakes can be made ahead of time and frozen. Make the sauce on the day of use.

2 eggs

1 cup sugar

1 cup flour

1 tablespoon baking powder

½ teaspoon salt

1 tablespoon butter

½ cup milk (hot)

Sauce

1 cup brown sugar

1 cup water

1 cup granulated sugar

1½ tablespoon butter

½ cup rum

Beat the eggs and sugar very lightly. Sift together the flour, baking powder, and salt. Fold the sifted mixture into the eggs and sugar. Melt the butter into the hot milk. Fold the butter mixture into the other mixture as gently and quickly as possible.

Cook in greased muffin tins for 20 minutes at 375°F.

To make the sauce: Mix the brown sugar, water, granulated sugar, and butter. Boil for 5 minutes. When the mixture has cooled, add the rum. Baste the cakes with the sauce. When serving, top with whipped cream.

MAKES 18 MINIATURE CAKES

SOUTHERN BARBEQUE CHICKEN

NINA M. PHELPS

¼ cup white vinegar

½ cup water

2 tablespoons sugar

1½ teaspoon cayenne pepper

¼ cup butter

¼ cup chopped onion

1 tablespoon prepared mustard

1 thick lemon slice

1½ teaspoon salt

½ cup catsup

½ cup chili sauce

2 tablespoons Worcestershire sauce

2 fryers, 2½ pounds each, split in halves

2 tablespoons flour

2 tablespoons butter

Combine the first nine ingredients in a saucepan and simmer for 15 minutes, stirring occasionally. Blend in the catsup, chili sauce, and Worcestershire sauce. Bring to a boil and remove from heat. Place the chicken halves flat in roasting pan, skin side up. Spoon half of the sauce over the chicken. Cover the roasting pan and cook in the oven at 350°F for 30 minutes. Spoon more sauce over the chicken and cook, uncovered, for 30–45 minutes, adding more sauce and basting several times until the chicken is tender. Transfer the chicken to a heated platter. Heat the butter in a saucepan, stir in the flour and heat until the mixture bubbles. Blend this mixture into the sauce in the roaster. Cook over low heat, stirring constantly until the sauce thickens. Spoon the sauce over the chicken and serve.

MAKES 4 SERVINGS

THE POWER OF RICE

KIM CLIETT LONG

Love is like rice. Plant it everywhere and it grows.
—Malagasy proverb

THE MOST COMMON FOOD EATEN among all cultures, nationalities, and nations, rice transcends all boundaries: social, cultural, economic, and ideological. The origin of South Carolina's former staple crop was firmly rooted in the engineering expertise and cultivation knowledge of enslaved West Africans toiling under the extreme conditions of the South Carolina coastal plain during the early eighteenth century. Over two hundred years, generations of Black Carolinians grew millions of pounds of rice for export, the proceeds of which resulted in unprecedented wealth for White Lowcountry planters.

The enduring legacy of African, European, and Native American people remain evident in the art, history, and culture of America, but especially in the South. There is no greater testament to this legacy than the region's foodways, especially in two traditional dishes—rice and greens and rice and okra. Similar to Sierra Leone's plasas and West African jollof rice, these dishes reflect the Rice Coast origins of the Gullah–Geechee culture established by West Africans enslaved on the largely insular rice and indigo plantations of the southeastern coast.

My first known paternal ancestor arrived in Charleston in 1705. Robert Clyatt was born in 1693 in Scotland. Later, census takers, midwives, and other recorders would spell Clyatt a multitude of ways, including our branch's Cliett. Family records and ancestry DNA confirm his descendants. On July 28, 1713, Robert Clyatt married Hannah Stone in Charleston. Hannah's parents were John Stone Sr. and Margaret Wilson Stone, also of Charleston.

One of Robert and Hannah's sons eventually made his way to Sapelo Island, Georgia, and this was the genesis of my branch of the Clyatt/Cliett family. This lineage also solidified my family's lifelong relationship with rice. Rice was served in many ways several times a week, not just at our home but among extended family and neighbors. Rice was found on tables at morning, noon, and night. It could be a side dish or the entire meal. The most common way I love rice is hot, salted, and buttered in a bowl. For me, that bowl of rice signifies home and all the love in the world. The next best way to have it was smothered in the gravy from an entrée like chicken, steak, liver, roast beef, or fish. Then, there was rice as the side dish: red rice, curried rice, black rice, rice and okra, rice pilaf, Rice-a-Roni, and yellow rice. Rice as the entire meal was Spanish rice with ground beef; stir-fried rice with meat and vegetables; rice, sausage, and okra; and my favorite, chicken and rice. When I was growing up, I looked forward to chicken and rice like it was a gourmet delicacy. It was and is my favorite meal. This food combination is just the ultimate comfort food for me. Loving family memories are contained in every spoonful.

While living in Naples, Florida, I met artist Jonathan Green and his partner, Richard Weedman. We became fast friends and often shared meals. Surprisingly and happily for me, Richard's favorite meal to cook and eat is chicken and rice. He says that his recipe is extremely easy to make, but I have never attempted to cook it, because I revel in the love that he puts into preparing it and sending some home with me. I am so thrilled that we are all reunited in Charleston, where I can once again dine on Richard's delectable chicken and rice. Hence, I am sharing his glorious recipe in this ode to rice, because it is prepared with the most magnificent and powerful ingredient of love, which makes meals so incredibly special.

RICHARD WEEDMAN'S SAVORY CHICKEN AND RICE

A favorite recipe that is southern comfort food at its best.

4 chicken thighs with bones and
  skin
Salt and pepper
1 can Campbell's cream of
  chicken soup
1 can Campbell's cream of
  mushroom soup
1 can Campbell's cream of
  celery soup
1 soup can water
1¼ stick unsalted butter
1 small jar button mushrooms,
  or 8 ounces fresh sliced
  mushrooms sauteed in butter
  until brown
1 small jar red pimentos
4 small celery stalks, thinly sliced
1 cup uncooked yellow rice

Remove the skin from the chicken. Lightly salt and pepper the chicken on both sides and place in a slow cooker with the bones facing down.

In a saucepan, combine soups with water, add butter, and bring to a low boil. Add the mushrooms, pimentos, and celery, and stir together for 4 minutes. Then add the uncooked yellow rice and stir for 3 more minutes. Pour the sauce and rice over the chicken. Cover the slow cooker and cook at 300°F for 2 hours, or until the rice is tender.

To enhance the presentation of the chicken and rice casserole, serve it over chopped lettuce and sliced baby tomatoes.

MAKES 6 TO 8 SERVINGS

KUSHKIE AND KISHKA

FAYE GOLDBERG MILLER, AS TOLD TO LYSSA KLIGMAN HARVEY

———

*Charlestonian Faye Miller speaks with Lyssa Kligman Harvey about her
mother's kosher kitchen and growing up on St. Philip Street.*
Kushkie *and* kishka *are traditional Jewish recipes
for duck and stuffed derma.*

———

MY NAME IS FAYE GOLDBERG MILLER, and I grew up in Charleston on St. Philip Street in
the early 1940s. My father, George Goldberg, had a men's clothing store on King Street,
a few doors down from Firetag's Furniture Store. My family is from Kaluszyn, Poland.
My grandfather`s name was Chaim (Charles) Altman; he left Kaluszyn around 1918 to
work in Argentina making furniture, where he made enough money for a new future. In
1920, he was able to bring his wife, Wittle, and their eight children to Charleston, where
they both had relatives. Two years after Wittle and the children arrived, Chaim passed
away of a heart attack. Wittle had a brother in Charleston, A. M. Solomon. He bought
her a grocery store on Radcliffe Street so she could earn a living to feed her children and
become independent. Wittle was a good businesswoman; although she could not speak
a word of English, she knew how to make money. My mom, Jeanette Altman, immigrated from Poland in 1920 and was one of eight siblings. My parents met and married
in 1933 in Columbia and then returned to Charleston.

In 1957, I met and married the love of my life, Ivan Miller. We worked together 24/7
in the deli business Groucho's in Columbia. We raised three great children: Shira, Robert, and Bruce. Working with my partner, Ivan, raising my kids was my life.

My mom only cooked food that she was raised on; everything was kosher! As a little girl, I would go to Zalkin's butcher shop and pick up chickens for my mom. Also, I
would have to get sweetbreads, lung, cow brains, and flanken. Susan Zalkin Hitt, who
is a good friend of mine, was also originally from Charleston. It was her grandfather,
Joe Zalkin, who owned the kosher butcher store. As a child, I would go to the butcher
store with a basket and pick up whatever Momma ordered. On Sundays, Momma would
bake a delicious duck "kushkie," always with farfel as a side dish. Stuffed baked derma
was another specialty of hers. I remember Momma cooking cow brains in boiling water

**Toba Goldberg Gelbert,
Mogieinica, Poland, n.d.**
COURTESY FAYE GOLDBERG MILLER.

with celery and carrots, salt, and pepper. Another favorite was lamb testicles; that was baked in the oven. Liver was another favorite cooked with onions. I remember the fish soup, and the fish head would be bobbing in the water—not a favorite. My mom could not drive a car, so after school on Fridays, as a teenager, I would drive her to Carroll's Fish Market on East Bay Street, where she would pick out a fresh fish, still moving, take it home, dump the fish in a black bucket, and let it wiggle around until it died. The maid cleaned it and Momma baked it! We had fresh fish for Friday night Shabbat dinner.

My sweet mother-in-law, Ethel Miller, taught me how to cook. She was a great cook, I might add. When I married my beloved Ivan, it was Ethel who introduced me to southern Jewish cooking.

DUCK, OR "KUSHKIE"

This is not my grandmother's recipe. Unfortunately, I don't have that, but this is the recipe I use to honor her "kushkie."

4- to 5-pound duckling, cut into serving pieces

½ cup plus 2 tablespoons sweet red wine

Orange peel

1 clove garlic, minced

3 tablespoons oil

1 tablespoon potato starch

1¼ cup orange juice

1 tablespoon honey

¼ teaspoon ground ginger

⅛ teaspoon pepper

1 cup fresh orange sections

Puncture the duck skin generously with a fork and place it in a roasting pan. Pour ½ cup red wine over the duckling pieces. Roast at 325°F, basting occasionally, allowing about 25 minutes per pound.

To make the sauce: In medium saucepan, lightly sauté the orange peel and garlic in oil. Add the potato starch, stirring until smooth. Slowly add the orange juice, 2 tablespoons wine, and honey. Simmer for 1 minute.

Stir in the ginger, pepper, and orange sections. Simmer 5 minutes longer. Serve the sauce hot with roasted duck.

MAKES 4 TO 6 SERVINGS

STUFFED DERMA, OR KISHKA

JEANETTE ALTMAN

6 feet kosher beef casings from the butcher

⅔ cup chicken fat

2 cups all-purpose flour, sifted

1 medium onion, grated

½ cup grated carrots

2½ teaspoons kosher salt, divided

½ teaspoon black pepper

1 teaspoon paprika

In a large pot, heat the water and 1 teaspoon of salt. Have enough water to cover the casings. Cut the casings into 12-inch pieces. Sew up one end and turn inside out; do this to all the casings.

Combine the chicken fat, flour, onion, carrots, 1½ teaspoons salt, pepper, and paprika. Stuff each casing with the filling. Sew up the ends.

Put the stuffed casings into the boiling water. Reduce the heat to low-medium. Cook for 10 minutes. Meanwhile, preheat the oven to 325°F. Grease a large sheet pan that will hold the kishka. Remove the kishka from the boiling water and drain. Put the kishka on a sheet pan and bake for 2 hours. Remove from the oven. To serve, cut into 1- to 2-inch pieces.

Kishka can be frozen. When they are defrosted, just reheat them in the oven. While still frozen, they can also be put on a plate and reheated in the microwave; heat for about 1 minute, turn over, and heat for another 30 seconds.

MAKES 8 SERVINGS

KREPLACH, MATZO BALLS, AND THE SOUP LADY

LILLY STERN FILLER

Lilly Stern Filler, MD, is the daughter of Holocaust survivors, Jadzia and Ben Stern. Making kreplach was a holiday tradition for her mother, who passed it down to her children.

MY MOM, JADZIA SKLARZ STERN, was the ultimate cook and homemaker. The fourth of eight children of Hadassah and Zev Sklarz of Poland, she learned by watching her mother care for the family of ten. How and why my mother learned to cook remains a mystery to us all today, because she was separated from her parents at age thirteen, never to see them again. Although she lost her formative years with her parents, my mother survived the Holocaust. She didn't just survive, she thrived. Although she never had any formal education, she was the home executive, excelling in cooking, sewing, flower arranging, and caring for her family. Her culinary skills were known throughout the community.

Her specialties were many, but no one could make a soup like my mom. She was "The Soup Lady." When one of her four children would bring

Jadzia and Ben Stern with daughter Lilly, Munich, Germany, 1948.
COURTESY LILLY STERN FILLER.

home an unexpected guest, there was always plenty of soup to go around. Without recipes, she made split pea, barley, vegetable, and, of course, chicken soup. Her "recipe" was tasting, smelling, and touching the food. My mom would tell stories about her mom, Hadassah, always welcoming her children's many friends to join them at the kitchen table. Despite living very modestly, my grandmother always had a pot of soup on the stove; for more people, she added more water, seasoning, and maybe a potato or leafy greens.

Jadzia's chicken soup was renowned and continues to be made by her daughters, Lilly (me) and Helena, and her daughter-in-law, Linda Cherry Stern. It was our good fortune that Mom provided Linda with a recipe for her glorious kreplach, the king of all soup add-ins.

Kreplach is a meat dumpling involving a laborious process to arrive at a delectable delicacy. As children, we often crowded around Mom to watch and to count the number of kreplach she made. We calculated how many we each could eat and made sure no one "overstepped" that number. When my younger brother, Herb, was about ten years old, he intently watched Mom make kreplach and began pacing around the room. She noticed his obvious "concern" and questioned what was wrong. He sheepishly asked, "Do one of my sisters have the recipe for the kreplach, so that just in case you [Mom] were not around, they could they make them?" We laughed for years about that story, so it was fitting that Linda (married to my brother, Bill) went to help Mom in the late 1980s, right before the High Holidays and before Herb was to be married. Jadzia had undergone foot surgery and needed some assistance. Thus began a cherished tradition of one of the girls working with Mom to prepare the delicious dumplings.

KREPLACH

AS TOLD BY JADZIA STERN TO DAUGHTER-IN-LAW, LINDA CHERRY STERN

Dough
5 eggs
1¼ teaspoon salt
10 tablespoons water
5 pounds all-purpose flour

Filling
2 pounds chopped onion
2 tablespoons chicken schmaltz
4 pounds ground beef

To make the dough: Beat the eggs, and add salt and water. Add the flour gradually and knead to a smooth loaf until it does not stick to the hand. Cut in half and roll out into a round or square. With each half, cut into four strips down and across, like a grid, until you have about 70 3-inch squares.

To make the filling: Sauté the onions in the schmaltz until clear. Mix the onions with the meat and cook through.

Assembly: Place the meat mixture on the dough squares (kreplach) and fold into triangles. Pinch the edges together and close. Bring points up together to form a little purse. Boil a large pot of water with a little salt, and drop the kreplach in and cook for 15 minutes or until they float to the top. Remove and place on a cookie sheet. To finish, brush with chicken fat and bake at 350°F for 10–15 minutes until light brown.

MAKES ABOUT 70 TO 75 SERVINGS

KNEIDLACH (MATZO BALLS)

Because of the enormous time spent making the kreplach, occasionally kneidlach (matzo balls) were made. The discussion among many (not the Stern family, however) was "What is the correct texture of kneidlach?" Were they to be soft or hard, fluffy or firm, small or large, from a box or "homemade"? The debate continues today. Jadzia's matzo balls were homemade, firm, and large—no debate there!

4 tablespoons vegetable oil

3 to 4 large eggs, slightly beaten (more eggs make a harder matzo ball)

4 tablespoons chicken soup (you can add club soda if you prefer lighter, fluffier balls)

1 to 2 teaspoons salt

1 cup matzo meal

Mix the oil, eggs, soup, and salt before adding matzo meal. Mix well and place covered in a bowl in the refrigerator for at least 1 hour.

Boil 3 to 4 quarts salted water. Form the chilled matzo balls with a teaspoon and your hands, making each ball about 1 inch in size, and drop them in the boiling water. Cover and cook for 1 hour.

Once cooked (they will double in size), the matzo balls can be frozen on a cookie sheet and stored in an airtight container in the freezer, or gently dropped, one per person, into a bowl of warm chicken soup.

MAKES ABOUT 16 SERVINGS

CHICKEN SOUP

This soup is best if made at least 1 day before eating.

1 large baking hen

1 to 2 tablespoons of salt and pepper to taste

3 to 4 tablespoons Osem Consommé seasoning mix

1 large leek, chopped

6 to 8 large carrots, sliced

4 to 6 stalks celery, sliced

Fresh parsley and/or dill to taste

Clean the hen and salt well. Boil 2 to 3 quarts of water and then add the hen. Bring to a boil again and skim the fat off the top. Cover and boil for about 1 to 2 hours, depending on the size of the hen.

Add 3 to 4 tablespoons of Osem seasoning mix to the soup. Salt and pepper to taste. Slowly add all vegetables to soup, put on low heat, and simmer for another 2 hours, covered. After cooking, cool the soup and refrigerate.

Skim the fat off the top of the soup and remove the hen before rewarming. Take the chicken off the bone or cut the cooked chicken into small serving sizes and add to the soup.

MAKES 12 SERVINGS

YOU ARE GOING
TO REMEMBER THIS

MINDA LIEBERMAN MILLER, RITA MILLER BLANK, AND ESTHER GOLDBERG GREENBERG

———

Holocaust survivor sisters, Cela Miller and Bluma Goldberg are remembered by their children. Minda remembers her mother-in-law and her love of family. Esther recalls her mother's tireless work making special holiday meals.

———

Remembering Cela Miller, Holocaust Survivor

MINDA LIEBERMAN MILLER AND RITA MILLER BLANK

CELA AND DAVID MILLER ENJOYED nothing more than being surrounded by their family sharing a meal. For Cela, cooking traditional Jewish dishes brought back loving memories of her childhood in Poland and being in the kitchen with her mother. These foods became a link to the past, present, and future, and a segue for us to share their story of surviving the Holocaust.

Cela Tyszgarten was born in the small town of Pinczow, Poland. Her father was a leather merchant, and the family lived behind the shop in the center of town. Cela was the second of six siblings. Life was happy and comfortable, until the war changed everything. In 1939, the Nazis invaded Poland and burned down their town. The family moved in with relatives on the outskirts of Pinczow for three years. During that time, the situation for Jews grew increasingly difficult.

In 1942, the situation became far worse, with Polish Jews rounded up and sent to Treblinka, an extermination camp. Cela's parents were forced to make hard choices. Her mother, fearing the worst, made a decision that no parent should be forced to make. She stuffed what little money she had into Cela's pocket and literally forced Cela and her next youngest sister, Bluma, to flee to the woods nearby. In her wisdom, she was giving her teenaged daughters a chance to live. The girls, crying, walked into the for-

Sisters Cela Tishgarten Miller (right) and Bluma Tishgarten Goldberg (left), 1940s.

COURTESY MINDA MILLER.

est where they hid for several weeks. After being captured, they worked as slave laborers in Nazi ammunition and airplane factories. Each day was a fight for survival. Conditions were horrid. They clung to life, for neither could bear leaving the other. Later, they were transported to Bergen Belsen and finally liberated by the Americans at Kaufering. Both were extremely sick. They were taken to a hospital to recover. While in the displaced persons camp in Landsburg, Germany, the sisters learned that the rest of their family had perished.

David Miller was born in Warsaw, Poland, in 1921, the only son in a family of six. In September 1939, German troops began to occupy Warsaw, and in October 1940, they established the Warsaw Ghetto. Conditions in the ghetto were unbearable: overcrowding, disease, starvation, and death made life a daily struggle. From the ghettos, Jews were being sent to extermination camps. The month-long Warsaw Ghetto Uprising began on April 19, 1943. David escaped through the sewers as one of the last of the Jews to leave the ghetto alive. He was captured the next month and taken to Auschwitz. Instead of being sent to the gas chamber, David was assigned to harsh labor in the coal mines nearby. In the final weeks of the war, he was sent on a death march to Buchenwald. Among the prisoners with David was his close friend, Felix Goldberg, who had worked with him in the coal mines. Although weak and brutally emaciated, they both managed to survive the march by locking arms together and encouraging the other to hang on.

With the war finally over, David and Felix were sent to the displaced persons camp in Landsburg, Germany. This is where the friends would regain their strength. David would confirm that he was the sole survivor of his family. It was at the displaced persons camp where he and his buddy, Felix, met the two sisters. Cela and David and Bluma and Felix were married in a double wedding in July 1946.

After surviving the horrors of the Holocaust and over five years of brutality under the Nazi regime, Cela and David were finally able to immigrate and begin new lives in the United States. They were the first survivors to arrive in Columbia, South Carolina, in May 1949. Beth Shalom Synagogue, their sponsor, welcomed them with open arms, and the couple cherished the lifelong friendships they made. The city's Jewish community provided housing, jobs, and English lessons and assisted them in adapting to their new country. Shortly after their arrival, Cela encouraged Bluma and Felix to join them. They focused on rebuilding their lives and starting a family.

David was given a job in the warehouse of Columbia Liquor Distributors. Encouraged by Bob Burg Sr., he saved his money and opened several downtown liquor stores. His first store on Gervais Street stood across from the State House and adjacent to the Capitol Newsstand and the Marmack Hotel. Politicians often stopped in. Cela ran the Lady Street store. Helen Silver, who owned a retail store downtown, would often come by to "kibitz" with Cela.

We lost Cela in 2000 and David in 2011. They are greatly missed, but we cherish all our happy family memories. Our family is dedicated to carrying on their legacy by teaching the lessons of the Holocaust and promoting tolerance and justice for everyone. They were so proud of their children and grandchildren and always stressed the importance of family. When sharing her story in schools, Cela would conclude with these words: "Do not take your family for granted: Keep them close to you. No matter how we feel today, what we lived through can happen again. We must never forget."

SPONGE CAKE

Our family continues to prepare and enjoy these favorites, which always bring to mind happy memories of being at the table with Cela and David.

10 eggs, separated
1½ cups sugar
¾ cup matzo cake meal
¾ cup potato starch
6 ounces orange juice
Fresh strawberries and
  whipped cream (optional)

Add the sugar to the beaten egg yolks. Combine the cake meal and potato starch. Add the cake meal mixture to the sugar and beaten egg yolks. Add the orange juice and beat.

In a separate bowl, beat the egg whites until stiff peaks form. Fold this into the meal mixture.

Place in an ungreased tube pan. (Do not grease the pan, as it will ruin the cake.) Bake for about 50 minutes at 325°F.

After removing from the oven, turn the cake upside down while still in the pan to cool. Allow to cool for a couple hours. Serve with fresh berries and whipped cream (optional).

MAKES 12 TO 16 SERVINGS

A Loving and Happy Home

ESTHER GOLDBERG GREENBERG

My parents, Bluma and Felix Goldberg, met in a displaced persons camp after surviving the concentration camps of Nazi Germany. Mom's sister, Cela, also met her future

Brothers Leon, Felix, and Bernard Goldberg, Columbia, SC, 1970s.
COURTESY ESTHER GOLDBERG GREENBERG.

husband, David Miller, at the camp. The two couples shared a wedding ceremony on July 8, 1946. After applying to immigrate to the United States, Cela and David settled in Columbia, with the help of the Hebrew Immigrant Aid Society and the Columbia Jewish community. After a few months, Mom and Dad also applied to leave Germany, along with their baby, Henry. They arrived in Columbia in December 1949. About ten years later, Dad's brother, Bernard, left Israel to join our family, along with his wife, Luba, and two children, Esther and Norman.

Holidays, especially Rosh Hashanah and Yom Kippur, were a special time for our family. Our parents lost most of their family during the war. We spent most holidays with our aunts, uncles, and cousins. Yiddish was the language of choice in those days, with lots of conversation late into the night around the holiday table. Our parents were so extremely happy to be free and living in the United States. They loved the Columbia Jewish community and were so thankful to be a part of it. They were determined to give us a loving, happy home, and that is exactly what they did. On one memorable holiday, Dad's brother, Leon, visited from Israel. It was wonderful to see Dad and his two brothers reunited, doing their best comedy routine. There was a huge table that extended into the living room. We still talk about memories of that Yontov holiday today.

Mom worked tirelessly to prepare for our holiday meals. Many hours were spent preparing gefilte fish, matzo ball soup with homemade egg noodles and kreplach, chopped liver, brisket, and apple cake. We remember Mom grinding livers by hand to prepare chopped liver, recreating what her mother had done in Poland. To us, each dish she made was fabulous, and we anticipated the flavors of the holiday meal.

GEFILTE FISH

2 pounds whitefish (such as pike or haddock), ground; reserve the bones

3 eggs

1 cup matzo meal (should be a moist texture)

1 onion, finely grated

1 onion, cut into rings

Sugar, salt, and pepper to taste

8 carrots

In a large bowl, mix the fish, eggs, matzo meal, grated onion, and seasonings by hand.

Bring to boil a large pot with 6 to 8 cups of water. Wash the fish bones well and place in the pot. Put the onion rings in the pot.

Form the mixture into small 4- to 6-inch-long ovals, and place gently into boiling water. Boil for 2 hours. Cut the carrots and add to the water after the fish has cooked for 30 minutes.

Allow the fish to cool. Remove the gefilte fish carefully and place on a large oval plate. Put the cooked carrots on top of each piece of fish.

MAKES 12 SERVINGS

Bluma Goldberg and granddaughters, Columbia, SC, 1980s.
COURTESY ESTHER GOLDBERG GREENBERG.

FEEDING THOUSANDS

LARISA GERSHKORICH AGINSKAYA, AS TOLD TO LYSSA KLIGMAN HARVEY

———

Larisa Aginskaya is the kitchen director of Beth Shalom Synagogue,
Columbia. She and her husband immigrated to
the United States in 1979.

———

LARISA GERSHKORICH AGINSKAYA considers Beth Shalom Synagogue's kitchen her second home. Since 2000, the culinary maven has planned, shopped, and cooked for thousands of people attending Sabbath meals and Jewish holidays, bar and bat mitzvahs, and special events.

Born in Kazakhstan in 1944 to Romanian Holocaust survivors, Miriam and Moishe Gershkorich, Larisa grew up feeling like a hidden Jew in Kharkov, Ukraine, a town with no synagogues, rabbis, schools, or Jewish businesses. She rediscovered her Judaism after her parents passed away. As a young woman, Larissa moved to Uman, Ukraine, where Jews from all over the world visit Hasidic Rabbi Nachman's grave during Rosh Hashanah. At the Hasidic Center, she and her husband, Khaim, worked as kosher chefs, providing meals for the nearly forty thousand sojourners.

Larissa in the Beth Shalom Synagogue Kitchen, Columbia, SC, 2019.
COURTESY HISTORIC COLUMBIA.

Economic unrest and supply shortages in Ukraine exacerbated persecution of Jews during Larissa's time there. Aid from the Hebrew Immigrant Aid Society brought thousands of Jews and Christians from the Soviet Union to the United States during the 1970s. Among them were forty of Larisa's family members who immigrated to Columbia. Sponsored by her sister, Raisa Rabinovich, Larisa and Chaim came to America in 1979. They arrived in New York before being welcomed to Columbia, where the Jewish community provided housing, jobs, and financial and emotional support. Larisa said that she was shocked at the huge apartment stocked full of food and linens that the Jewish community provided for her family.

Larisa loves to feed people. She says that "the synagogue kitchen feels like my home, and I invite everyone over for a meal and cook. It nurtures me and is a warm giving feeling of belonging. I am part of a community."

Larisa doesn't measure. She knows the amount of ingredients from experience. This is whether she is cooking for three or hundreds of people. Larisa cooks by taste, texture, and memory, but she also loves creating new recipes. Her experience as a cook allows her to taste and see if the recipe is going to turn out well. She now cooks these same dishes that she served in Ukraine—egg salad, tuna salad, kugel, and cholent—for Beth Shalom Synagogue for Kiddish luncheons, served after Saturday morning Sabbath services. The Jewish dishes she serves today—kugel, eggplant, and soups—remind her of her home in Ukraine and her parents, but they have never been written down.

LARISA'S MUSHROOM BARLEY SOUP

Larisa usually makes this hardy soup for three hundred people, but here is the recipe for four people.

1 onion, chopped

1 tablespoon oil

1 pound white button mushrooms thinly sliced

1 carrot, peeled and diced

1 can cream of mushroom soup

6 cups chicken stock or chicken bouillon

½ cup instant barley

Salt

Pepper

In a large soup pot, sauté the onions, mushrooms, and diced carrots in oil. Cook until slightly browned and the onions are translucent. Add to the pot the cream of mushroom soup and chicken stock or chicken bouillon. Bring to a boil and add the instant barley. Return to a boil, and then simmer for up to an hour. Add salt and pepper to taste. And that's it!

MAKES 4 SERVINGS

THE LATKE KING

JANIS DICKMAN

———

Max Dickman, cook extraordinaire, was the bastion of Jewish food events in Columbia. His daughter, Janis, remembers his contributions.

———

IF YOU ASK ME TO DESCRIBE our father, I will tell you that Dad was like a Boy Scout. He was kind, generous, and industrious. Dad could fix things and build things and grow things, and he could cook for a crowd. So how did a Jewish boy from Newark, New Jersey, become the Latke King of Columbia?

Dad's mother, who emigrated from a small village in Russia, is remembered as a wonderful cook of Ashkenazi cuisine. In his late teens, Dad spent his summers as a waiter at a Jewish hotel in the Catskills, otherwise known as the Borscht Belt. When the United States entered World War II, Dad was an airplane inspector at Shaw Army Airfield (today's Shaw Air Force Base) in Sumter, South Carolina. This was Dad's introduction to the South. Dad volunteered for the Army Air Corps and was

Max Dickman.
COURTESY JANIS DICKMAN.

immediately sent to England for thirty-one months to repair war-weary airplanes. After D-Day in June 1944, when there were no planes to be repaired, Dad took over as sergeant of the soldiers' mess. Last, when Dad returned to New Jersey, he owned a bakery. Dad even baked his own wedding cake!

In 1949, Max Dickman, with Selma Dickman (from New York City), moved to Sumter and a year later to Columbia. Max Dickman, together with Oscar Seidenberg, founded Columbia Steel & Metal, originally on Assembly Street across from the old baseball park. As transplants from up north, my parents were warmly welcomed by the established southern Jewish families. Mom and Dad quickly became part of the fabric of Columbia's Jewish community and made the very best forever friends. Their friends were a marvelous and colorful lot—some from large southern families, some transplants like my parents, and some who had survived the Holocaust—all joining together to raise their children in a close-knit Jewish community.

On special occasions, such as Hanukkah and Passover, they shared meals at the Columbia Jewish Community Center with Jewish soldiers bused in from Fort Jackson, where they were undergoing basic training. Dad was the sergeant of a crew of men and women turning out hundreds of hot, crisp latkes. For years, Dad was also the head latke cook for the Tree of Life Temple Hanukkah parties. For the Jewish holidays, the Columbia Jewish community also organized home hospitality for Jewish soldiers. Long before cell phones and Skype, homesick soldiers spent as much time calling home from kitchen phones as they did enjoying the Passover meal. Only now do I appreciate what bringing soldiers into our home for the holidays must have meant to my dad, who himself had been a soldier far from home.

POTATO LATKES

This recipe is adapted from my much loved, tattered copy of The Stuffed Bagel, *published by the Columbia, South Carolina, chapter of Hadassah, 1975–76. This recipe can be easily multiplied.*

2 cups grated potato
2 well-beaten eggs
Pinch of pepper
2 tablespoons matzo meal
1 teaspoon grated onion
½ teaspoon salt
Pinch of baking powder

Mix all ingredients and form into patties. Fry in hot oil until crisp on both sides. Serve plain, with applesauce or sour cream.

MAKES 8 TO 12 SERVINGS

PICKLED CORNED BEEF OR TONGUE

This is the only recipe I have found in Dad's tiny, neat handwriting.

3 **pound beef tongue**

½ **cup salt**

⅓ **cup sugar**

1 **teaspoon saltpeter**

1¼ **cup mixed pickling spices**

2 **bay leaves**

6 **cloves garlic**

1 **teaspoon paprika**

2 **cups water**

Mix all the ingredients well. Place the meat in this brine and add water to cover the meat halfway. Place a plate or heavy article to hold meat well into brine. Refrigerate for up to a week. Turn meat over every 2 days.

To cook, simmer in water, to which has been added 2 cloves garlic, paprika, pepper, and 2 bay leaves. Simmer for 2½ to 3 hours. Slice.

For tongue, cool in liquid 15 minutes, remove skin, and slit along length.

MAKES 4 TO 6 SERVINGS

THE JEWISH SPEAKER OF THE HOUSE AND SMOKED BEEF TONGUE

MICHAEL TONQUOR

———

Michael Tonquor now resides in Washington, DC, but is forever tied to his Barnwell roots because of a unique food arrangement between the South Carolina Speaker of the House and his father.

———

I AM THE FIRST PERSON in my family to be born in the United States—specifically, Barnwell, South Carolina. Unlike typical "Barnwellians," my parents got there circuitously—from Russia to France, to Romania, to Turkey. They were both born in Russia around the time of the Bolshevik Revolution, which began in 1917. As a young girl, my mom left Russia with her mother and lived in France, Romania, and then Istanbul. My father and his family fled Russia for Istanbul with a division of the anti-Bolshevik military forces. That is where my parents met during World War II, married in 1945, and had a daughter, my sister, Nadia.

They were in a small minority of Russian emigres in Istanbul and in an overwhelmingly Muslim country. Their close friends were Jewish, Armenians, Greeks, and other Russians. Of course, they developed a great fondness for Jewish cuisine (who wouldn't?), or maybe that was already part of their DNA. Much later in life, as a grown man, I learned that our family tree also included Jewish ancestors.

My parents wanted badly to immigrate to the United States. Through some family connections, a Russian-born, Jewish-American owner of zipper manufacturing plants offered my father a job with his New York-based company, and he sponsored our family's immigration in 1950.

Around that time, long-time South Carolina House Speaker Solomon Blatt and Senate pro tempore and Finance Committee Chair Edgar Brown, the core of the powerful "Barnwell ring" political force, were encouraging industries with locations in the North to move to South Carolina, and they especially pushed to have industries relocate to Barnwell, which before then was a mostly farm-based economy. The company Dad worked for, National Fasteners Corporation, was the first manufacturer to move to Barnwell, but the company's headquarters remained in New York.

My father was supposed to work in the New York office, but he became manager of the Barnwell plant and lived there until 2012—the year both my parents died. Dad regularly traveled to New York to meet with his boss. He would take the overnight train from either Barnwell, Denmark, or Columbia, and spend a few days there three or four times a year. He was a city boy and loved those trips. Dad loaded up as best he could with gifts and food (especially hard-to-find Jewish deli fare, like whitefish, lox, beef tongue, herring, corned beef, and chopped liver) for the return trip home. Today's generation takes for granted that you can buy almost anything, including food, from anywhere and have it delivered to your home with just a few clicks of a mouse. Of course, when my dad made his business trips to New York, these days were far in the future.

Always among the Barnwell beneficiaries of his deli shopping was the Honorable Solomon Blatt. Blatt was the son of Russian Jewish immigrants. His father, who came to South Carolina in 1893, began as a peddler selling wares from Charleston to Augusta and Savannah. He established a small store in Blackville, which was on the Southern Railway line. Solomon was born in 1896. Exemplifying the great American immigrant story, Blatt became a lawyer in 1917, served in World War II, and was elected to the South Carolina House in 1932. He served in the House until he died in 1986. For thirty-two of those years, he was the powerful House Speaker, and for twelve years, he was the Speaker Emeritus. He was also a senior partner in his hugely successful law firm, which enjoyed an excellent reputation even at the national level. Speaker Blatt never forgot his cultural roots, and apparently that included his love of Jewish cuisine, especially smoked beef tongue. My father always made a point to gift the powerful Barnwell politico with a smoked tongue upon his return from New York.

Michael Tonquor and father, Jack Tonquor, Barnwell Library, SC, 2007.
COURTESY MICHAEL TONQUOR.

All of that provides context for a couple of thank-you notes I recently found in my dad's papers. In one note from 1970, on the speaker's official stationery, he thanked my dad for having delivered to him the smoked tongue because "I can never get any and only have it when you are kind enough to send it." Moreover, Blatt assures that he will enjoy eating it and will "think of you as I do." That conjures some wonderful imagery. The gifts of tongue helped to cement the relationship between my family and the powerful Speaker.

With our families' relationship firmly entrenched with these annual food gifts, I was pleased to receive a nice high school graduation gift from the Speaker. Even though I was accepted to Stanford University, I ultimately ended up at the University of South Carolina under the tutelage of Sol Blatt. Thanks to his guidance, I worked as a page in the South Carolina Senate and attended the University of South Carolina Law School. As I reflect on the many things for which I am thankful, including my family and my career, I am grateful to Solomon Blatt, who was instrumental in my career path, and, of course, to my visionary father, whose generous gifts of smoked tongue ingratiated our family to the Speaker of the South Carolina House, who, fortunately for us, lived in a town with no Jewish deli!

A JEWISH KID FROM LONG ISLAND LANDS IN MYRTLE BEACH

DONALD SLOAN

———

"Best not to know" is Donald Sloan's mantra on kosher food, as he
and his wife have made a home in Myrtle Beach.

———

NO ONE WOULD HAVE BEEN MORE astonished than my parents to hear that I am being asked to write about food. To be brief, when growing up, I had serious food-as-control issues, and my diet consisted of carbs and dairy products. I hated meat, including poultry, and neither eggs nor fish passed my smell test. So, I could not tell you about my mother's brisket or stuffed cabbage. My family didn't keep a kosher home but ate mostly kosher foods (with the addition of shellfish). Eventually, as I left home and traveled, I learned to eat omelets and fish.

A few years after I got married, I realized that we had a mostly vegetarian/pescatarian diet, with my wife Renée also eating turkey breast or chicken dishes occasionally. We decided that there was really no excuse not to keep kosher. She kept a few plates for the turkey or chicken that she might bring into the house, and we had to give up shellfish, but living in Akron, Ohio, we found that shellfish wasn't exactly a local delicacy. We still went out to restaurants and did not order anything that clearly was not kosher. As for the rest, we had to adopt a "don't ask, don't tell" policy. Was that risotto cooked in a shrimp broth? Did that soup use chicken stock? Best not to know.

In 2008, I took a job at Coastal Carolina University, and we moved to Myrtle Beach. It was the first time I had ever been to the South (and South Florida doesn't count, of course). I was surprised at the large number of New Yorkers already here and somewhat amused by the local accents of the others, as though central casting sent a few character actors here to make sure we had enough Southern flavor.

We were pleasantly surprised that, unlike in Akron, we actually had a few kosher restaurants in Myrtle Beach. Because of the small but prosperous community of Israelis who owned most of the beachwear shops up and down Kings Highway, there was the Jerusalem Restaurant, the fleichig eatery, and Cafe M, the milchig one. Both were modest places—a counter and a few tables—but kosher. They have since closed, but there always seems to be another kosher place popping up, and today, the Pita Planet is the "meat" place for the kosher set. We still ate out in other restaurants, and if our "don't ask, don't tell" policy was in effect in the Midwest, it was even more necessary here. Even the breads (that is to say, the biscuits) and desserts often were made with lard, and we wondered if there was anything that didn't have pig products in it. Best not to know.

So rather than try to share some amalgam of kosher and southern food for you, I'd like to fall back on one of my mom's best pastry recipes. She called them schnecken, which most Eastern European Jews know as rugelach. These were so good that once, when a month passed while I was away at college without a care package from home, one of my friends picked up our phone when my mother called and asked her if everything was okay—after all, she had a whole set of college kids waiting for the next tin of schnecken to arrive.

GLORIA SLOAN'S SCHNECKEN, OR RUGELACH

Like most recipes, these were jotted down on scraps of paper or index cards, and what was there was not always one hundred percent like what she actually baked. My sister verified the necessary requirements: margarine, not butter, and real sour cream, not the low-fat version.

Dough

3 cups flour

1 package dry yeast

2 sticks margarine

2 egg yolks

1 cup sour cream

Filling

1 cup ground pecans

1 cup sugar

1½ to 2 teaspoons cinnamon

¼ cup white raisins (optional)

To make the dough: Mix the dry yeast and the flour. Cut pieces of margarine into this mixture. Add the egg yolks and sour cream and combine. Form into a ball, put clear wrap around it, and refrigerate at least two hours.

To make the filling: Mix the filling ingredients.

To prepare: Roll the dough out into flat disks, cut into wedges, put the filling on top, and roll into crescents. You'll have to experiment with how to split the dough for these disks as well as how large these crescents should be. My recollection is that each batch made 2 to 3 dozen pastries, each 2 to 3 inches long.

Bake on a cookie sheet at 325°F until golden brown (30 to 45 minutes).

MAKES 2 TO 3 DOZEN

SOUTHERN ROOTS 2

WE ATE LIKE OUR SOUTHERN NEIGHBORS 49
Rhetta Aronson Mendelsohn and Carol Aronson Kelly

Henrietta Block Rich's Matzo Balls
Mrs. Aronson's Noodle Kugel

A PASSED-DOWN SOUTHERN RECIPE FOR A JEWISH TABLE 53
Lyssa Kligman Harvey

Annie Gailliard's Okra Gumbo

OUR SOUTHERN JEWISH FOOD IDENTITY 57
Laura Moses, Natalie Moses, and Robert Moses

Artichoke Pickles
Sumter-Style Scratch Biscuits
Scones
Eliza Gregg's Fried Chicken
Pecan Nut Cake
Wine Jelly

EUTAWVILLE FOOD MEMORIES 63
Ernie Marcus and Ellen Marcus Smith

Fig Preserves
Brandied Peaches
Watermelon Preserves

FOOD THRILLS FROM ROCK HILL 68
Judy Kurtz Goldman

Chicken Liver Pâté

MY JEWISH CONNECTIONS 71
Judge Casey Manning

Hot Milk Cake
Chicken Dressing

A JEWISH MERCHANT'S CHRISTMAS IN SUMMERTON 75
Rachel Gordin Barnett

Ethel Glover's Squash Casserole

FLORIDA MAE BOYD, THE BEST JEWISH CHEF IN COLUMBIA 77
Janis Dickman, Jacquelyn Dickman, and Sheryl Dickman

From shelling peas on a back porch in Sumter to fishing the banks of the Little Pee Dee River in Dillon County, contributors to this chapter share their love of local foods that were staples on the family table. You may say the farm-to-table movement had its beginnings in small farming communities such as these!

The stories and recipes in this chapter come from families who lived in small towns and urban centers. Robert Moses, born in Sumter in 1921, reminisces about churning buttermilk, peeling shrimp, and shelling peas. Ernie Marcus remembers that there was always a seat at the table in Eutawville. Judge Casey Manning, born and raised in Dillon, recalls his summers in the Catskills at Kutscher's basketball camp. Their memories of food remind us of the origins of southern traditions. A confluence of food sources that define our southern roots followed the people who settled in the South—Sephardic Jews from Spain, Portugal, and the Mediterranean; enslaved Africans from West Africa and the Caribbean; Ashkenazic Jews from Eastern Europe; and indigenous Native Americans. Each brought knowledge and skills that shaped today's southern Jewish food.

Climate, soil, and waters also shaped the southern palate. Growing conditions yielded crops with global origins, such as tomatoes, okra, collards, rice, and corn. Peach orchards, fields of peanuts, and seasonal row crops dotted the landscape of the Palmetto State. Most South Carolinians in the nineteenth century and earlier cooked what they grew in their gardens and on their farms; raised livestock; and purchased coffee, flour, canned goods, and sugar from local merchants and commissaries. They fished where they lived—from the coastal Grand Strand to the Lowcountry marshes and Upstate and Piedmont rivers. Their nets, poles, and rods yielded fish and seafood of all kinds, including shrimp and crab. Backyard coops provided eggs and fowl, and nearby pastures often a milk cow. South Carolina Jewish households came to host meals that were distinctly southern and distinctly Jewish, although many immigrants avoided shellfish and pork because of kosher laws.

More often than not, South Carolina Jews were merchants and generally one step removed from the farms located around the towns and cities where they lived. The Palmetto Pigeon Plant, founded in Sumter in 1923 by Wendell Levi and Harold

Moïse, and Barnett's Peaches, established in Dalzell in 1956, reminds us of exceptions to that rule. The people who cooked in Jewish homes and synagogue kitchens were often African Americans, both women and men, who brought their own culinary expertise and indiscriminately turned out traditional Jewish dishes and southern specialties.

As Orangeburg native Rhetta Mendelsohn remembers, "Truly we ate like our southern neighbors but with a few notable exceptions. Granny and Mother did not cook with bacon grease. . . . Our menus included things our neighbors never knew about like chopped liver, herring, blintzes, lox, brisket, potato, and noodle kugel." In his recollection about life in Eutawville, Ernie Marcus recalls, "The most palpable memories revolved around food (what else?) a mix of traditional southern fare like fried chicken, rice and gravy, okra and tomatoes, and dishes passed down from Eastern Europe." Their recipes and those of other contributors feature Ashkenazic staples while reflecting the availability of South Carolina ingredients, including peaches, figs, cucumbers, watermelon, blackberries, hickory nuts, pecans, corn, squash, and okra.

Sunset on Fishing Creek, Edisto Island, SC, 2015.
COURTESY RACHEL BARNETT.

WE ATE LIKE OUR SOUTHERN NEIGHBORS

RHETTA ARONSON MENDELSOHN AND CAROL ARONSON KELLY

———

*Rhetta Mendelsohn and her sister, Carol Kelly, reminisce about growing up
Jewish in a small South Carolina community and about their
mother, who was known as the best cook in town.*

———

GROWING UP IN ORANGEBURG in the 1950s and '60s, we were southern and Jewish and totally a part of the community. After World War II, our parents worked very hard to establish a successful business—Aronson Awning Company. We lived in a small house before moving to a more affluent neighborhood in 1960. Our grandparents lived close by.

Our grandmother, Henrietta Block Rich, spent her life as a homemaker, sharing her special matzo balls with friends and neighbors. She visited all the local farmers markets and spent her time sitting on the front porch, shelling butter beans and peas while our grandfather, Lipman Philip Rich, cracked the pecans. Granny, as we called her, took us to her friend's homes to pick figs that she made into wonderful preserves, cucumbers that she turned into dill pickles, and chestnuts that she put into the Thanksgiving turkey. Every Saturday morning, Papa, as we called him, appeared at our door with boiled peanuts and a Coke for us. Until she passed away in 1984, Granny never failed to send us home with something wonderful from her kitchen—most notably, her smothered chicken that everyone loved. We still use her tattered copy of *The Settlement Cook Book* and her recipes written in pencil on scraps of paper and on the backs of checks.

Following in her mother's footsteps, our mother became known as the best cook in Orangeburg. In addition to working every morning at Aronson Awning Company, she cooked three meals a day. We mostly ate at home, only sometimes going to the country club or a local restaurant, Berry's on the Hill. Dinner was in the middle of the day, when she and Daddy came home to eat. Daddy went back to work, but Mother stayed home. On Saturdays, we had fried chicken and macaroni and cheese, prepared with the expert help of Jessie Mae Palm. Jessie Mae lived in her home near an enclave of relatives with her husband and daughter Terri. She taught me how to iron and clean windows—a job we always did together.

On Sundays, we had rib roast or steak prepared on the grill by Daddy's hands. We enjoyed the bounties of the southern seasons—corn, butter beans, white acre field peas, peaches, figs, and pecan desserts. Also, we all enjoyed barbeque from the locally famous Dukes' establishments. We ate bacon and ham along with chicken and fish that Papa caught in the nearby lakes and the Edisto River. We ate grits, canned salmon, and Vienna sausages.

Truly, we ate like our southern neighbors, but with a few notable exceptions—Granny and Mother did not cook with bacon grease or store it in a special little can on top of the stove. They always used Fleischmann's margarine. Our menus included things our neighbors knew nothing about—chopped liver, herring, blintzes, bagels, lox, brisket, potato and noodle kugel, matzo balls, matzo brei, and more. So, when we went to the beach every summer, we took along fried chicken, barbeque, and deviled eggs as well as chopped liver, herring, and brisket. Mother could put on a lovely dinner party at a moment's notice and prepare fabulous bite-size hors d'oeuvres and sweets for cocktail parties. Her recipes reflect a slower pace of life—with time to put love and labor into her cooking. Our Jewish heritage is still very much a part of how we cook today. Although we cook fewer casseroles and sweets, we fall back on Granny and Mother's recipes as delicious and dependable for family meals as well as for company.

In the 1950s, Granny and Mother sold cookies to raise money to build Orangeburg's Temple Sinai. It was no secret that we were one of about twenty Jewish families in Orangeburg. We personally never experienced anti-Semitism in our small South Carolina community.

HENRIETTA BLOCK RICH'S MATZO BALLS

Granny's unique recipe for matzo balls. We think they are the best, but we have yet to perfect them. We will keep trying!

1 to 2 chopped spring onions

2 tablespoons margarine

2 tea matzos or the thinnest available

Salt and pepper to taste

2 egg yolks, beaten

2 egg whites

1 tablespoon matzo meal, plus more for rolling balls

1 handful chopped parsley

Sauté some chopped spring onions in margarine (you can substitute butter, but the balls don't hold together as well).

Soak 2 tea matzos in water. Squeeze really well and crumble into pan with onions. Add salt and pepper and remove from heat. Stir in 2 egg yolks.

Beat 2 egg whites until stiff and fold into the matzo mixture. Fold in 1 tablespoon of matzo meal and parsley. Put into the refrigerator to cool. Make into balls and roll in matzo meal.

Can be frozen. Thaw and roll again in matzo meal before using. Add to soup just before serving. When the balls float to the top, the soup is ready to enjoy. The matzo balls only take a few minutes to cook.

MAKES APPROXIMATELY 12 MATZO BALLS

MRS. ARONSON'S NOODLE KUGEL

This recipe for noodle kugel made mother a finalist in the first South Carolina Dairy Association cookoff. It made the newspaper, but she unfortunately didn't win.

4 ounces egg noodles

2 large eggs

2 tablespoons milk

2 teaspoons sugar

1 teaspoon baking powder

Pinch of salt

1 (18-ounce) can or jar applesauce

1 (12-ounce) carton cottage cheese

1 (8-ounce) carton sour cream

½ cup raisins

½ stick butter

3 tablespoons brown sugar

1 cup crushed corn flakes

Boil the noodles in a quart of water for four minutes and set aside.

Beat the eggs lightly and add the other ingredients as listed (from 2 tablespoons milk through ½ cup raisins). Add the mixture to the noodles and stir to mix.

Put the ½ stick butter in a 9 × 13-inch Pyrex dish and melt it in oven while heating to 350°F. Take the dish out of the oven and sprinkle 3 tablespoons brown sugar in the bottom of the dish. Pour the noodle mixture over the brown sugar and butter and add 1 cup of crushed corn flakes to the top. Bake at 350°F degrees for 45 minutes to 1 hour.

MAKES 12 SERVINGS

A PASSED-DOWN SOUTHERN RECIPE FOR A JEWISH TABLE

LYSSA KLIGMAN HARVEY

―――――

This favorite southern dish, included in many Jewish holiday menus, was created by Charlestonian Annie Gailliard and was passed down to her employers, the Firetags.

―――――

THANKSGIVING IS A WONDERFUL American tradition of gratitude with feasting and festivities that, for us, means sharing the day (from early afternoon into the evening) with family and friends. I love to set a fancy fall table and prepare the turkey and a couple of my favorite dishes. Family members bring their Thanksgiving meal specialties—a mixture of Jewish recipes and southern foods: challah, turkey, corn pudding, mac and cheese, sweet potato casserole, apple pie, and rugelach, and I have added Annie Gailliard's recipe for okra gumbo!

Annie Gailliard (1904–2003) lived in Charleston with her husband, Walter Gailliard, and their children, Walter Jr., Elizabeth, and Lorraine. They lived in the building next door to (and shared a backyard with) my grandparents, Joe and Mildred Reznick Firetag, at the intersection of St. Philip and Morris streets. At the time, St. Philip Street was home to many Jewish and Black families. Annie began working for my grandparents in 1933. She was an excellent cook. My aunt, Lynda Firetag Denberg, recalls her delicious fried chicken, macaroni salad, and okra gumbo—just a few of the southern foods she introduced to our family. Aside from my grandmother's requirement that she keep kosher, Annie controlled the kitchen, cooking three meals a day. She eventually moved to Concord Street and became known in her neighborhood for selling chilly bears (frozen Kool Aid) in

Annie Gaillaird, Charleston, SC, 1994.
COURTESY LYNDA DENBERG.

little Dixie Cups and sweet potato pies. Annie was an active member of Mother Emmanuel AME church on Calhoun Street. She lived to be ninety-nine years old, and I attended her funeral with Lynda and other family members. All of Annie's family members, including a granddaughter, Rita, have since passed away.

Annie shared her recipe for okra gumbo with my Aunt Lynda, who subsequently shared it with me. Lynda is my mother, Helene Firetag Kligman's, youngest sister. Only ten years older than me, she is and has always been my favorite aunt. After leaving home, she didn't know how to cook, and this recipe was one of several that Annie later shared with her. Like many great cooks, Annie cooked by taste, and so none of her recipes were written down. For our family, she kept the dish kosher, which meant no bacon or bacon grease. Instead, she used vegetable oil to sauté the vegetables. She might have made this gumbo for her own family a little differently! Although traditional gumbos have a roux base, Annie's recipe is more like a succotash, but she—and our family— have always called it okra gumbo.

Lynda made this recipe for the Friday night Sabbath meal, and it still is a family favorite. I am excited about serving this passed-down "told" recipe for our Thanksgiving meal. I hope it lives up to Annie's and Lynda's long-loved recipe.

ANNIE GAILLIARD'S OKRA GUMBO

Annie Gailliard shared this recipe with my Aunt Lynda Firetag Denberg, who then told it to me. It was a spoken recipe until now. Lynda changed the recipe slightly by using a mix of fresh and frozen vegetables and adding a dollop of ketchup. This recipe calls for lima beans, though not all recipes for okra gumbo do. I have given the recipe a Jewish touch, with a dollop of schmaltz and olive oil, served with a Jewish grain dish called kasha varnishkes rather than white rice.

The okra gets very slimy when you cut it. Sautéing the okra over high heat or blanching it before sautéing can lessen the slime. Or you can soak the okra in vinegar for half an hour before cutting. Rinse and pat dry. Annie used vegetable oil to sauté the onions and okra. I add schmaltz to give it extra flavor with a Jewish touch!

1 tablespoon olive oil

1 tablespoon schmaltz
(rendered chicken fat)

1 large onion, chopped

1 garlic clove, crushed

1 pound fresh okra, chopped

3 ears fresh corn, cooked and
kernels taken off the cob

1 pound baby lima beans
(fresh or frozen)

1 large can diced tomatoes or
4 fresh tomatoes, diced

2 tablespoons ketchup

Salt and pepper to taste

Cover the bottom of a large heavy skillet with olive oil and a tablespoon of schmaltz. Cook on the stovetop on medium temperature. Caramelize the onions and garlic together. Put aside.

Sauté the chopped okra on medium temperature to cook off the slime. Cook until tender. Add the corn and lima beans to the okra. Stir until well mixed and cook until tender. Add the tomatoes and the ketchup and cook on low until the vegetables are tender. Salt and pepper to taste.

MAKES 6 TO 8 SERVINGS

OUR SOUTHERN JEWISH FOOD IDENTITY

LAURA MOSES, NATALIE MOSES, AND ROBERT MOSES

———

*Generations of the Moses family have resided in Sumter
and share their generational recipes.*

———

Sumter Musings

ROBERT MOSES

I am sure that all of us feel closely related to food! Early on, I enjoyed helping my mother with her cooking. I remember assisting her with churning buttermilk, making curd, and trying to help manage the damp towel used to roll the cake for chocolate rolls. Later came peeling shrimp and shelling peas. As an adult, most of my cooking efforts centered on baking. My all-time favorite was buttermilk English tea scones. For several years, I grew a large volume of mushrooms underneath the back porch and ordered many pounds of soil inoculated with mycelium. We ate them as another table vegetable! It wouldn't surprise me to find out that two favorites of my mother were particular to Sumter, never being seen outside of the city. These two are her cured fish roe and pecan nut cake. I've never known anyone except my mother to cure the roe, whereas all of her wide circle of friends made almost identical nut cake recipes.

A Menu of Memories

NATALIE MOSES

Like many southern Jews, our Jewish food identities are pretty diluted, as our family was and is an assimilated Jewish one, including intermarriage as well. Our immediate family was based in Sumter, and we spent a fair amount of time at Pawleys Island, in the Lowcountry. Our family grew up eating pork and plenty of shellfish. As a child, Daddy spent hours in the salt marsh creek and deep-sea fishing off the coast. We also enjoyed many hours with him on the creek. These were often social occasions where we were joined by houseguests. He was known to wake his daughters at five o'clock in the morning, in time to catch the tide to get through the inlet out to open water. My mother was never particularly comfortable on the water and did not accompany us on fishing trips.

Daddy also took us shrimping in the creek. We had long rectangular shrimp nets attached to tall, sturdy poles at either end, weighted at

Robert Moses and Laura Moses, Sumter, SC, July 2011.
COURTESY LAURA MOSES.

the bottom. Daddy would take one end (probably the deeper end), and the children would hold the other. We'd walk through the sucking pluff mud, dragging the shrimp net stretched out between us. When Daddy thought we'd probably caught some shrimp, the person on the far, deep edge would start to walk toward shore, keeping the pole hugging the bottom. Both poles were brought together with the shrimp caught in the middle. These tender, sweet, and very flavorful small creek shrimp were served with grits for breakfast. Another treat from the creek was crab, caught carefully with hand lines. The picked crab was made into cakes by mixing in Ritz crackers and egg and then pan frying in butter, served with grits.

Eliza (Liza) Gregg worked for our parents, Robert and Harriett Moses, starting before the oldest daughter, Natalie, was born and continuing through when Elizabeth, the youngest, was in grade school. During that time, Liza had three children of her own who were of similar ages as we were. She helped our mother with cleaning, cooking, ironing, and childcare. Carol once asked Liza what she had wanted to be when she grew up, and she said a teacher. Carol says that, in fact, she was a great teacher—to us, to those around her, to her own family.

Our family didn't eat much beef. The exception to this was brisket, a low-cost cut, which was rubbed with ground coffee and slowly roasted. We ate brisket frequently. Years later, my mother said she had never known how to cook meat and so avoided it by cooking elaborate side dishes. Once we were invited to dinner at a friend's home. This hostess was known for being a very fine cook, and sure enough, we had a magnificently succulent meat dish as a main course. I'd never eaten meat like that. When leaving, I asked Daddy what it was, and he cryptically replied, "expensive." It was pork tenderloin. The friends were Jewish. All the southern Jews I knew ate pork.

ARTICHOKE PICKLES

NATALIE MOSES

This recipe was from my grandmother, Charlotte Emanuel Moses, in 1970. If unable to get clean artichokes, you may need to scrape, scrub, and wash to clean them.

3 pounds brown sugar

1 small box dry mustard

2 ounces turmeric

1 cup salt

1 ounce celery seed

1 gallon white vinegar

1 peck artichokes (¼ bushel), cut into bite-size pieces—trim the sharp points and stem

1 small head cabbage, shredded coarsely (optional)

6 green peppers, cut into strips and slices (optional)

1 quart seed (pearl) onions, or 10 medium onions cut into chunks

1 head cauliflower, cut into bite-size pieces

1 lemon, sliced thin

Mix the brown sugar, mustard, turmeric, and salt really well in a crock. Add the celery seed, slowly add the vinegar, and stir until all dissolved. Add the vegetables and stir well each day for ten days. Store covered in a cool place. Pickles keep well in a cool crock or in jars with the brine liquid, in a refrigerator.

MAKES 5 TO 7 QUARTS

SUMTER-STYLE SCRATCH BISCUITS

ROBERT A. MOSES

Note: If using plain flour, add 4 teaspoons baking powder and 1 teaspoon salt

6 tablespoons Crisco

1 cup milk

Sifter full—approximately 3 cups full of self-rising flour

Mix the Crisco and milk, and add the flour slowly, holding back a little for dusting and rolling out the biscuits. Cut out the biscuits with a biscuit cutter or round cookie cutter. Bake at 400–450°F until golden brown.

MAKES 24 BISCUITS

SCONES

NATALIE MOSES

Daddy has always been the scone maker in the house, and these are gently fought over! He has given baking lessons to daughters, sons-in-law, and grandchildren to pass on this important responsibility.

2 cups all-purpose unbleached flour

2 rounded tablespoons sugar

2 level teaspoons baking powder (if using regular milk instead of buttermilk, use 3 teaspoons baking powder and no baking soda)

¼ rounded teaspoon baking soda

¼–½ teaspoon salt

5⅓ tablespoons (⅓ cup) butter

1 beaten egg

¾ cup buttermilk

Dates, frozen blueberries, currants, pecans, or cranberries, etc. (optional)

Preheat oven to 425°F. Grease a cookie sheet.

Sift or whisk together the flour, sugar, baking powder, baking soda, and salt.

With a pastry blender, cut in the butter until the mixture resembles coarse corn meal. Stir in the beaten egg.

Gradually stir in ¾ cup buttermilk to form a stiff ball of dough that comes away from the side of the bowl. Knead 15–17 times on a floured board. Divide into two equal balls.

Fold in the dates, etc., if desired.

Use flour as necessary on hands and the counter to prevent the balls of dough from sticking. Press the dough out into circles ¾ inches thick. Turn them over and flatten into circles ½ inches thick. Cut into eight wedges each.

Place the wedges, flipped over, onto a greased cookie sheet. Bake 10–12 minutes.

Store the leftovers in an airtight container to keep them from getting too hard.

MAKES 16 SCONES (NOT THE GIANT SIZE).

FOR 32 OR 48 SCONES, JUST DOUBLE OR TRIPLE THE INGREDIENTS, RESPECTIVELY.

ELIZA GREGG'S FRIED CHICKEN

NATALIE MOSES

Here's what Liza showed me: Put some flour and salt and pepper in a brown paper bag. Put the chicken pieces in and shake it well. Shake off the excess flour, and fry in a large cast iron pan (most likely in bacon grease) on medium high heat, adjusting as necessary. Don't crowd the chicken pieces. She would have gone light on the salt and heavy on the pepper. I know that's not a recipe, *per se*, but fried chicken like this doesn't get too complicated!

PECAN NUT CAKE

ROBERT MOSES

Notes from Natalie: According to Daddy, he has never seen this recipe outside of Sumter. It is finicky and time consuming; it is also dense, moist, and serves many. We often had this with wine jelly; it pairs nicely. Daddy's recipe below, as written. He made this every year, taking precise notes each time. Several years ago, he brought me one and said "Sweetheart, this is my last one. It's up to you to make them from now on!" I stretched out that last cake for weeks. I make a slightly different recipe now, that seems to have more consistent results.

1 pound pecans, cut fine (just under 4 cups chopped pecans)

1 pound white seedless raisins, cut
in half

1 pound sugar (2 cups, slightly rounded)

3½ sticks butter

7 eggs

4 level cups sifted flour (from 1 pound plain flour)

1 teaspoon baking powder, sifted with above

4 ounces wine or bourbon

Mix the pecans and raisins lightly but thoroughly and toss with a smidgen of flour.

Cream the sugar and butter until the sugar is dissolved. Add the eggs one at a time. Add the flour and baking powder mixture alternately with wine or bourbon, begin and end with the flour mixture (do not overbeat). Fold in the pecans and raisins.

Line the bottom and sides of a 10-inch tube pan with wax paper, or lightly greased brown paper, or a butter wrapper. Grease and flour the sides of the pan. Put the batter into the pan.

Bake for 2 hours at 300°F. Under the cake pan, place some water in a pan on a lower rack while baking. Cover the top of the cake pan with foil when browned.

MAKES 12 TO 16 SERVINGS

WINE JELLY

BASIC RECIPE: FROM *THE SETTLEMENT COOK BOOK* BY LIZZIE BLACK KANDER

(FEBRUARY 20, 1977)

1 ounce gelatin

½ cup cold water

1½ cup boiling water

⅓ cup orange juice

¾ cup wine and ¼ cup bourbon
  (or sherry, port, brandy, in
  whole or in part), to make
  1 cup

3 tablespoons lemon juice

1 cup sugar

Add cold water to the gelatin, and let stand for 5 minutes to soften. Add boiling water, and stir until dissolved; add sugar, dissolve, and when cooked, add the orange juice, wine mixture, and lemon juice. Pour into a bowl, and let it cool. When it is hardened, cut up into cube-like pieces and spoon into individual bowls. Top with whipped cream.

EUTAWVILLE FOOD MEMORIES

ERNIE MARCUS AND ELLEN MARCUS SMITH

———

Siblings Ernie and Ellen recall the love, laughter, and great food that were
felt at generations of family occasions. Their essay includes recipes
for homemade local products like watermelon preserves.

———

Henry and Louise Marcus's wedding party, Eutawville, SC, 1949.
COURTESY ERNIE MARCUS.

WE ARE GREAT GRANDCHILDREN of Harris Nathan and Sarah Basza Cohen, from the
Russia-Poland borderlands near Bialystok, who immigrated around 1880 to New York
City and then moved on from the tenement houses of the Lower East Side to the South
Carolina farming communities of Mayesville and then Eutawville. Thus began nearly
a century of our family's presence in small-town South Carolina with family members
working as merchants. Memories shine bright of the closeness of family, encouraged by

Cohen/Karesh/Marcus family reunion, Eutawville, SC, 1986.
COURTESY ERNIE MARCUS.

special cooks in the kitchen; meals together with those in the town; and frequent visits from the Eutawville diaspora in Charleston, Columbia, and up north. There was *always* a seat at the table.

If physical closeness breeds emotional closeness, it is no surprise how the ties became so strong. It is hard to appreciate just how many relatives lived together in the same modest house. First, there were Harris and Sarah with their three sons and five daughters (Moses, Isaac, Abe, Katie, Janie, Gertie, Leah, and Mary). Katie married Abraham Karesh, adding six Karesh children to the house. When those children became adults and had their own families, there were, at one time, fourteen adults and children in the house from the Katie Karesh line alone. In addition, for a time, Moses's family of four lived there, and Janie and her two children (she was widowed by Morris Marcus) were also in the house. There was even Sam Zaks, a Russian immigrant, who escaped from the Czar and lived in the house for decades and had a store in town. This truly was another crowded tenement house, the only difference being that this one was in a Lowcountry shtetl!

All of the family members of a certain age remember the outhouse in the backyard in Eutawville, baths in a tin tub, the barrel outdoor shower heated by the sun, and the giant fig tree. But the most palpable memories revolve around food (what else?)—a mix of traditional South Carolina fare like fried chicken, rice and gravy, okra and tomatoes, and dishes passed down from Eastern Europe. The eldest daughter of Sarah, Katie, who was born in New York City during those early tenement years, was the food maven whom most people mention. However, Katie's daughters, Rita, Jeannette, and Marie, and sister-in-law Corinne (wife to her youngest brother, Abe) were also culinary stars. Corinne later created a handwritten recipe book for each of the Karesh sisters. The recipes reflected Ashkenazi staples but also included special foods native to Eutawville, such as peaches, figs, cucumbers, watermelon, blackberries, hickory nuts, pecans, corn, squash, and okra. Dinners were often supplemented by herring, kosher pickles, bagels, and lox brought back from visits to Charleston delis like Harold's Cabin and Zinn's.

The scene at holidays and big Sunday dinners in Eutawville was a long table groaning with course after course, brought in with a flourish from the wood-burning stove. The kids sat at one end of the table and were sent off to play outside after the meal so the adults could play poker, sometimes with non-Jewish shopkeepers sitting in on the low-stakes penny ante games.

The days of a Jewish presence in small, rural towns in South Carolina are mostly over. As the family is now in its fifth generation, recipes are an invaluable way to stay connected to our unique and special past.

FIG PRESERVES

Consult canning manuals for safety instructions.

5 pounds figs
3¾ cups sugar
3 lemons
Ground ginger to taste

After washing carefully and draining, put the figs in a large pan and lightly mash. Mix them with ¾ pound of sugar for every pound of figs, and slice thinly 1 lemon for every 2 pounds of figs. Let the mixture sit for 5 or 6 hours or until the sugar has drawn out most of the juice from the figs.

Cover and put the pan on a stove on low heat until it comes to a boil. Then remove the cover and stir every few minutes. Raise the heat if you are going to stand over the stove and stir continuously. Cook until thick, and then add ground ginger to taste (start with 1 teaspoon) and stir well.

Put into sterilized jars. Leave a gap of 1 inch from the top of the jar when filling. Place rings and lids on snugly. Put the jars into a boiling bath of water submerged for 12–15 minutes. Remove the jars from the water and let them cool.

MAKES APPROXIMATELY 6 TO 7 PINTS OF PRESERVES

BRANDIED PEACHES

Easy and so good. Consult the canning manuals for safety instructions.

1 cup water

1 cup sugar

1 pound peeled and halved peaches

3–4 tablespoons brandy

Boil 1 cup water and 1 cup sugar together for 1 minute. Add 1 pound peeled and halved peaches to the mixture, and then boil the syrup and peaches for 5 minutes. Put the peaches into the prepped jars and fill until ¾ full. Fill the jars mostly up with syrup. Add 3–4 tablespoons brandy. Leave in the jars for 3–4 months before serving.

MAKES 1 QUART

WATERMELON PRESERVES

Consult the canning manual for safety instructions.

6–7 cups of watermelon rind, finely cut

4½ cups sugar

2 lemons, thinly sliced

2 teaspoons lemon juice

1 teaspoon cinnamon

2–3 teaspoons ground ginger

Mix the rind, sugar, and lemons, and lemon juice together, and let stand overnight.

Next morning, boil until the rind is clear, remove the rind, and boil the syrup down until thick.

Add cinnamon, ginger, return the rind, and bring to a good boil. Use an immersion blender to blend together ingredients.

Place into jars and seal. Process in a boiling water bath for 10 minutes.

MAKES APPROXIMATELY 2½ PINTS OF PRESERVES

FOOD THRILLS FROM ROCK HILL

JUDY KURTZ GOLDMAN

————

*Judy Kurtz Goldman explores the reasons behind her mother's
reimagining of Jewish chopped liver into chicken liver pâté.*

————

MOTHER'S FRIEND SENT ME a copy of *Food Thrills from Rock Hill,* a cookbook published by the women of the Episcopal Church of Our Saviour in 1964, the year after I graduated from college. Her inscription, in her curled cursive: "Judy, do try my corn dressing on page 42! Fondly, Duff." In the cookbook, there is no accent over the "e" in her recipe for chicken pate. And no explanation as to how you render fat from a chicken. For sure, she did not refer to chicken fat as "schmaltz." More on that later.

Peggy Kurtz was my mother. She did not cook at all. She had never even boiled water for tea. She turned on the stove for the first time when she was in her sixties and learned how to fry an egg. Oh, how she bragged when she slid a perfect over-light egg onto my father's plate on Sunday mornings when Mattie Culp, the Black woman who cooked for my family (and had lived in) for years, now lived on her own and had weekends off. How I heard about those yolks, so plump and intact.

The reason Mother gave for not cooking was that she had always worked. Of course, a person who works can cook, but none of us questioned her explanation. She had been the only female majoring in accounting at the University of South Carolina, on her way to becoming a certified public accountant. However, Grandpa Bogen, her rascally father who owned a department store in Denmark, South Carolina, gambled; he either won big or lost everything, which meant the family moved from town to town in the Carolinas, sometimes in the dark of night (I don't like imagining what they were avoiding by moving). When my mother was a student at the University of South Carolina, her father again lost at the poker table, and she had to drop out, return home to Denmark, and get a job keeping the books for South Carolina Electric & Gas.

After she married my father, she was the bookkeeper for his two clothing stores, The Smart Shop and King's Men's Shop. Mattie, who came to work for our family in 1944, did the cooking. It was Mattie who chopped the liver, rendered the chicken fat, and stirred it in along with eggs and onion. It was Mattie who served the chopped liver on iceberg lettuce or between slices of toasted white bread—always for lunch, never as an hors d'oeuvre.

My father's mother, Grandma Kurtz, a large diabetic woman who traveled from Atlanta to visit us fairly often, taught Mattie how to "cook Jewish." Mattie was known for her fried chicken, biscuits, candied yams, cornbread, and chicken pie. She was also known for her matzo ball soup, brisket, kreplach, matzo brei, and chopped liver. So, the question becomes: Why did my mother transform this Jewish delicacy into a French delicacy? Was she trying to hide her Jewishness? Or was she simply making the dish palatable to Gentiles? The second explanation makes more sense with what I know about my mother.

Everyone in Rock Hill understood that we were Jewish. It was no secret. Mother invited my class, my sister's class, my brother's class, *and* my sister's Girl Scout troop to our home to light Hanukkah candles with us. When my sister and I were confirmed,

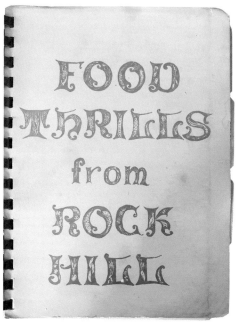

Food Thrills from Rock Hill cover, Rock Hill, SC, 1964.
COURTESY JUDY GOLDMAN.

Mother invited everyone we knew to the ceremony, because she wanted our friends and neighbors, teachers and classmates, shopkeepers on Main Street, even the saleswomen and customers in my father's stores to learn about Jewish rituals. Our house was so decorated for Christmas, it was on the Rock Hill Tour of Homes.

The reasoning behind what we would do and would not do was ironclad. And emotional. Because Mother's father had gambled, and because her childhood had been so unstable, she decided early in her marriage that our family would live in one town and develop roots in that town. Developing roots meant being a part of the community. Being a part of the community meant celebrating our own religious holidays and everyone else's. Our Hanukkah candles flickered in the shade of a very tall Christmas tree, silvery with tinsel icicles, heavy with satin balls. We poured a glass of wine for Elijah on Passover, and we dyed eggs and bought pink and lavender baby chicks on Easter. The student rabbis who rode the train from the Jewish Theological Seminary in New York City to lead High Holy Days services for our temple always stayed with us. I played basketball for the youth team at the Episcopal Church of Our Saviour. I knew the words to both "Amazing Grace" and "Adon Olam."

I can picture Mother at her desk in the den, Mattie standing over her and explaining how to make chopped liver so that Mother could send in the recipe for the church cookbook, Mother's handwriting so straight-up-and-down—this many years later, I can still duplicate it exactly. Mother was probably thinking, *I believe I'll call it Chicken Liver Pâté. Yes, people will be more likely to try it. And let's just not use the word "schmaltz."*

CHICKEN LIVER PÂTÉ

PEGGY KURTZ (MRS. B. F.)

1 pound chicken liver
1 medium onion, minced
4 hard-boiled eggs
Rendered chicken fat

Sauté the chicken liver and onion. Grind with the eggs and mix with chicken fat. Salt and pepper to taste. May be used for sandwiches or for a salad.

MAKES APPROXIMATELY 12 SERVINGS, AS AN APPETIZER

MY JEWISH CONNECTIONS

JUDGE CASEY MANNING

———

L. Casey Manning Sr. served as the Fifth District circuit judge from 1994 until his retirement in 2022 and was the first African American to play basketball for the University of South Carolina. He has been called "Voice of the Gamecocks," with his radio program broadcast during every University of South Carolina basketball game. Judge Manning is in The South Carolina Hall of Fame. This essay is adapted from Judge Manning's transcripts of his Jewish connections and food stories growing up in Dillon.

———

I WAS BORN IN DILLON COUNTY on December 7, 1950. My father was Paul Manning Sr.; my mother was Harnetha Manning. They got married on May 6, 1939. My mother was Pentecostal Holiness, and my father was United Methodist. They had seven children. Six of us have survived, and the six are Paul Manning Jr., my oldest brother; Glenn; Joe Melvin; Linda; me; and my youngest sister, Sandra. I have three kids, Casey, Charlotte, and Morgan. Casey Jr.'s wife is Jewish, and their sons, Ajax and Felix, are Jewish. They are my "kugels and collards."

My mother was a great cook. My father was probably a better cook. Both of them, but my mother especially, made sure that all her children could cook. So, I've been cooking since I was in high school. Before I was a teenager, I knew how to cook. I remember asking, "Mother, why do you want us to learn how to cook?" I said, "I'll get married one day." She replied, "Well, son,

Manning family on the porch of the family home, Latta, SC, ca. 1982.
COURTESY MANNING FAMILY.

your wife may not know how to cook, so it's best to learn." And so, all the children, all six of us, were required to learn how to cook before we finished high school and left home. My mother prayed all the time. She always prayed for herself, for her children, for the neighbors, for everybody. People always say grace before you eat, to bless the food, and I learned to bless food a long time ago from my mother.

My first really close experience with Jewish food was when I went to Monticello, New York, to attend Kutschers' Sports Academy and Camps. I was a junior in high school. Kutschers' was an established resort in the Catskills—the "Borscht Belt" or the "Jewish Alps," as it's called—and I had my first expe-

Casey Manning, Coach Frank McGuire, Alan Schafer, unidentified tennis player, 1970s.
COURTESY CASEY MANNING.

rience with lox and bagels, not mixing meat and milk, and all the other Jewish delicacies, as well as what was permissible—and not permissible—to eat.

Dillon, where I grew up, had a strong Jewish presence. J. B. Bernanke, who opened a drugstore in 1947, was the father of Mort and Phil Bernanke and the grandfather of Ben Bernanke, who later became head of the Federal Reserve. The Bernankes were my landlords when I came back home in 1979 to practice law after attending the University of South Carolina Law School. Then there was Alan Schafer, who owned South of the Border. His brother, Joe Schafer, was the father of Judge Diane Schafer Goodstein. I got to know Alan Schafer very well, and he became a dear friend. Coincidentally, he was good friends with Coach Frank McGuire, my basketball coach at the University of South Carolina. Every year, the team's first trip was to South of the Border. I spent several summers working as a waiter at South of the Border's Sombrero Room. I watched people cook and got tips on how to do things.

My mother was a great cook. She really was. I learned as a little kid by watching her. I learned by watching her peel and chop vegetables, how long she let them simmer on the stove, and when to add salt and pepper, so, it's not as if you have a recipe that you absolutely go by. If I make a gumbo, I always put in shrimp, okra, and hot sausage. I don't always use turkey. I use chicken. I've made rabbit gumbo and quail gumbo. You want to boil the bones, throw them away, and drain it. Add anything you want to your onions, celery, bay leaves, salt and pepper, and a little Cajun seasoning.

We had a garden every year, and we grew a little bit of everything. Anything you can imagine that people ate down south, we pretty much grew. There were always string beans, butter beans, peas, okra, corn, squash, and mustard greens. We would pick them fresh out of the garden. My favorite greens are mustard and turnip greens. I learned how to cook all these things before I graduated from high school. I did a lot of cooking—breakfast, lunch, and dinner—and I still do. It's in my DNA.

I love to fish. I grew up fishing with my father and my brother. We knew every little hole along the Little Pee Dee River in Little Rock, where my father was born and raised, Harllees Bridge Road. We knew where all the catfish and the red breasts hung out. I can remember one morning I got up, and I was at Lake Murray before the sun came over the pine trees in the east. I caught twenty-two stripers in a row—*twenty-two in a row*. I had a cooler full of stripers that I gave my parents that day. They ate for two or three months. But you talk about fishing. I cooked the fish that I caught. I baked them, and I fried them. I learned how to make a catfish stew. I remember, one day my father and I caught fifteen two-and-a-half-pound catfish. My Aunt Helen was down visiting, and she took about seven or eight of them and cooked them slowly in a casserole with onions and seasoning and everything. It was the best catfish stew I ever ate in my life—and I can really cook catfish stew. We always made a white stew rather than a red stew. The secret of cooking a catfish stew is the heads and the bones: That's where you get the flavor.

I've been a trial judge since 1994 and a Circuit Court judge for over a quarter of a century. I look forward to the day when I ride off into the sunset and don't have litigants or lawyers in front of me anymore. Just a pole and a line fishing somewhere. I'm going to fish here; I'm going to fish there. I'm going to fish the ocean. I'm going to fish the rivers. I'm going to fish the ponds. I'm going to fish on the East Coast and West Coast and down in the Bahamas. That's what I plan to do if I'm fortunate enough—knock on wood—to live so long.

HOT MILK CAKE

Linda Manning shares her mother's recipe.

4 eggs
2 cups sugar
2 cups sifted cake flour
2 teaspoons baking powder
Pinch of salt
1 cup milk
1 stick butter
1 teaspoon vanilla extract
1 teaspoon almonds

Beat the eggs until thick and add the sugar gradually. In another bowl, mix together the cake flour, baking powder, and salt. Melt the stick of butter (do not boil) and mix with 1 cup milk. Add to the egg mixture and add the vanilla and almonds. Then add together with the flour mixture. Mix well. Bake at 350°F at 25 to 30 minutes.

CHICKEN DRESSING

This is my mom's dressing; she would use as many homegrown ingredients as possible, including the chicken, onions, and sage. Some people like a wet dressing, and some like a dry crispy dressing. I would say, go by taste.

4 boiled chicken backs

2 onions, chopped

2 stalks celery, chopped

1 pound sausage, diced

¼ pound cooked chicken
  gizzards, chopped

Cooked cornbread from a box
  mix or homemade

Black pepper

Fresh sage

In a deep saucepan, cover the chicken backs with water. Add the chopped onions and celery and bring to a boil; then turn the heat down. Add the diced sausage and let simmer for about 30 minutes.

Drain the liquid (saving some if you think the dressing is too dry). Pick the chicken off the bones. Mash the cornbread in with the chicken, vegetables, sausage, and cooked chopped gizzards in Pyrex dish. Add black pepper and sage. Bake at 350°F for 35 to 40 minutes or until the top is nicely browned.

A JEWISH MERCHANT'S CHRISTMAS IN SUMMERTON

RACHEL GORDIN BARNETT

———

*Jewish merchants were prevalent in small towns across South
Carolina in the late nineteenth and twentieth centuries.
Rachel remembers the biggest selling season of the year
mixed with love of family and food.*

———

**Gordin holiday preparation,
Summerton, SC, 1970s.**
COURTESY RACHEL BARNETT.

WHEN I WAS A KID GROWING UP in a small, rural town in South Carolina, Christmas
was a big deal. Not so much in a religious sense to my family, since we are Jewish, but
we were merchants, so it was an important holiday because so much of the store's sales
occurred at Christmas time.

My family operated three stores in the tiny town of Summerton. In the early 1900s,
my grandfather, Morris, and his brothers made a home there for their families. My
dad took over Gordin's Dry Goods when his father passed away and, as he was a phar-
macist, he also operated Rowe-Tomlinson Drugs. My maternal grandmother sold her

Army-Navy store on upper King Street in Charleston and moved to Summerton in the 1960s to be near her only child, my mother. Gran was a businesswoman, and she immediately went into business opening a "better" ladies' store. She and my mother went to Charlotte, North Carolina, for the apparel market to keep Summerton women in the best of fashion. With three stores in the family, my three siblings and I didn't lack for work. Once we were old enough, we worked in the various stores on Saturdays and holiday vacations.

Everyone worked long hours and was happy when we were able to close at nine o'clock at night on Christmas Eve. Mrs. Ruth Furse, the manager of Gordin's, was a wonderful cook and would drop off boxes of homemade chocolate fudge, divinity candy, fruitcake, salted pecans, and chow chow for us. Her delicacies made for a special and sweet holiday. On Christmas Day, our extended family from around the state gathered at my parents' home for a holiday meal that Mama and Ethel Glover, who worked for our family, prepared. As everyone was in the schmatta (clothing) business, this was a day to relax and enjoy what they hoped had been a good holiday season. Ethel arrived early in the morning so she could open her presents. There was always a new church dress, hat, and items for her home. I loved selecting a special dress and hat combo for her from Gordin's.

The menu was the same each year, a combination of Jewish and southern dishes. Brisket, turkey, kugel, squash casserole, rice, sweet potatoes, succotash, and the requisite Jell-O mold graced the dining room table. There was a kids table. I never made it to the grownups' table. Once the four of us grew up and left home, we returned each year for Mama's and Ethel's holiday dinner. In 1989, I took over preparing the holiday meal. Each year, I prepare the same menu, and the next generation is now at the table as we continue this tradition.

ETHEL GLOVER'S SQUASH CASSEROLE

5 pounds yellow squash
3 beaten eggs
½ cup half and half
2 cups grated cheese
Salt and pepper to taste

Slice the squash and place in a pot of water. Cover and cook until tender. Drain the squash and mash to get the water out.

Beat the eggs with the half and half and pour into the squash. Add the cheese, and salt and pepper to taste. Mix well.

Spoon into a 9 × 13-inch baking dish and bake at 350°F until bubbly and set.

MAKES UP TO 12 SERVINGS

FLORIDA MAE BOYD,
THE BEST JEWISH CHEF IN COLUMBIA

JANIS DICKMAN, JACQUELYN DICKMAN, AND SHERYL DICKMAN

———

The three Dickman sisters share their memorable impressions
of Florida Boyd's food legacy.

———

**Florida Mae Boyd and the
Dickman family, Columbia,
SC, 1990s.**
COURTESY
JACQUELYN DICKMAN.

FLORIDA MAE BOYD WAS AN AMAZING woman with great talent, intelligence, heart, faith, and dignity. She was a much-admired member of the Columbia Jewish community, known as the go-to cook and caterer for Jewish holiday dinners and events. Her kugels—and her collards—were exceptional.

Florida came to work for our family in 1956, when she was twenty-four years old. She became part of our family and enriched each of us emotionally and spiritually. Our mother, Selma Dickman, and Florida developed a dear friendship which lasted until our mother's death at age one hundred! Florida and her two daughters attended our family celebrations, and we shared in theirs. Her strong, soulful voice enriched family bar and bat mitzvahs, wedding and birthday celebrations, and especially our mother's ninetieth and one hundredth birthday festivities. Florida sang a beautiful rendition of the Twenty-Third Psalm at our mother's funeral.

Florida was an amazing cook, treating our family to the most delicious southern specialties—the world's best fried chicken, peach pie, banana pudding, okra and tomatoes, and mac and cheese. She would bring Dad containers of the catfish stew she made for her family, which was far too spicy for the rest of us and definitely not kosher.

Our parents introduced Florida to Ashkenazi Jewish cuisine. Many think that it was our mother who taught Florida to cook "Jewish foods," but it was actually our father, Max Dickman, a wonderful cook and volunteer caterer in the Jewish community (see chapter 1). For our family holidays and parties, Mom did the planning and worrying, while Dad and Florida did the cooking. Florida's specialties included the best kugel, creamy with a crispy Kellogg's Corn Flake topping; huge, fluffy matzo balls; juicy, perfectly sliced brisket; and her famous chopped liver.

Born and raised in Prosperity, South Carolina, Florida had a rich family life and was devoted to her church. With her husband, L. B. Boyd, she raised her two daughters, Bertha Miller and Mary Irby, and her sister's three sons. She is survived by fourteen grandchildren, thirty-eight great grandchildren, eight great-great grandchildren, and sixty-one nieces and nephews. An elder of Chappell Memorial African Methodist Episcopal Church, Mother Boyd, as she was known, held many offices and received many honors. She and her husband were talented gospel singers and mainstays of several church choirs. Our family attended numerous church services and ceremonies when Florida was honored by her community. Janis recalls one dinner during Black History Month, when Florida was on the dais, dressed in a full-length, green sequined gown (although she favored red), being honored along with the president of the Columbia Urban League and a professor in the School of Social Work at the University of South Carolina. Florida attended countless funerals, including many for members of the Jewish community. Wearing her beautiful funeral outfits and fabulous hats, she was definitely the best dressed woman. Our mother used to say that attendance at Florida's funeral, when the day came, would fill the Township Auditorium. Indeed, "Mother Boyd's Homegoing" was amazing and well deserved, with eight hundred mourners and several choirs.

Florida eventually took over the catering at the Jewish Community Center. She catered Yom Kippur break-the-fasts, second night Passover seders, Bris and other Jewish family events, and onegs for bar mitzvahs at the temple.

Steve Savitz, longtime leader and past president of the Tree of Life Temple, stated, "Florida was known as the best Jewish chef in Columbia." In her later years, Florida sat on a stool in the temple kitchen, directing her staff. Although Florida learned to cook

Jewish specialties from our dad, telling people what to do and how to do it was a skill she learned from our mother. Florida's daughter, Mary Irby, reminisced about her mother preparing Jewish specialties for the Lourie, Kline, Baker, and Kligman families, among others. We remember Florida's phone calls from Jewish women asking how to make traditional dishes her special way. We're not sure that they ever got a precise recipe. We never did. But we do have many wonderful memories and gratitude for this remarkable woman and her deeply important role in our family and community.

SOUTH CAROLINA JEWISH FOODWAYS 3

THE STRONG WILL OF A JEWISH IMMIGRANT WOMAN 83
Olivia Brown

PIGEONS AND PEACHES 85
Henry Barnett, as told to Rachel Gordin Barnett

Barnett's Baked Stuffed Squab
Peach Cobbler

GROUCHO MILLER'S RUSSIAN BLINTZES 89
Bruce Miller

Groucho's Blintzes

**PUMPERNICKEL SPECIALIST SAM ZUSMAN AND
HIS COLUMBIA BAKERY** 92
Katharine Allen and Ronald Port

HYMAN'S SEAFOOD STORY 95
Eli Hyman and Aaron Hyman, as told to Lyssa Kligman Harvey

Hyman's Fried Green Tomatoes
Hyman's Seafood Salmon and Grits

JACK KAHN, THE PICKLE MAN 99
Sharon Kahn

Deli Style Pickles in a Day

HAROLD'S CABIN 102
John Schumacher, as told to Lyssa Kligman Harvey

Savoure Cheese

LASH'S KOSHER MEAT MARKET 104
Barry Lash, Ira Lash, and Lori Lash Samuels, as told to Lyssa Kligman Harvey

Lizzie's Meatloaf

"EAT SOMETHING—YOU'LL FEEL BETTER!" 107
Teri Bernstein Lash and Sandy Bernstein D'Antonio

Brisket Nita

THE SOUTH CAROLINA STATE FAIR JEWISH FOOD BOOTH 111
Jerry Emanuel and Jacqueline Dickman

Flanken and Barley Soup

JEWISH FOOD FUNDRAISERS 115
Debbie Bogatin Cohn, Shelley Spivak Kriegshaber,
and Joe Wachter

Aunt Sophie's Stuffed Cabbage
Chopped Herring Salad
Butterflies

Each summer, one of the favorite smells at the Barnett family's Edisto Island home is that of Old Bay seasoning added to steaming baskets full of crabs recently pulled from the deepwater creek. Little did we know that a Jewish immigrant, Gustav Brunn, was responsible for our favorite summer aroma of blend of herbs and spices. Brunner immigrated to Baltimore in the 1930s to escape the Nazis.

Like Brunn's ubiquitous Old Bay seasoning, so much of what we buy, cook, and order comes from Jewish entrepreneurs, grocers, restaurateurs, and bakers. South Carolinians who have built strong food-based businesses are the backdrop for the stories that follow. Even as *Kugels & Collards* largely examines Jewish cooking through a South Carolina lens, it also reveals the Jewish influence on southern food sourcing and foodways.

Early immigrants opened neighborhood grocery stores, as noted in this chapter, in Olivia Brown's story, "The Strong Will of a Jewish Immigrant Woman." Through their delis, Jewish proprietors brought Old World Jewish tastes, smells, and foods to South Carolina. Groucho's in Columbia and Harold's Cabin in Charleston provided specialty foods. What would Jewish life-cycle events be without a Jewish caterer? Sandy Bernstein D'Antonio and her sister, Teri Bernstein Lash, remember their family's kosher catering business: "At one time, they were the only caterers in Charleston who knew how to cater a kosher affair." Operating from their family's former dry goods building on Meeting Street in downtown Charleston, Eli and Aaron Hyman have, for thirty-five years, plied customers from around the country with South Carolina staples, such as fried shrimp and fried green tomatoes.

Jewish bakers, too, brought their talents to South Carolina. Skilled Russian baker Sam Zusman arrived in Columbia in 1921 at the behest of Barnett Berry, proprietor of B. Berry's mercantile store on Assembly Street. As Columbia did not have a Jewish baker of its own, Berry felt that Zusman would be perfect for the job.

From these stories, we have come to realize how integrated our Jewish forebears, their businesses, and the items they supplied have been and continue to be in our contemporary South Carolina communities, urban and rural.

Previous page: Wendell Levi and Patty Levi Barnett, Sumter, SC, 2000.
PHOTOGRAPH © BILL ARON, COURTESY JEWISH HERITAGE COLLECTION, SPECIAL COLLECTIONS, COLLEGE OF CHARLESTON LIBRARIES.

THE STRONG WILL OF A JEWISH IMMIGRANT WOMAN

OLIVIA BROWN

———

According to her granddaughter, Lorraine Lourie Moses, "'Miz' Clara was no-nonsense, hard-working, witty, smart, dedicated, stubborn, selfless, and altogether wonderful." Laurie Baker Walden contributed a family history that is the basis for this story.

———

IN 1912, CLARA KLIGERMAN and her younger sister, Esther, boarded a ship to New York City; the girls—seventeen and twelve years old, respectively—set sail for America, leaving behind their parents and nine other siblings in Nikolaev, Ukraine. While living with an aunt and uncle in New York, Clara met Frank Baker. Frank lived with his father and brother in Mount Pleasant, where he convinced Clara and Esther to visit. By 1917, Clara and Frank married and moved to Estill. It was after the Bakers relocated to Columbia that they opened a grocery store at 931 Park Street in 1926, in the heart of the city's African American community, a neighborhood known as Ward One.

Once they settled in Columbia, the Bakers had to decide the extent to which they would embrace their Jewish culture and customs. Clara's Jewishness did not always align with her role as a business owner and operator in Columbia. The Bakers did not live or work near a synagogue or Jewish neighborhood. In fact, Clara and Frank Baker were one of very few non-Black families on their block. By 1967, when Clara Baker sold the store to Oscar Shealy, a long-time employee, Baker's Grocery had become a respected and valued part of its surrounding community.

Clara Kligerman Baker, Columbia, SC, n.d.
COURTESY LARRAINE LOURIE MOSES
AND LAURIE BAKER WALDEN.

**Painting of Baker's Grocery by
Edmund Yaghjian, ca. 1977.**
HISTORIC COLUMBIA,
HCF2016.9.1.

Although Baker's Grocery was listed under Frank Baker's ownership, Clara truly ran the business on a daily basis. Her steadfast dedication to the store is remembered most by family and friends. John Bell, a long-time customer and close family friend, described Clara as "one of the hardest working women you've ever seen in your life," working twelve- to fifteen-hour days at the grocery. She opened the store early and closed it late to best serve the needs of her customers.

The relationships Clara built with her clientele made her a well-known figure in Ward One. Although she was a white, Jewish woman serving an almost exclusively African American clientele, through forty-one years of reliable service, relationship building, and the generous lending of credit to those in need, she became a protected and respected member of her community. In a quick look around Baker's Grocery, a customer might see a section of fresh produce with onions, collards, and turnip greens; milk and butter; eggs bought from an elderly woman in the neighborhood; and dry goods such as tobacco, first-aid items, clothing goods, and a meat counter. Baker's advertised a slew of non-kosher meats, including ham hocks, pig ears, and pickled pigs' feet. Despite the store's treyfe (non-kosher) goods, the Baker family was still very familiar with Old World Jewish food traditions, and Clara often made borscht, strudel, and homemade dill pickles at home for her family.

PIGEONS AND PEACHES

HENRY BARNETT, AS TOLD TO RACHEL GORDIN BARNETT

———

Barnett's Peaches and the Palmetto Pigeon Plant were forerunners of the farm-to-table movement. Barnett's Peaches stopped operations in the mid-1990s. The Palmetto Pigeon Plant is still in operation from its original location on Broad Street in Sumter.

———

Henry "Bubba" Barnett; Mr. Smith, manager of Barnett's Peaches; Mr. Bowen, SC Department of Agriculture, Dalzell, SC, n.d.
COURTESY SUMTER COUNTY MUSEUM.

TODAY, SUMTER IS A MIDSIZED CITY in the Midlands of South Carolina, but its history reveals that it was also home to some of the Palmetto State's earliest Jewish families. Sephardic family members became merchants and professionals after making their way inland from Charleston between 1815 and 1820. Later, during the mid-1800s Jewish immigrants arrived from Germany and Prussia. Among them were members of the Levi and Barnett families. Starting out as merchants and farmers in rural Clarendon, Sumter, and Lee counties, they eventually made their way to the town of Sumter to open stores and continue farming. Later generations became professionals, but agriculture remained at the heart of the family business.

In 1923, Wendell M. Levi and Harold Moïse established the Palmetto Pigeon Plant. During World War I, Levi was in charge of the pigeon section of the US Army Signal Corps for the South Eastern Division, and his knowledge would prove beneficial. Located on Broad Street in Sumter, the facility was the largest producer of squab in the United States. President Franklin Delano Roosevelt served squab from the Palmetto Pigeon Plant to King George VI on his 1939 visit to Washington, DC. Another royal, King Charles III (then-Prince Charles), enjoyed squab from the Palmetto Pigeon Plant so much that he ordered more to be shipped to him while he was visiting Florida.

Upon Levi's passing, his daughter, Patty Levi Barnett, joined the board of directors and later took over management of this unique and important family business. Patty immediately tackled marketing. She contacted *Southern Living* and other magazines to familiarize epicureans with the delicacy of squabs. She prepared a squab dinner, and her recipe was printed in the magazine and its 1982 *Annual Recipes*. Meticulous, honest, and driven, Patty used her smarts to put the Palmetto Pigeon Plant on a profitable path. She remained at the helm for several years. An article from January 17, 1982 in *The State* described Patty's delicious lunch of "tomato aspic with artichoke hearts and black olives, baked squab with wild rice stuffing, a peach and grape salad, sweet potato casserole, biscuits and a light, delicate chocolate mousse for dessert." The article also noted that Barnett's husband, Henry, was a peach grower.

Henry D. Barnett—"Bubba," the son of H. D. Barnett Sr.—came to farming naturally. His grandfather, B. J. Barnett, arrived in the country in the mid-1800s, opened a rural store, bought acreage, and began farming. After his duty during World War II, Bubba returned to Sumter to take over the family farms. He and Patty Levi were married in 1950 and settled in the family home on Warren Street. Bubba's love for farming and interest in innovative crops led him to peach farming. He planted his first peach tree the year his oldest son was born. Barnett explained that a horticulturist urged him to experiment with peach crops because the underground water levels and contour of his land made it conducive to peach farming. The year was 1956. Barnett's Peaches grew to become one of the largest peach orchards in the state.

BARNETT'S BAKED STUFFED SQUAB

Patty's recipe for baked stuffed squab appeared in Southern Living *magazine and* The State *newspaper.*

1 (6-ounce) package long grain
  and wild rice
6 squabs
Salt and pepper
¼ teaspoon ground ginger
¼ cup sliced fresh mushrooms
¼ cup chopped parsley
¼ cup chopped celery
¼ cup butter
1 tablespoon soy sauce
2 teaspoons Worcestershire
  sauce
½ cup white wine

Preheat oven to 450°F.

Cook the rice according to directions. Set aside.

Remove the giblets from the squabs, and reserve them for another use. Rinse the squabs with cold water and pat dry. Season with salt, pepper, and ground ginger. Sauté the mushrooms, parsley, and celery in butter until soft. Mix in the rice. Stuff the squabs with the rice mixture; sprinkle with soy sauce and Worcestershire sauce.

Place the squabs in a 4½ quart baking dish. Add ½ inch water. Cover and bake at 450°F for 45 minutes. Remove the cover and reduce heat to 350°F. Add white wine and bake an additional 30 minutes.

MAKES 6 SERVINGS

PEACH COBBLER

A tried-and-true favorite South Carolina cobbler recipe.

1 stick butter (½ cup)
1 cup flour
2 cups sugar
1 tablespoon baking powder
1 cup milk
4 cups peaches, peeled and
  sliced

Melt the butter in a 9 × 13-inch baking dish. Mix together the flour, 1 cup sugar, the baking powder, and the milk. Pour the batter over the melted butter. Do not mix.

Add peaches. Do not mix. Sprinkle the remaining cup of sugar over the peaches. Bake at 350°F until the crust forms and browns.

Serve warm or cool.

MAKES 8 TO 12 SERVINGS

GROUCHO MILLER'S RUSSIAN BLINTZES

BRUCE MILLER

———

*Groucho's Deli, founded by Harold "Groucho" Miller in 1940
as Miller's Deli, is still operating today.*

———

Miller's Delicatessen, forerunner of Groucho's Deli, Columbia, SC, ca. 1942.
COURTESY BRUCE MILLER.

HAROLD "GROUCHO" MILLER, my grandfather and founder of Groucho's Deli, was the son of Russian immigrants who arrived in America in 1899. The history of Groucho's name is a story unto itself and one that can only be told as follows.

Harold "Groucho" Miller came to Columbia in 1940 with a handful of original recipes for potato salad, coleslaw, and various salad and sandwich dressings, most of which were thought up during his childhood in a Philadelphia orphanage. Groucho's son, Ivan Miller, recollected in an interview with *The Columbia Record* in 1986: "When Pop first opened this store, Columbia was a small town, and everything had a label. Here he [Harold Miller]

Groucho Miller, Groucho's Deli, Columbia, SC, 1940s.
COURTESY BRUCE MILLER.

was this really crazy kind of guy. Always, joking. Always had a big cigar. A mustache. He looked like Groucho Marx, he talked like Groucho Marx, and to Columbia, he was Groucho Marx. So that is how the name came about."

Throughout the generations, Groucho's Deli has used only the highest quality products and ingredients, which has, in turn, led to Groucho's legendary status. One recipe that never made it to Groucho's Deli menu was learned by Groucho Miller during a stint as a vaudeville emcee in Philadelphia in the 1920s. He befriended a Russian Jewish comedian who taught him one of his favorite recipes—blintzes—a time-consuming and labor-intensive dish. They were available for sale at Miller's Deli on opening day in 1940. A year later, the name was changed to Groucho's Deli.

GROUCHO'S BLINTZES

Pancake ingredients

1¼ cups milk

⅔ cup water

1 cup flour

1 egg

½ teaspoon salt

½ tablespoon oil, plus more for greasing the pan

Filling

16 ounces cottage cheese

8 ounces cream cheese

½ cup sugar

Zest of 1½ lemons

3 egg yolks

A few drops vanilla extract (optional)

¾ cup currants or raisins soaked in a little rum for ½ hour (optional)

2–3 tablespoons melted unsalted butter

Topping

Cinnamon and confectioners' sugar to sprinkle

Sour cream

To make the pancakes: Add the milk and water to the flour gradually, beating vigorously. Add the egg, salt, and oil. Beat the batter until smooth. Leave the batter to rest for 1 to 2 hours.

Heat a nonstick frying pan with a bottom not wider than 8 inches, and grease very lightly with oil. Pour about half a ladleful of batter into the frying pan, and move the pan around so the entire surface is covered with batter. The batter and the resulting pancake should be thin. As soon as the pancake is slightly browned and detached, turn it over with a spatula and cook a moment only on the other side. Continue until all the batter is used, and put the pancakes in a pile.

To make the filling: Blend the cottage cheese and cream cheese with sugar, lemon zest, egg yolks, and vanilla in a food processor. Stir in the raisins, if you are using them.

Take each pancake, one at a time, and put two heaping tablespoons of filling on the bottom half. Fold the edge of the pancake over the filling, tuck in the sides carefully, and roll, making a slim blintz. Place the blintzes side by side in a greased oven dish. Dot with butter and bake at 375°F for 20 minutes.

Serve hot, dusted with confectioners' sugar and cinnamon, and pass the sour cream for people to help themselves.

MAKES 12 BLINTZES

PUMPERNICKEL SPECIALIST SAM ZUSMAN AND HIS COLUMBIA BAKERY

KATHARINE ALLEN AND RONALD PORT

———

According to Sam Zusman's grandson, Ron Port, the bakery's famous recipes were kept in a little notebook behind the counter that was lost when the bakery burned in 1963.

———

Born in White Russia [Belarus], he learned his trade while serving in the British merchant marine[s] and by working as a baker's assistant in Austria, Hungary, and Germany. As a result of his skill and wide experience, his bread and rolls have a highly prized continental flavor which gourmets associate with the best of European cooking.

—"Pumpernickel Specialist," *The State,* October 3, 1954

RUSSIAN NATIVE SAM ZUSMAN arrived in Columbia in 1921 at the behest of merchant Barnett Berry, proprietor of B. Berry's on Assembly Street. According to Zusman's daughter, Jane Zusman Eneman, Berry and Zusman met in Birmingham, Alabama, where Zusman was managing a local bakery. At the time, Columbia did not have a Jewish baker, and Berry knew that Zusman was perfect for the job. A few months later, Zusman arrived in town with his new wife, Pauline.

He opened his new business, The Columbia Bakery, at 1914½ Main Street and established himself as the only baker with a brick oven. Advertisements in the 1920s and 1930s touted his specialties of rye and pumpernickel breads sold at the Main Street storefront and at the Assembly Street market. By 1936, the bakery's goods were also available at Rivkin's Delicatessen and at 1330 Assembly Street, where Zusman briefly opened a second location.

Zusman's shipped breads across the Southeast and supplied multiple Columbia-area hospitals. For decades, The Columbia Bakery was the most popular among Jewish

George Port, son Ron Port, and
employees, Columbia Bakery,
Columbia, SC, 1957.

Columbia Bakery, bakers Odell Cody (left) and Andrew Green (right), Columbia, SC, n.d.

merchants on Main and Assembly Streets, and it also had loyal customers from the Greek, Syrian, and Italian communities. Downtown shoppers stopped at The Columbia Bakery to purchase their breads, rolls, cookies, and cakes, as well as to enjoy conversations enriched by the aroma of fresh baked goods.

Pauline and Sam Zusman had three children while living in Columbia: Ansel Zusman, Celia Zusman Port, and Jane Zusman Eneman. Celia's husband, George Port, joined the business after their marriage and became owner after Sam Zusman's death in 1957. The business remained a family affair until 1963, when lightning struck a nearby electricity pole and the bakery was destroyed in the resulting fire. Ron Port, eldest son of George and Celia, shared his memories of that day: "We were having dinner at home before Dad went back to close up and received a call that the bakery was on fire. Dad immediately left, and we saw the fire on the local news that night. When Dad got back home much later that night, he told us what had happened." That was the end of The Columbia Bakery, but there are still people who remember Sam Zusman and his bakery, and memories don't end.

HYMAN'S SEAFOOD STORY

ELI HYMAN AND AARON HYMAN, AS TOLD TO LYSSA KLIGMAN HARVEY

———

In an interview with two favorite cousins, Aaron and Eli Hyman,
to find out the story of their well-known
restaurant in Charleston.

———

**Hyman's Seafood,
Charleston, SC,
2000s.**

MY FIRST COUSINS, Aaron and Eli Hyman, are blessed with a good business brain or *kuph*; a father, Maier Hyman, who believed in supporting his children's dreams; a loving, generous mother, Phyllis Firetag Hyman; and an ideal location for their famous Charleston seafood restaurant, Hyman's Seafood. The brothers established their business in the same Meeting Street building in which their great-grandfather, Wolf Maier Karesh, a Jewish immigrant from Eastern Europe, founded Southern Wholesale in 1890. The story of the brothers' restaurant success began nearly a century later, in 1987, when Aaron opened Aaron's Deli and Eli debuted Hyman's Seafood in the family's long-held Meeting Street property.

When Aaron returned home from living in Israel, he wanted to open a restaurant. With plenty of experience working in southern kitchens from Camp Maccabee to the Medical University of South Carolina, he opened a deli in North Charleston and then moved the business to his father's building in 1986. Aaron's Deli quickly became a destination for New York deli-style foods—pastrami, salami, corned beef, tongue with homemade potato salad, and coleslaw, along with southern dishes. The restaurant originally served breakfast, too—eggs, hash browns, bacon, and grits. Several dishes were named after relatives, such as the "Melton Kligman Omelet," named for my father who loved to put peppers, onions, and hot sauce in his eggs. Customers flocked to Hyman's Seafood for its fried green tomatoes, hush puppies, boiled peanuts, crab cakes, fried seafood platters, crispy fried flounder, crab cakes, and Carolina Delight, their version of shrimp over grits. Although not a kosher restaurant, Hyman's provides for its observant patrons by serving salmon over grits.

As young children, Eli and Aaron remember catching blue crabs on Sullivan's Island with their grandfather, Joe Firetag. Aaron recalls, "We were not allowed to bring the crabs in the beach house, which had a kosher kitchen, but we steamed them and ate them outside on newspaper out of respect for our great grandmother." Their memory mirrors that of other southern Jews who negotiated the conflict between Jewish dietary laws and regional cuisine.

Family recipes, including some from Sarah Jane Wiley, filled the menu at Hyman's Seafood. Her fried chicken, collards, and okra gumbo, like her strong African American Christian values, shaped the brothers' lives as small children. Eli says, "Sarah taught me how to treat all people, and to this day, I practice what I learned from her in the restaurant and in life." Now the sole owner of the establishments, Eli continues to run his business with a basis in his strong Jewish values and education. Chief among those values is sharing with others. After Hurricane Hugo in 1989, when much of Charleston was devastated and most businesses closed downtown, their kitchens provided three hundred to five hundred free meals a day to those in need. He often serves free lunches to the less fortunate, who need a decent meal. Eli believes, the more you give away, the more that will come back to you to help others. Although the food at Hyman's Seafood and Aaron's Deli is the star, the restaurants have been an opportunity for the Hymans to extend their love with others, show respect for all, and share their southern and Jewish hospitality, treating their guests like family. This is the formula for a success story. Eli says, "Our restaurant is a place where people gather, eat, laugh, share ideas, and make memories."

Fried green tomatoes.
PHOTOGRAPH BY BEN REITZ,
COURTESY HYMAN'S SEAFOOD.

HYMAN'S FRIED GREEN TOMATOES

4 cups milk

4 eggs

4 large green tomatoes

1 cup flour

½ cup cornmeal

1½ cup vegetable oil (add more
   if necessary)

Beat the milk and eggs together in a large bowl. Slice the tomatoes thick so they won't become soggy when fried. Mix the flour and cornmeal together, and drop the tomato slices into the mixture until they are covered. Dip breaded tomatoes into milk and egg mixture. Dip in breading again and let sit for 30 minutes. Pan fry until golden brown.

MAKES APPROXIMATELY 16 PIECES

HYMAN'S SEAFOOD SALMON AND GRITS

This dish is the first cousin to the popular shrimp and grits on the menu and was created for customers who do not eat shellfish. It has become very popular. Eli says that the trick to this dish is to cook "the grit out of the grits" and to cook low and slow, making sure that the grits do not burn.

4 fresh salmon filets
1 teaspoon kosher salt
Cajun seasoning (optional)
1 tablespoon olive oil

Grits
1 cup locally milled grits
2 teaspoons salt
2 cups of water or milk
2 tablespoons butter
1 beaten egg yolk
Any fine-grained breading or cornmeal and flour

White sauce
½ cup chicken broth
½ cup milk
½ cup heavy cream
1 stick of butter
2 teaspoons minced garlic
Salt and pepper
1½ cups grated Parmesan cheese
Paprika

To make the salmon: Sprinkle the salmon filets with kosher salt (and Cajun seasoning, if using), and drizzle the olive oil on to the filets. Broil or bake the filets in a conventional oven for 8–10 minutes. Be careful not to overcook the salmon.

To make the grits: Put 1 cup of grits into 2 cups salted boiling water until the water returns to a boil. Turn down to simmer, add butter, and cook slowly, stirring constantly and adding water so that it doesn't burn.

To make a grit cake: Prepare the grits and put the grits in a greased sheet pan overnight. Once it has hardened, you can cut out round cakes. Brush the beaten egg yolks over both sides of the grit cake. Dip into the breading. Fry the grit cake in a cast iron skillet.

To make the white sauce: Add the broth, milk, cream, and butter to a large saucepan. Simmer over low heat for 2 minutes. Whisk in the garlic, Cajun seasoning, salt, and pepper for 1 minute. Whisk in the parmesan cheese until melted.

Put the salmon over grits or grit cake. Pour the sauce over the salmon. Shake a little Cajun seasoning or paprika on top for color.

MAKES 4 SERVINGS

JACK KAHN, THE PICKLE MAN

SHARON KAHN

———

Jack Kahn was passionate about creating kosher-style dill pickles that met his high standards. It's no surprise that he became Charleston's renowned Pickle Man.

———

MY FATHER, JACK KAHN, was the ultimate foodie years before people spoke with a knowledge and appreciation of food. I sometimes thought of him as a "mad food scientist." He was passionate about food and was interested in appearance, texture, taste, and smell, and he would pore over his substantial collection of cookbooks during his spare time. As my sisters and I grew older, we started our own collection of cookbooks. Whenever he found one that he particularly liked, we each received a copy in the mail.

As children, we were often the lucky beneficiaries of his passion. I remember when he was focused on the proper way to enjoy whipping cream. One night, he used vanilla extract. Another night, he combined vanilla and almond extract, with or without confectioners' sugar. It went on and on. This was his modus operandi for all his food endeavors. My father was introduced to the business of food, through coffee and spices, at an early age. His father, Morris, owned Monogram Coffee and Tea Company on Prioleau Street in Charleston during the early 1920s, and a grocery store on Adgers Wharf that my grandmother ran. I have vivid memories of the pungent sting of pepper in my nose, which they ground and packed there—five hundred pounds of pepper in an hour.

My father drove a semi-truck to New York to pick up tons of black pepper. I remember seeing his truck parked on St. Philip Street, where we lived until shortly before my sixth birthday. He also brought back kosher and other specialty

South Windemere, Charleston, SC, n.d.
COURTESY SHARON KAHN.

foods that we didn't have in Charleston at that time, like barrels of kosher-style pickles. If you grew up in Charleston in the 1950s, '60s, and '70s, then you remember those barrels of garlicky pickles at Harold's Cabin on Wentworth Street. It was a symphony for the senses.

Being a food perfectionist, my father grew dissatisfied with both the quality and the burden of transporting barrels from New York and decided to make his own pickles. The "food scientist" got to work developing and perfecting the right formula and timing to make the ultimate pickle. Freshness and timing were critical. My father spent a great deal of time gathering the ingredients for his pickling cucumbers, which later arrived by truck from Mexico, Arizona, Florida, and Texas. If a truck arrived at midnight, my father was there to begin production. After discarding the unwaxed cucumbers that didn't meet his standards, the remainder were put in the walk-in icebox—which he built himself—and the cukes were then placed in fifty-gallon barrels. Next, he covered them with his specially developed formula of brine, vinegar, and spices. After a few days, he moved the pickles into buckets where fresh garlic, more spices, and brine were added. During the summer, he purchased his cucumbers locally grown for him on Johns Island, South Carolina. Then began the angst over rain: Too much rain or too little rain would negatively affect the crop. Our family's preoccupation with weather can be traced to worrying about the cucumbers. My father did not use preservatives, nor did he pasteurize the cucumbers. Once again, he was ahead of this time.

During the last few years of his involvement with pickle production, my father developed a business relationship with Alexis Van de Weil, and together they produced not only pickles but also pickled okra. These products were in restaurants all over town as well as in the Charleston Farmers Market in Marion Square. Earth Fare, at one time, also carried his pickles and advertised them on their marquee. They were a favorite at the Kahal Kadosh Beth Elohim synagogue's annual bazaar.

Although many around Charleston knew my father as the "Pickle Man," he engaged in several other food enterprises. Before the war, he was trained as a mechanical engineer and built his own smokehouse. He smoked lox and sturgeon, calling sturgeon "the Cadillac of fish." During the 1960s and 1970s, he made kosher-style pastrami, corned beef, salami, and hot dogs. He co-owned a deli named Patrick's on the north side of Liberty Street. During the mid-1970s, he owned a restaurant called Country Cove, just off the City Market. In addition to his meats, Country Cove served fried chicken. During the 1970s until the early 1980s, my mother, Marisha, ran Oliver's Sandwich Shop on King Street. During lunchtime, a line of hungry customers stretched from the front of the restaurant to the street. My sisters and I remember our clumsy attempts to help our mother when she needed to run an errand. All of these establishments served our fathers' crispy, fresh pickles as well as the meats from his smokehouse.

Anyone who had the good fortune to spend time with my father could see that he was a Renaissance man. He was interested in people, food, music, science, nature, and travel. He could fix anything, grill the best steaks, and build anything. He loved learning from books and people. Although he was an avid storyteller and never forgot a joke, he was an intent listener as well. He was always available to help a friend, and many restaurateurs sought him out for advice. I was very fortunate to spend quality time with my father during his later years. We enjoyed many hours in rocking chairs on the front porch of my house in Sullivan's Island. There was never a shortage of conversation. He was a proud, native Charlestonian, and together we marveled at her natural beauty. A bird, a particular food, or the sound of Ella Fitzgerald conjure memories of him.

DELI STYLE PICKLES IN A DAY

JACK KAHN

As said in his "How to Prepare Pickles in a Day" pamphlet, "Pickles prepared to please the pickle palate."

2 one-quarter glass containers with lids1 package of dry pickling mix
1 (3-ounce) cups of white vinegar
1 pound fresh pickling cucumbers
Cold tap water

To make the pickle brine: Empty one package of dry pickling mix into a one-quart container. Add 3 ounces of white vinegar and enough cold water to make one full quart of pickling solution. Mix well. This will make enough brine for 2 quarts of pickles.

To make the pickles: Wash and cut the cucumbers into chips or spears, and fill the empty quart container. Pour approximately half of the pickling solution over the cucumbers until fully covered. Use the remaining pickle solution to make a second quart of pickles, or you can refrigerate the rest of the pickle brine to use later.

Seal with lids and refrigerate at least overnight before eating.

2 days refrigerate: ½ sour pickle

5 days refrigerate: full sour pickle

Pickles must be refrigerated and will keep up to 3 months.

Tip: Try adding yellow squash, green tomatoes, or pearl onions to the pickle brine instead of cucumbers. Add fresh garlic to taste.

HAROLD'S CABIN

JOHN SCHUMACHER, AS TOLD TO LYSSA KLIGMAN HARVEY

———

*John Schumacher, one of the present owners of Harold's Cabin,
says, "Many Charlestonians remember the tastes and smells of Harold's
Cabin specialties like 'Savoure' Cheese, Jack Kahn's pickles, and other
gourmet delicacies. Harold Jacobs had his finger on the pulse of
what was new and upcoming in the food world."*

———

**Harold Jacobs,
Charleston, SC, n.d.**
COURTESY JEWISH
HERITAGE COLLECTION,
SPECIAL COLLECTIONS,
COLLEGE OF CHARLESTON
LIBRARIES.

HAROLD JACOBS, the only child of Sam and Mignonette Cohen Jacobs, was born in Charleston in 1913. Harold's grandfather, Isaac Jacobs, emigrated from Eastern Europe and settled in Charleston, running a dry goods store on King Street. Harold was raised by his parents in the St. Philip Street neighborhood. They later moved to Hampton Park Terrace. The first shop at 247 Congress Street looked like a small log cabin. In 1929, they began to sell snowballs, which soon became a popular summer icy treat. The shop offered three "snow" flavors—chocolate, vanilla, and strawberry—in sizes small for a penny, medium for a nickel, and large for a dime. The only person who ever purchased the large snowball, one of the store's earliest loyal customers, was Ernest "Fritz"

Hollings, who later served as a US senator from South Carolina and as the state's one hundred sixth governor. Here began Harold's lifelong career in specialty and gourmet foods in Charleston.

Shortly after the snowball shop opened in 1929, the Jacobs family transformed the business into a neighborhood grocery store called Harold's Cabin in the 1930s. As business grew, they added a section for gourmet and specialty foods. With the help of a forward-thinking banker, Harold was the first entrepreneur to own a freezer in Charleston.

Under the ownership and guidance of Harold and his wife, Lillian Breen Jacobs, Harold's Cabin thrived in Charleston, moving to a larger downtown space at 84 Wentworth Street in the 1950s. Here, the selection of gourmet foods grew, including three hundred different cheeses. The store became a stop on tours of historic Charleston. In 1964, Harold's Cabin was sold to Piggly Wiggly, but Harold and Lillian were invited to stay on and manage the "Harold's Cabin Gourmet Department." There, you could still buy pickles from a barrel and the delicious Savoure cheese made with cream cheese, garlic, and poppy seeds.

Throughout his life, Harold played an active role in Charleston's Jewish community. He died in 2009 at the age of ninety-six, leaving a legacy as a respected entrepreneur and pioneer in the Charleston gourmet foods market.

Yarrum Properties partners John Schumacher, Mike Veeck, and Bill Murray opened a reimagined corner store and café concept under the Harold's Cabin name, in homage to the original, at the corner of President and Congress streets in early 2016. *Food and Wine* magazine awarded them the "coziest restaurant in South Carolina" designation in 2018.

SAVOURE CHEESE

Savoure is a recipe created by Harold's Cabin.

3 (8-ounce) packages cream cheese

2 parts scallion cream cheese (instructions follow)

1 part relish cream cheese (instructions follow)

½ teaspoon poppy seeds

Lawry's Seasoning Salt to taste

To make the scallion cream cheese: Mix 2 (8-ounce) packages of cream cheese, softened, and ¼ cup finely chopped scallions. Mix well.

To make the relish cream cheese: Combine 1 (8-ounce) package of cream cheese and 2 tablespoons of sweet relish. Mix well.

Make each style of cream cheese, add the other ingredients in a mixer, and blend well.

MAKES 24 OUNCES OF DIP

LASH'S KOSHER MEAT MARKET

BARRY LASH, IRA LASH, AND LORI LASH SAMUELS, AS TOLD TO LYSSA KLIGMAN HARVEY

––––––––

Lash's Kosher Meat Market, owned and operated by Lila (Winter) and Alex Lash, was a historic and successful landmark in Charleston for more than forty-three years. They were the go-to business for kosher meats for much of the state for nearly forty-five years. Lash's Kosher Meat Market was one of the last in South Carolina.

––––––––

OWNING A KOSHER MEAT MARKET in Charleston was Lila and Al Lash's destiny. Al's paternal family had been butchers in Lithuania for four generations. In fact, Al was only five years old when his father, a New York butcher, first put a knife in his hand and told him to help him cut up a piece of lamb. Lila's grandfather, who was originally from Poland, came to Charleston and worked as a kosher butcher before moving to New York. Lila spent her childhood in both Charleston and New York. Their families' lives weaved in and out of the kosher butcher business for decades.

After Lila and Al married in 1947, they moved to Charleston and opened Lash's Kosher Meat Market in 1949 at 605 King Street in a district known as "Little Jerusalem" because of the many Jewish businesses in the neighborhood. They worked long hours to provide Charleston's Jewish community with the finest kosher meats and poultry. It wasn't an easy business. Tedious work was required to kosher meats properly and to adhere to strict regulations. Later, they moved the shop to 617 King and then to 1107 King Street. The business closed in 1993.

When the Lashes first came to Charleston, there was another kosher butcher shop called Baker's Kosher Market, which closed in 1958. An African American butcher from Baker's, Sam Coaxum, had learned to speak Yiddish and came to work for the Lashes for many years. Barry Lash, the eldest of the three Lash children, remembers his father and Sam talking in Yiddish at the store. Al worked side by side with Sam to kosher and cut all the meat.

The only day the store was closed was Saturday, the Jewish Sabbath. However, every Saturday night, Al and Lila would go to their store to make sure that the refrigeration

Lila Lash, Charleston, SC, 1992.

COURTESY JEWISH
HERITAGE COLLECTION,
SPECIAL COLLECTIONS,
COLLEGE OF CHARLESTON
LIBRARIES.

was working properly. In fact, one Saturday evening while checking the meat freezer, Lila accidentally locked in Al. Luckily, Lila had told him to always keep a coat in the freezer, "just in case." She let him out when she realized, while sitting in the car waiting for him, that she had not seen him for quite a while!

For many years, Al and his father-in-law, Louis Winter, went to Augusta, Georgia, every Tuesday at three o'clock in the morning to purchase meat. This often led to a stressful situation because there was a seventy-two-hour window to kasher the meats. The ritual included washing and salting the meat and fully draining the blood. If not done correctly within the time period, they had to send the meat back. People used to have salt boards at home to kasher their own meat and chickens before kosher butchers took over these tasks. Kosher butchers have to answer to a strict local Kashrut Council, a governing board from the local synagogues. The rabbis and mashgiachs (kosher inspectors) oversaw the standards of Kashrut and oversaw compliance.

At first, Lash's Kosher Meat Market slaughtered and koshered chickens bought from local farmers. Ira, Al's son, remembers going with his father out to the country to buy chickens from farmers rather than sourcing them from out of town.

Some of Lash's biggest customers were Syrian Jews from Myrtle Beach. They bought enough kosher meat to last from Passover to Rosh Hashanah. Barry Lash remembers going to Myrtle Beach to deliver large orders of meat packed in coolers in their family car. These large orders helped keep the business afloat during some tough times.

Lori Lash Samuels remembers, "Since Mama worked all the time, my grandmother, Fay Winter, and an African American domestic worker, Elizabeth Mack, affectionately known as "Lizzie," helped raise us and cooked the most wonderful kosher meals for our family. Lizzie even made my wedding cake." Ira reflects, "Shabbat dinners bring back cherished memories for us. Our parents worked very long hours, and we did not see much of them during the week. It was such a treat to be together and eating the most delicious food ever on Friday nights. Many times, we had guests over as well to enjoy our weekly feast with us."

It was a match made in kosher culinary heaven when Ira Lash married Teri Bernstein in 1976. Teri's mother, Anita Bernstein, was Charleston's premiere kosher caterer. Ira remembers the food from their wedding being "over the top." They had grilled steaks and lamb chops, and every kosher cut of meat you can think of—all made to perfection. In addition, the desserts were to "die for," and all the food was beautifully arrayed as far as the eye could see.

LIZZIE'S MEATLOAF

LAURIE LASH SAMUELS

Meatloaf and mashed potatoes were served every Monday at the Lash home. Lizzie would add a special design with ketchup on top of the meatloaf. Laurie continues to prepare this recipe.

1½ pounds highest quality
   ground beef
1 egg, beaten
¼ cup chopped onion
1 cup breadcrumbs
Salt and pepper to taste
1 teaspoon minced garlic
1 teaspoon paprika
¼ cup ketchup
2 tablespoons tomato paste

In a large bowl, combine the ground beef, egg, chopped onion, and breadcrumbs. Season with salt, pepper, minced garlic, and paprika. Add the ketchup and tomato paste. Mix together well.

Bake at 400°F for an hour in a greased loaf pan.

MAKES 6 TO 8 SERVINGS

"EAT SOMETHING— YOU'LL FEEL BETTER!"

TERI BERNSTEIN LASH AND SANDY BERNSTEIN D'ANTONIO

———

The Bernstein family name has been synonymous with food for as long as we can remember. We love to reminisce about how our parents and grandparents could find a way to make food the center of every occasion. If we complained to our mother about anything, her standard answer was, "Eat something and you'll feel better!"

———

THE LEGACY BEGAN with our grandmother, Mildred Bernstein. She was a wonderful cook. Growing up in Philadelphia, she would often help at her mother's restaurant. After she married our grandfather, Manning Bernstein, and they moved to Charleston, they volunteered weekly to cook meals for soldiers during World War II at The Daughters of Israel Hall, where the Jewish USO was located. What began as a volunteer effort eventually turned into three generations of family catering.

In 1944, Mildred was asked by her friend, Corrine Cohen, to help her prepare food for her son Harris's bar mitzvah. As her popularity grew, Mildred enlisted the help of her close friend, Minnie Weinberger, to join her in business. Mildred and Minnie went on to cater generations of bar mitzvah onegs, cocktail parties, and weddings. People fondly referred to them as "M & M."

Mildred and Minnie's claim to fame was the annual KKBE Temple Bazaar, where they sold their famous stuffed rolled cabbage, award-winning brisket, chicken dinners, homemade chopped liver, cabbage soup, and bean and barley soup. It was also where they earned a reputation for making the best pecan pie and cheesecake people had ever tasted. Eventually, our mother, Anita Bernstein, began to help them. It must be told that our mom was not always a great cook!

Mom never imagined that one day she would be a sought-after local Jewish caterer. Before getting married, she was extremely uncomfortable in the kitchen. Dad loved to share the story of the very first meal Mom prepared for him as a newlywed. "Anita

Mildred Bernstein (fourth from left) and Minnie Weinberger (third from left), Daughters of Israel Hall, Charleston, SC, 1940s.
COURTESY BERNSTEIN FAMILY.

thought she would make me homemade spaghetti. She bought pre-made sauce, poured it into a pot, then emptied the box of uncooked noodles directly into the sauce. As she proudly stirred her first pot of spaghetti, she could not understand why the noodles were so crunchy," he would say while laughing. Mom began helping Mildred and Minnie, and the rest is history.

Years later, we watched in awe as our mom entertained and cooked for famous celebrities—the likes of Liberace and Dizzy Dean—in our home. During the Jewish holidays, Mom carried on Mildred's tradition of inviting young Jewish cadets from the Citadel to join the family for meals. Although neither my two sisters nor I ever dated or married these eligible bachelors, it was not for her lack of trying!

In 1970, after our grandmother passed away, Mom became Minnie's official sidekick. In addition to catering private events, Mom and Dad eventually opened a fine dining restaurant, the Harbor House, in downtown Charleston. They included the family brisket on the menu and fondly called it "Brisket Nita." They also opened the Deli Den on Market Street and, later, Bernstein's Bagel Factory and Deli. Our brother, Hal, and sister, Lynn, helped run the delis.

Lash wedding dessert table, Charleston, SC, 1976.
COURTESY TERI BERNSTEIN LASH.

On Minnie's passing, our oldest sister, Lynn, began helping our mother. Lynn proved to be a quick study. She always told Mom, "You can't die until I learn how to make your famous babka!" Thankfully, many years passed before Mom felt the need to teach her! My sisters and I were blessed that Mom lived long enough to cater all three of our weddings. Teri's was first. She and Ira Lash were high school sweethearts. Ira's parents owned Lash's Kosher Meat Market in downtown Charleston. Anita knew that the kosher caterer's daughter was a perfect match for the kosher butcher's son. One guest famously left our wedding with an entire smoked whitefish hanging out of his coat pocket.

Mom passed away in 1998, but her legacy did not die with her. Our sister, Lynn, immediately took charge for the next generation, and she learned to make the babke before Mom passed away. After many years of catering, Lynn sadly died in 2012 at the young age of sixty, almost ending the catering tradition.

We all know that traditions never completely go away. The legacy has continued in a very small way, as I still make the famous Bernstein stuffed rolled cabbage every year for the local annual Jewish food festival known as "The Nosh." Teri continues to make our mom's famous New York style cheesecake. It is arguably the best cheesecake found south of New York City.

After Anita and Lynn both died, Teri and I were left with an abundance of passed-down recipes. The task of organizing those makes us laugh together. Many are incomplete because Anita would only write down the part she could not remember. She always said the magic to a good recipe was in her head, hands, and heart. She never measured anything; Anita's idea of a great recipe included a handful of this and a pinch of that. We would ask, "How do you know it is the right amount?" Mom would say, "Because I know . . . and if you want to be good cooks, just watch and learn!"

BRISKET NITA

Brisket Nita was one of the most sought-after recipes in Anita's vast collection. Although the recipe that follows is exactly how she made it, it has been said that no one can make a brisket as good as Anita did. First-cut heavy kosher briskets are recommended, although any fresh brisket will do.

3 large onions, sliced
1 large brisket, up to 12 pounds
Garlic
Salt
Pepper
1 (12-ounce) bottle ketchup
1½ quarts water
1½ pounds dark brown sugar
2 cans white potatoes or 2
  pounds fresh small red or gold
  potatoes, washed and boiled

Cover the bottom of a large roasting pan with sliced onions. Place the brisket in the pan on top of the onions. Sprinkle the brisket generously with the garlic, salt, and pepper mixture on both sides. Pour the bottle of ketchup over brisket. Wash out the ketchup bottle with water and pour the water into the pan. Generously sprinkle the brown sugar over the entire brisket.

Cover the roasting pan well with aluminum foil, sealing all sides. Bake at 400°F for approximately 3 hours. Uncover and baste well.

Add two cans whole drained white potatoes or fresh boiled potatoes to gravy. Cook uncovered for another hour, basting occasionally.

Always slice the brisket *against* the grain, starting from the front end. When you reach the back of the brisket, turn and slice the back end in the other direction against the grain.

MAKES 12 TO 14 SERVINGS

THE SOUTH CAROLINA STATE FAIR
JEWISH FOOD BOOTH

JERRY EMANUEL AND JACQUELYN DICKMAN

———

*Jerry recalls that the Jewish Food Tent at the South Carolina State Fair,
sponsored by B'nai B'rith Women, was a popular destination for
the traveling carnies in the 1950s and 1960s, and Jacquelyn
shares Florida Boyd's flanken soup.*

———

LIKE THE CRY OF "Meet your party at the rocket"—heard on the public address system if someone is lost or looking for someone—food has been equally synonymous with South Carolina State Fair patrons who gather each October for the sights, sounds, smells, and tastes of fall. In the late 1950s or early 1960s, the fair not only included commercial food booths on the midway but also others sponsored by charitable organizations, including one by the local chapter of B'nai B'rith Women. The fair lasted ten days, and members of the Jewish community would cook and bake, sometimes beginning weeks before the event. Volunteers from B'nai B'rith Women, B'nai B'rith and BBYO, the youth organization, worked the booth in some capacity.

Located near the bandstand, the B'nai B'rith Women's booth catered to the "carnies," the working people who traveled with the entertainment and food trucks to carnivals and fairs across the country. "They came to our booth because we served corned beef and brisket, salami and eggs," reminisced Heidi Golden. "It was good old New York delicatessen style." Other favorite dishes included matzo ball soup and lentil soup and chopped liver. Helen Coplan recalled, "Many of the carnies were Jewish, and they just worshipped the food. They were like wolves. We didn't have a kosher restaurant in Columbia, so there was no place to get decent Jewish food except at the fair."

Florence Berry was one of the leaders who planned and supervised the event. Florida Boyd, a Black housekeeper, who had learned how to "cook Jewish" by her employer, Selma Dickman, worked as the booth's primary cook. Florida was in the booth kitchen every day, and she also prepared dishes like omelets and sandwiches on the spot. The cooks prepared the gamut of traditional Jewish cuisine.

South Carolina State Fair, Columbia, SC, 1955.

There were times when working in the booth was a challenge. Sometimes it would become crowded because too many volunteered that day, so they would take turns walking around the fairgrounds. "When it rained on a Big Thursday, the day of the University of South Carolina-Clemson football game, water came into the booth, sometimes horizontally, and everyone got soaked," said Helen Silver. Once, she remembered, "one fellow who was 'in charge' of the booth saw the portions we were giving and said, 'From now on, when we sell soup and *kneidlach* (matzo balls), we only give one and a little bread to go with it.' I did that with one of the carnies, and he looked at the food and said, 'Oh, you're charging more and giving less?' I went to Florida and asked her to give me a hot bowl of soup, two *kneidlach*, and plenty of bread, which she did. I took it to the carnie, who remarked, 'That's more like it!'"

FLANKEN AND BARLEY SOUP

Jacquelyn reminisces: "Florida was a mainstay at the fair. One of the dishes especially enjoyed by the traveling carnies was her flanken (beef short ribs) and barley soup. Although I do not have Florida's recipe, I know this hearty soup was made with cellophane tubes of Manischewitz soup mix to start, with added carrots, celery, onions, maybe potatoes and powdered garlic, and, of course, short ribs. I havc combined what she told me and a little research to create a recipe. Now I am motivated to prepare this soup for a cold winter's night and think of the fair, my parents, and Florida."

3 pounds or 8 pieces of flanken (beef short ribs)
1 roll of vegetable Manischewitz Soup Mix
1 roll of split pea and barley Manischewitz Soup Mix
1 cup each of chopped carrots, celery, onion, and potatoes
Bay leaves
Garlic powder
Salt and pepper to taste

In a large pot, cover the flanken with water; bring to a boil for 2 minutes; then change the water to the full amount (4 quarts). Bring the water with the flanken to a boil, then simmer covered for 1 hour.

Add the Manischewitz soup mixes (but leave the spice package to add later). Add the chopped carrots, celery, onions, and potatoes. Simmer covered for another hour. While cooking, stir occasionally and thoroughly, and add water if needed. You may need more or less cooking time.

Mix in the contents of seasoning packets, a few bay leaves, and garlic powder, salt, and pepper as needed. Simmer covered for 15 minutes.

MAKES 8 TO 10 SERVINGS

Tree of Life Sisterhood, Columbia, SC, 2000.

PHOTOGRAPH © BILL ARON, COURTESY JEWISH HERITAGE COLLECTION,

SPECIAL COLLECTIONS, COLLEGE OF CHARLESTON LIBRARIES.

JEWISH FOOD FUNDRAISERS

DEBBIE BOGATIN COHN, SHELLEY SPIVAK KRIEGSHABER, AND JOE WACHTER

———

For decades, Jewish congregations have shared Jewish customs and cuisine with the larger community through annual fundraising food events.

———

The Big Nosh

DEBBIE BOGATIN COHN

To nosh is to have a snack or nibble and comes from the Yiddish word nashn.

For years, the congregants of Columbia's Tree of Life synagogue prepared traditional Jewish treats and baked goods for the annual fundraiser. Soon after becoming chair of the event's fundraising committee, I assumed the task of taking this much-beloved fair to the next level. "The Big Nosh" was born (and trademarked) as a signature event in Columbia that brings people together to celebrate Jewish culture and food.

From an early age, I became cognizant of my Jewish roots through traditional meals when my family and friends celebrated Jewish holidays and rituals. I always wanted to educate others about my Jewish culture, and The Big Nosh is a fun and educational way to access Jewish culture. People come for the food but also can visit the synagogue; meet the rabbi; learn to make a matzo ball; participate in a mock Passover Seder, a bar/bat mitzvah, or a Jewish wedding ceremony; and dance the Hora, a traditional Israeli dance. It's the smell of those sizzling latkes that brings people in, but they leave with a better understanding of "everything Jewish."

The Big Nosh offers an astonishing array of mouth-watering Jewish delicacies to eat in or take out from Bubbe's Kitchen, The New York Deli (sponsored by Groucho's Deli), an Israeli Tent, and our famous Bakers' Bakery. Everyone enjoys delicious Jewish favorites, ranging from fresh hot latkes to bagels, chicken soup (Jewish penicillin), chopped liver, stuffed cabbage, New York kosher-style brisket, kugel, pastrami, hot dogs, falafel and pita bread, challah, strudel, rugelach, and cheesecake.

AUNT SOPHIE'S STUFFED CABBAGE

DONNA STERN MAGARO

The go-to recipe, enjoyed by all.

1 head large cabbage

1 cup chopped fine onion

2 tablespoons butter

1 cup Minute Rice

2 pounds ground chuck

½ teaspoon parsley flakes

Salt and pepper to taste

1 (14.5-ounce) can tomato soup

½ cup brown sugar

To prepare the cabbage: Core the cabbage, put it in a pot, and cover the cabbage with water. Bring the pot to a boil, then turn off the heat and let the cabbage sit for 10–15 minutes. Drain the water and peel the cabbage leaves. They should be soft and easy to manage. Let sit on a paper towel to drain.

To prepare the meat mixture: Sauté onions in two tablespoons of butter. Cook the rice and mix well into the raw chuck. Add salt, pepper, and parsley flakes to taste. Add the onion to the mixture. Make golf-ball-sized meatballs with the meat mixture.

To prepare the stuffed cabbage: Use a 9 × 13-inch casserole dish. Take a cabbage leaf at the thickest part. Roll the cabbage leaf around the meatball, taking the thinnest part of the leaf and tucking it under the whole ball. It should be a nicely wrapped meatball. You can also use two of the smaller leaves to make a makeshift roll. When you finish a meatball wrapped in cabbage, place it with the fold down in the bottom of the dish. Add tomato soup and sprinkle with ½ cup brown sugar.

Bake at 300°F for 2½ hours.

MAKES 16 CABBAGE ROLLS (8 SERVINGS)

First Bubbie's Food Festival

SHELLEY SPIVAK KRIEGSHABER

The handwritten recipe for chopped herring salad had been ignored in my recipe box for years. But, on September 13, 2009, I dusted it off and knew it was headed for greatness. That was the day of Beth Shalom Synagogue's inaugural Bubbie's Brisket Bakeoff, and I was entering my recipe in the appetizer category. Some of our synagogue's best cooks were busy preparing their briskets, matzo ball soups, challahs, des-

Bubbie's Jewish Food Festival, Columbia, SC, 2000s.
COURTESY BETH SHALOM SYNAGOGUE.

serts, and other delicacies for the competition. Everyone had to make ten batches of their recipe to be able to offer samples to those attending. Two well-known chefs and a food critic in the community judged each entrée. The winners were announced, and I was delighted to hear that the chopped herring salad won for best appetizer! Next, the winners of each category gathered to learn which recipe was the best overall . . . and yes, the chopped herring salad won first place! I was thrilled. What no one knew at the time was that this was the only year there would be a competition, so I have the great honor of being the first, last, and only overall winner of the Bubbie's Bakeoff.

CHOPPED HERRING SALAD

2 (8-ounce) jars of herring in wine sauce

2 hard-cooked eggs

1 tart apple, pared

1 small onion, diced fine

2 tablespoon lemon juice or 3 tablespoons vinegar

2 tablespoons oil

2 tablespoons sugar

3 tablespoon bread or cracker crumbs

Pepper

Drain the herring and reserve the liquid for spreadability. Chop the herring and eggs into a smooth pulp.

Grate in the apple. Add the onion, lemon juice, and oil. Add the sugar. Stir in the dry crumbs. Add pepper. Cover and refrigerate.

Serve cold on crackers. Garnish with olive or pimento. Stir before spreading on crackers as the liquid tends to settle out.

MAKES 12 SERVINGS, AS A DIP

Since that day, the bakeoff has transitioned from a competition into a popular community food festival. Bubbie's Brisket and Bakery Extravaganza, sometimes referred to simply as "Bubbie's," is the only kosher food festival in South Carolina. Volunteers begin cooking briskets and baking challahs months before the fall event, so they are well prepared to feed the large crowds who come to satisfy their cravings for Jewish food.

My chopped herring salad recipe card is back in my recipe box, now stained with dribbles of herring oil. It has joined the ranks of my most beloved and often used recipe cards. Those recipes, along with ones written in my late mom's and my late mother-in-law's handwriting, make my recipe box one of my most valued possessions.

Challahs at Beth Shalom Synagogue, Columbia, SC, 2017.
COURTESY HISTORIC COLUMBIA.

Spartanburg Sisterhood Bake Sale

JOE WACHTER

Over the years, Spartanburg's B'nai Israel Synagogue has been more than simply a re-vered place of worship. It has served as the venue for all manner of programs from din-ners to game nights and entertainment of all sorts. The annual Sisterhood Bake Sale stands out as one of the most popular events. Begun in 1950, the same year when the Sisterhood was organized, the Sisterhood members bake for months ahead of time to prepare for the event. Dot Frank, a founding member of the Sisterhood, has participated in the Sisterhood's bake sale since it started. The annual bake sale is one of her favorite and most enjoyable activities. One of her treasured recipes is for Miami Sweet Rolls, a pastry made with nuts and powdered sugar that Dot and others call "Butterflies." There are now more than one hundred bake sale items that are made and sold each year.

Temple B'nai Israel Sisterhood, Spartanburg, SC, 1964.
COURTESY TEMPLE B'NAI ISRAEL.

BUTTERFLIES

4 cups flour

½ teaspoon salt

1 cup (2 sticks) butter

1 package active dry yeast

¼ cup of water at 105°F plus
  1 teaspoon of sugar to bloom
  the yeast

3 eggs, separated

½ teaspoon vanilla

½ teaspoon almond extract

¾ cup sour cream

Powdered sugar

Filling

¾ cup sugar

¼ teaspoon vanilla

½ teaspoon almond extract

1 cup chopped nuts (½ cup
  pecans and ½ cup walnuts)

Powdered Sugar

Sift the flour and salt into a large bowl. Cut in the butter as for pie crust.

In another bowl, dissolve the yeast into very warm (105°F) water with sugar; combine with the egg yolks, vanilla, almond extract, and sour cream. Add to the flour mixture and, using a wooden spoon, stir until well blended. Cover and chill for 1–2 hours— overnight is even better.

To make the filling: Beat the 3 egg whites until foamy; gradually add ¾ cup sugar and beat until stiff. Fold in ¼ teaspoon vanilla, ½ teaspoon almond extract, and 1 cup chopped nuts.

When ready to bake, divide the dough into 6 parts. Sift the powdered sugar over the surface. Roll each piece of dough into a circle 9 inches in diameter, and then cut into 8 wedges. Place a teaspoon of filling on each wedge and roll up, beginning at the wide edge. Place the pointed edge down on greased baking sheet; shape into crescents and bake at 375°F for 15 to 20 minutes. Remove the rolls from the pan immediately. Sift powdered sugar over them while still warm.

MAKES 4 DOZEN

South Carolina Jewish Foodways

AROUND THE JEWISH TABLE 4

SAVORY SABBATH DINNERS IN KINGSTREE 125
Lisa Collis Cohen

SHABBAT AROMAS OF OUR PAST 127   Deacon Joe Powell's Challah
Marilyn Schaeffer Arsham, Michele Schaeffer Cline,
and Jack Schaeffer

ALWAYS ROOM FOR ONE MORE 130   Susan and Nancy Lourie's Brisket
Susan Reiner Lourie   Helene Kligman's Brownies

THE ART OF SOUTHERN JEWISH ENTERTAINING 134   Lemon Meringue Pie in a Meringue Shell
Harold J. Brody and Sheila Brody Cooke   Bing Cherry Mold with Sour Cream Topping
        Cornbread Dressing with Optional Oysters

HOPPIN' JOHN AND COLLARDS: Lyssa's Hoppin' John
CELEBRATING NEW YEAR'S TRADITIONS 139
Lyssa Kligman Harvey

PASSOVER CHOPPED LIVER WARS 143   Chopped Liver Three Ways
Jake Bialos and Stefanie Levinson

PASSOVER IN ST. MATTHEWS 146
Brenda Yelman Lederman

MY ISRAELI FOOD JOURNEY 148   Israeli Hummus
Risa Strauss   Debby Harrison's Boreka

SHARING CHALLAH 151   Heidi's Challah
Heidi Kligman Lovit

In the Harvey household, the kitchen table is where we find our way together. It is where we gather to sustain body and mind. Meals awaken our senses—the images, smells, tastes, and voices of our past and present fill our hearts and stomachs. We leave the table nurtured, physically sated, and spiritually fulfilled. Stories from around the Jewish table are the inspiration for this book.

Early South Carolina Jews brought to their tables a mix of Central European, Eastern European, and Mediterranean foods and traditions. From these southern Jewish tables come individual essays with common themes of the Sabbath meal and both Jewish and American holiday celebrations—Rosh Hashanah, Hanukkah, Passover, and Thanksgiving.

Every Friday night at sundown, an intersection of region and religion takes place at Jewish Sabbath tables across South Carolina. Traditional—and increasingly not-so-traditional—dishes and prayers mark the end of one week and the beginning of the next.

Thanksgiving, the American holiday celebrating an early communal table in our country's national narrative, prompted an entertaining story in this chapter. As Harold Brody writes in this chapter, "For the Brody family of South and North Carolina, a family grounded in retailing, Thanksgiving was such a holiday. It was also a prelude to the day after Thanksgiving, one of the three biggest days of the year in retailing." All of the Brodys were "foodies," who enjoyed fare for Thanksgiving of Ashkenazic origin, supplemented by southern ingredients.

As Jessica B. Harris, celebrated scholar and historian of African American foodways, says in the documentary *High on the Hog,* "Through food, we can find out that there is more that connects us than separates us. What we eat and what we discover is how we know who we are. The communal table is what brings us together."

SAVORY SABBATH DINNERS IN KINGSTREE

LISA COLLIS COHEN

————

Jewish families in small towns across South Carolina went to extreme lengths to keep kosher in their homes.

————

FOR THE FIRST EIGHTEEN YEARS OF MY LIFE, my Shabbat celebrations were nearly identical. My family was one of two families in Kingstree, South Carolina who kept a kosher—not kosher-style—home. Every Thursday, my mother, Jennie Goldberg Collis, would write the menu for Shabbat dinner. If the dinner was to include beef, it would be taken out to thaw. Our source for kosher meat, Lash's Kosher Meat Market, was seventy miles away in Charleston. Planning ahead was a must because all of our meat, purchased from Lash's, was frozen.

On Friday, Carrie Mattie Scott, our housekeeper for decades, prepared Shabbat dinner. Carrie began working for our family when I was less than a year old. She was born and raised in Hemingway, South Carolina—a small town 25 miles from Kingstree. She was one of five children, which included four daughters and a son. She and her younger brother, Jeffrey, moved to Kingstree as young adults.

Without fail, a challah—usually from Spanier's Bakery in Florence, picked up by Daddy, or from Gottlieb's Bakery in Savannah—would be taken from the freezer. Once the dairy breakfast dishes had been cleared and washed by hand (the dishwasher was for meat dishes), Carrie would trim and season the entree. Most of our Sabbath meals, with the exception of fish, were fleshig (meat). Having been taught by Momma, Carrie's knowledge of kashrut was impressive. A rare error when she would mistake a milk utensil for a meat utensil would result in a temporary backyard burial for the errant tool.

Our Shabbat dinners were a mélange of traditional Eastern European fare, such as roasted brisket with vegetables, cholent, stuffed cabbage, and roasted chicken, and southern delicacies, such as whole baked striped bass, fried flounder or bream, and fried chicken. My favorite Friday night dinner was barbecued stew beef, rice, and Le Sueur peas. A tasty side dish was coleslaw with homemade mayonnaise-based dressing. Jell-O with fruit capped off dinner.

Although I don't have Carrie's recipe for barbecued beef, I know that it began with seasoning the beef cubes with chopped onions and spices. She then added water and cooked the meat in a heavy roasting pan on very high heat for a good while. Once everything had cooked down, she added the barbecue sauce, tightly covered the pan with foil, and baked it low and slow. The rice was always Mahatma extra-long grain white rice, which Carrie skillfully prepared in a double boiler. That technique is truly a lost art. The peas were the easy part. No one made Jell-O with fruit as well as Carrie did. Never runny or too squiggly, the dessert was a family favorite. Everyone wanted the portion with the rare maraschino cherry.

Because my father, Moses Collis, was the cook in our family, he taught Carrie how to prepare many Jewish foods. Stuffed cabbage, chopped liver, kreplach, kneidlach, chicken soup, and kugel were in her repertoire, as were red rice, okra gumbo, cornbread, potato salad, macaroni and cheese, fried chicken, and fish. We ate more fish on Fridays than our Catholic friends did. Carrie baked from memory, and her coconut cake was divine. Her yearly holiday gift to my father was a dense fruitcake, which he would eagerly unwrap and liberally douse with Jack Daniels.

Once Shabbat dinner preparation was well underway, Carrie polished the candlesticks and kiddush cup and set the dining room table. Before ending her workday, she set out the wrapped challah on its tray. The oven was warm, and the stage was set for a delicious Sabbath meal.

Friday night dinner was served at 6:30 p.m. With our heads covered with embroidered scarves from Israel, my sister, Momma, and I would begin the Sabbath prayers by kindling and blessing the Sabbath candles before sunset. Daddy would don his yarmulke, raise his gleaming kiddush cup, and recite the blessing over the wine in flawless Hebrew. We said Hamotzi, a prayer over the challah, together. Only after the blessings did we enjoy the delicious dinner that Carrie had prepared. After dinner, the four of us would attend the half-hour-long services at Kingstree's Temple Beth Or. Observance was important to my mother, but assimilation to a degree, was significant to my father. As a teen, I was theirs until 8:30 p.m. on Sabbath evenings. After services, I could catch up with my friends at a football or basketball game or at a social event.

Growing up Jewish in rural South Carolina was unique. As I raised my own children in Atlanta, Georgia, I drew much inspiration for Shabbat dinners from my memories. I now bake challah on Fridays. We still use Daddy's simple but elegant kiddush cup. Although my home remains kosher-style, I do prepare many Ashkenazic and Sephardic foods. One dish that I still miss and haven't mastered is Carrie's barbecued stew beef. Someday, I hope to do that in her honor.

SHABBAT AROMAS OF OUR PAST

MARILYN SCHAEFFER ARSHAM, MICHELE SCHAEFFER CLINE, AND JACK SCHAEFFER

"That's what we Southerners do. It's just part of our nature: to make everyone feel at home." The Schaeffer home in South Windermere was a welcoming place for a meal for friends and visitors alike.

GROWING UP JEWISH IN THE SOUTH in the 1950s and 1960s may have had its challenges, but we southerners are resourceful when faced with challenging situations. When we were growing up, South Windermere was our Jewish haven in Charleston. It had only one glitch— on Shabbat and holidays, we had to walk over a mile, across the Ashley River Bridge, to get to the Orthodox synagogue (Brith Shalom Beth Israel, or "BSBI") on Rutledge Avenue. Several generous families bought a centrally located house in South Windermere to serve as a BSBI-satellite synagogue, which we called "the minyan house." Dad (Nat Schaeffer) took on the custodial chores, which included re-pairs, shopping for the Saturday Kiddush, and making tuna and egg salad to complement the herring, gefilte fish, potato chips, and bottle of

Lee and Nat Schaeffer, Charleston, SC, 2003.
COURTESY MARILYN SCHAEFFER ARSHAM.

Scotch he bought each week for the Kiddush. Every Saturday morning, he stuffed his pockets with lollipops for the kids. As the minyan house gained popularity, the same group purchased a second home, so that visiting rabbis could have a comfortable place to stay. Southern Jews are hospitable!

Mom (Lee Schaeffer) was a kosher caterer in Charleston and loved what she did. She also loved having guests. This worked for Dad, who loved bringing home unexpected guests from the minyan house, including soldiers from Fort Jackson. That's what southerners do. It's just part of our nature: to make everyone feel at home.

Imagine a Friday night and you are our guest. As the front door opens, you smell a symphony of delectable aromas. Mom's cooking—rich chicken soup simmering on the stove, sweet-smelling noodle kugel sitting alongside the bowl of fresh salad on the counter, and roasted chicken. Dad's sweet, homemade challah is warming up in the oven. The aromas continue through the night as Mom's rich cholent (flanken meat, potatoes, sautéed onions, carrots, beans, barley, and water) slowly cooks in preparation for a warm Saturday lunch. In South Windermere, there were always visitors on Shabbat; you never knew who would stop by.

Mom's chicken soup, filled with fresh root vegetables, was a favorite of her Jewish dishes. Like her mother, she gave the soup to her friends when they were sick. Back in the 1960s, we "modern thinkers" always thought that these medicinal claims for chicken soup were just old "bubbe-meises" (Yiddish for untrue stories or fables), but our Bubbies were right. Chicken soup nourishes our bodies: The chicken broth hydrates

DEACON JOE POWELL'S CHALLAH

AS TAUGHT TO NAT SCHAEFFER

1 cup warm water

2 packets dry yeast or 1 cake (2 ounces) yeast

5 eggs (reserve one for egg wash)

1 teaspoon salt

½ cup sugar for regular; ¾ cup for sweet challah

5 tablespoons oil

6–8 cups bread flour

Raisins (optional)

Poppy or sesame seeds (optional)

Spray oil or grease pans

Add the yeast to the warm water. Mix by hand until the yeast has been absorbed by the water. Let stand no more than 5 minutes. Add the eggs, salt, sugar, and oil, and mix.

Add 3 cups flour to the yeast mixture and mix. Add 3 more cups of flour. If the dough is still sticky, mix in ½ cup flour at a time until it holds together without sticking to your hands.

Knead the dough on a clean, flat surface until it is well mixed and feels smooth. For raisin challah, knead in the raisins. If the dough is sticky, add flour in small amounts and knead until consistency is soft but not sticky.

First rise: Place the dough in a large, greased bowl, cover with a towel, and let the dough rise for 1 hour, preferably in a warm, humid area. If living in a dry climate, you may want to boil water near (but

RECIPE CONTINUES ▶

the body and soothes the throat; onions contain protein, calcium, and sulfur, which reduces nasal congestion; salt improves the loss of taste when we have a cold; chicken (like turkey) contains tryptophan, which improves our moods; noodles have carbohydrates, which give us energy; carrots give us vitamin A, which helps our immune system; celery, onion, and carrots contain vitamins C and K, and other antioxidants and minerals, which also help our immune system. Chicken soup is a beloved family tradition, passed down over generations.

Dad made the challah, but he didn't learn the recipe from his family. He was taught by Deacon Joe Powell, a local African American preacher by day and a baker in Dad's South Windermere bakery by night. Joe was a special person to all he met. He always had a smile and a biscuit for us when we came to the bakery. In fact, when Dad passed away a few years ago, Deacon Joe, who was in his mid-nineties, came to the funeral.

As Mom was one of the valued kosher caterers in Charleston, and Dad owned the South Windermere bakery, you could say our family was rich in food and recipes.

not next to) the dough or let it rise in your laundry room while doing your laundry. After an hour, check the dough. It should have doubled in size. If not, give it more time or place it in a warmer area. (If it does not rise, check the expiration date of the yeast. It may no longer be viable.)

When the dough looks ready, sprinkle flour on a clean, flat, dry surface (e.g., table or counter) and place the dough onto the floured surface. Divide the dough in 2 halves, and then divide each half into 3 balls. This will give you 6 palm-sized balls of dough. Roll each ball into a log, its length matching the length of the baking pan. Place 3 logs side by side and braid, twisting into a challah loaf. Grease 2 loaf pans, add the braided dough, and cover with a towel.

Second rise: Let the braided dough sit in a moist area (e.g., near boiling water) for 20 minutes. Optional: When ready for baking, brush egg (yolk or whole) on top. It doesn't add to the taste, but it makes the bread shine. You can also sprinkle with poppy or sesame seeds.

Fill a small pan with boiling water and leave it in the oven, so that the bread will have moisture while baking. Or you can use a brick like our dad used, if you have one.

Bake for 30 minutes at 350°F. Some metal pans bake faster than others; therefore, the first time you make this recipe, check the bread after 22 to 25 minutes. If it looks golden brown and ready, it probably is done.

MAKES 6 TO 8 SERVINGS

ALWAYS ROOM FOR ONE MORE

SUSAN REINER LOURIE

———

Everyone was welcomed around the Lourie holiday table—
from visitors to family, the Jewish holidays
were celebrated with gusto.

———

ROSH HASHANAH HAS ALWAYS been one of my family's favorite holidays. We celebrated both days of the Jewish New Year. The table was a scene of family and dear friends. We had soldiers from Fort Jackson and students from the University of South Carolina join us, and there was always room for one more. There was never a dull moment at our table as the conversation moved between football and politics. It was fun to watch our family and our friends' families grow with boyfriends, girlfriends, in-laws, and grandchildren.

Isadore Lourie and I were married in 1959 in Savannah, Georgia. I am from Savannah, and Isadore was from St. George, South Carolina. I went to the University of Georgia, and Isadore attended the University of South Caro-

Susan and Isadore Lourie, Columbia, SC, n.d.
COURTESY SUSAN REINER LOURIE.

lina. Eleanor Rubin Neistat set us up on a blind date. The rest is history.

After moving to Columbia, we celebrated our first Rosh Hashanah with my in-laws, Annie (Lourie) and Hyman Simon. The Simons stayed at the Jefferson Hotel on Main

Street so they could walk to the Marion Street synagogue four blocks away. They were observant Jews, kept a kosher home, and did not drive on the High Holidays. We attended services and then celebrated our Jewish New Year's meal at a restaurant downtown. The Simons hosted Passover, and, for years, seder was at their home. In the 1960s and early 1970s, the entire Lourie family—our family, as well as Sol and Mick Lourie's family—gathered at the Passover table.

Eventually, Isadore and I began to host the holiday meal. We celebrated both days of Rosh Hashanah. The Louries closed their clothing store and Isadore closed his law office. We had lunch after services for the first day of Rosh Hashanah, and Nancy and Mick Lourie hosted the second day. Nowadays, we have an early dinner, which I cook and prepare, although Florida Boyd always made the chopped liver. Some of the holiday recipes are mine, and some are borrowed, like Rose Kline's pound cake and Helene Kligman's brownies, which were served for dessert.

Over the years, sitting around our table were our boys—Lance, Joel, and Neal—and their wives and their wives' families, the Baums and the Druckers; Mick and Nancy Lourie and their children' Mary Lourie Rittenberg and Alvin Rittenberg; my brothers David Reiner and Larry Reiner and their families; Arline and Gerald Polinsky and their family; Fran and General Bob Solomon and their family; and Carla Donen Davis and her family. There were other friends and family members over the years to fill the table and then some. My children and grandchildren would invite guests at the last minute. We included new Jewish people who moved to town; professors from the University of South Carolina; news reporters; soldiers from Fort Jackson; and, of course, University of South Carolina students, many of whom were fraternity brothers of the boys. We often had thirty or more people and moved furniture to seat everyone. It was a pleasure.

Today, I still host the first day of Rosh Hashanah. Joel and Becky (Baum) Lourie have Erev (evening before Rosh Hashanah) dinner. I host the Kol Nidre (evening services before Yom Kippur) dinner, and Neal and Robin (Drucker) Lourie host Break the Fast after Yom Kippur. I have now passed the Passover seder torch to the next generation.

SUSAN AND NANCY LOURIE'S BRISKET

My children's favorite dish is my brisket.

1 4- to 5-pound first cut brisket
2 cans cranberry sauce
1 can Heinz chili sauce
1 package Lipton's onion soup

Mix the cranberry sauce, chili sauce, and onion soup package contents all together. Pour the mixture over the brisket. Cover and bake at 350°F for 3½ hours or until tender. I refrigerate it when it is cool and slice it the next day. Freezes well.

MAKES 6 TO 8 SERVINGS

HELENE KLIGMAN'S BROWNIES

HELENE FIRETAG KLIGMAN

This recipe was well loved and used by all her friends.

2 sticks butter
2 cups sugar
1 cup flour
½ cup cocoa
4 eggs
1 teaspoon vanilla extract
Powdered sugar

Preheat the oven to 325°F. Melt 2 sticks of butter in a 9 × 13-inch Pyrex pan. Mix all ingredients together, except for the powdered sugar, and pour the mixture into the Pyrex pan. Bake at 325°F for 35 to 40 minutes. Let cool. Shake the powdered sugar on top of the brownies. Cut and serve in colored baking cups. Freezes well.

MAKES 16 MEDIUM-SIZE BROWNIES

THE ART OF
SOUTHERN JEWISH ENTERTAINING

HAROLD J. BRODY AND SHEILA BRODY COOKE

————

*This large southern Jewish family makes holiday
entertaining an enduring tradition.*

————

Brody cousins, Sumter, SC, 1960s.
COURTESY HAROLD J. BRODY.

FOR THE BRODY FAMILY of South Carolina and North Carolina, a family grounded in
retailing, Thanksgiving is a special holiday. It provides a chance for extended families
separated by distance to reconnect to their youth and for the younger cousins to learn
from their uncles and aunts. It was also a prelude to the day after Thanksgiving, one of
the three biggest days of the year in retailing for "hog-wild sales, clean-up sales."

In the 1950s and 1960s, the family alternated between homes every year. Sara Brody
(wife of Abram), Ethel Brody (wife of Reuben), Lorraine Brody (wife of Morris), Jackie
Brody (wife of Alex), and Ruth Brody Greenberg (wife of Abe Greenberg) provided
their homes for home cooking every four or five years. Abram, Reuben, and Alex were

in Sumter, South Carolina; Ruth was in Florence, South Carolina; and Morris was in Greenville, North Carolina. After Reuben's death in 1964, and with three of the nieces and nephews graduating from high school in 1966, the family then alternated mostly between Sara's and Jackie's homes in Sumter. All the Brody family members enjoyed dishes for Thanksgiving derived from Ashkenazi origins and supplemented by southern dishes.

Starting dinner at two o'clock in the afternoon gave everyone the chance to go to the movies or travel home and still have energy for the next day's important and exciting retail race. The young people of the family put together retail boxes, ran alterations up to the sewing room, or got snacks at the five- and ten-cent stores. At sixteen years of age, they began to sell shoes and clothing to their contemporaries in high school and to their families.

Food, of course, is accompanied by drink, and all the Brody brothers had well-constructed bars in their homes. I was the appointed bartender and mixologist from the time I was sixteen years old or so. As soon as I entered any home, it was "Harold, give me some Crown Royal on the rocks," or "Harold, give me a vodka and tonic." I found it interesting that alcohol enhanced but never interfered with the lives of the Brody brothers.

Jackie Brody was exceptional as a hostess among the women, because she truly loved to cook and entertain. Her talents for preparing appetizers from chopped liver to venison, along with mouth-watering desserts such as Bing cherry mold, lemon meringue pie, coconut meringue cake, cheesecake, and devil's food cake made her meals a festival of color and memory. She was also known for her squash casserole and cornbread dressing with oysters.

Homemade chopped liver was a staple of all the Brody women. After cooking the livers until they were just beyond pink and saving the schmaltz to mix with hard-boiled eggs and caramelized onions, the ingredients are blended together with salt and pepper by hand chopping or using a blender. There were no gribenes (crisp skin with fat) in this preparation. The chopped liver was smooth and tasty because of the addition of a dollop of mayonnaise combined with schmaltz. My mother, Sara, could judge chopped liver instantly by its texture and its taste. As an appetizer, a pound of chopped liver was not nearly enough for all that bourbon, vodka, and gin before the meal. I can still see the family members spreading it on Club or Ritz crackers thickly and liberally.

The Brody Thanksgiving table grew each year. One appetizer begat two or three the following year, and one dessert begat more as time went by. Every family has lost recipes, no doubt, but it was a pleasure to remember and refine these Thanksgiving recipes from notes of over fifty years ago.

LEMON MERINGUE PIE IN A MERINGUE SHELL

JACKIE BRODY

Jackie's lemon meringue pie was always a rave.

4 eggs, separated
1½ cups of sugar
¼ teaspoons cream of tartar
4 tablespoons lemon juice
1 tablespoon lemon rind
⅛ teaspoon salt
1 pint heavy cream, whipped

To make the meringue shell: Beat the egg whites stiff into a meringue with a whisk. Sift 1 cup sugar and cream of tartar together. Add the sugar mixture to the egg whites slowly. Place into a well-greased pie plate, using cooking spray or butter, leaving a hollow in the center of the meringue (shape it like a pie crust). Bake the shell for about 1 hour at 275°F until it is dried and crisp.

To make the filling: Beat the egg yolks slightly and put them in the top of a double boiler. Add ½ cup of sugar, lemon juice, the lemon rind, and salt. Cook for 8 to 10 minutes to thicken in the double boiler, stirring constantly. Let the mixture cool, and fold in ½ cup whipped cream. Put the custard into the meringue shell. Cool for 24 hours in the refrigerator. Cover the top with the remainder of the whipped cream.

MAKES 8 TO 10 SERVINGS

BING CHERRY MOLD WITH SOUR CREAM TOPPING

JACKIE BRODY AND SARA BRODY

This is a quintessential 1950s recipe, as gelatins are no longer popular but can be delicious. Sara has prepared it in individual servings, without the sour cream topping, with just a dollop of sour cream, and replacing some of the water with Mogen David wine equal to the amount of Bing cherry juice.

Top of the mold

1 package lemon Jell-O

1 cup hot water

1 cup sour cream

Bottom of the mold

2 cans of pitted Bing cherries, liquid reserved

Shelled walnut halves, inserted manually into Bing cherries, if desired

1 package lemon Jell-O

1 cup sour cream

2 packages of Sparkle Black Raspberry Jell-O

To make the top of the mold: Dissolve the Jell-O in hot water. Stir the sour cream into the Jell-O mix. Refrigerate in a greased mold to set.

To make the bottom of the mold: Measure the Bing cherry liquid and add enough hot water to make 3½ cups. Dissolve the Jell-O in the liquid. Remove the mold from the refrigerator and add nuts and cherries on top. Pour the liquid Jell-O on top. Put this all back into the refrigerator to set. Invert and serve.

MAKES 12 SERVINGS

CORNBREAD DRESSING WITH OPTIONAL OYSTERS

JACKIE BRODY AND SARA BRODY

2 medium onions, chopped

1½ cups chopped celery

1 stick butter, melted

¾ cup self-rising white corn meal

¾ of a loaf of white bread, in 1-inch cubes, toasted in the oven at 250°F for 1 hour

¾ cup chicken stock

4 eggs, beaten

Salt, pepper, and sage

Optional: 1 to 1½ cup walnuts or 1 to 2 containers fresh oysters, liquid drained

Combine the onions, celery, butter, and corn meal.

Mix the dry toasted cubes well by hand with the chicken stock until the mixture is near the consistency of uncooked cornbread. Add the onions, celery, butter, and cornmeal mixture.

Add the eggs. Season with salt and pepper; add sage, if desired. Add the walnuts or oysters, if desired. Bake at 350°F in a 9 × 13-inch casserole dish covered with foil for 40 minutes. Uncover and cook for 40 to 45 additional minutes for crispness.

MAKES 12 TO 16 SERVINGS

HOPPIN' JOHN AND COLLARDS
Celebrating New Year's Traditions

LYSSA KLIGMAN HARVEY

———

The Harvey family New Year's Day meal has morphed into a combination of southern and Jewish traditions.

———

THE JEWISH NEW YEAR, Rosh Hashanah, takes place in the fall of each year. To celebrate this holiday, I always make my Grandmother Ida's lokshen kugel. It is a sweet kugel with raisins and sour cream. It is traditional to eat something sweet for Rosh Hashanah to bring sweetness to the new year. For New Year's Day on the first day of January, I have eaten black-eyed peas and rice, or Hoppin' John, and collards for as long as I can remember. Little did I know, black-eyed peas are not only a traditional southern dish, but a long-standing traditional Jewish New Year dish. In an article for *Southern Living*, Hannah Hayes notes, "There is evidence that people ate black-eyed peas for luck as early as 500 A.D. as part of the Rosh Hashanah meal. But the tradition of eating black-eyed peas with rice is African in origin and spread throughout the South, especially in the Carolinas, in the form of pilaus (perlo) or rice dishes simmered for a long time with chicken or shrimp. When black-eyed peas were added to the pilau, it became Hoppin' John."

Eating Hoppin' John, a savory blend of rice and black-eyed peas drawn from West African culture and brought to America by enslaved people, is today a southern tradition that purportedly ensures prosperity and health in the New Year. The original ingredients of Hoppin' John are simple: one pound of bacon, one pint of peas, and one pint of rice.

My mother, Helene Firetag Kligman, and her family grew up with this New Year's Day tradition in Charleston. Annie Gaillard cooked Hoppin' John for her own family and brought it over to my mother's home to share, so naturally, Hoppin' John has seeped into my collective food conscious as a traditional food for New Year's. I make it several ways, depending on how industrious I am feeling. I use fresh ingredients for Hoppin' John, which includes fresh field peas like black-eyed peas, red peas, or cow peas—which need to be soaked overnight—and Carolina Gold rice, an early, much valued variety of

New Year's Day lunch on Fishing Creek, Edisto Island, SC, 2019.
COURTESY RACHEL BARNETT.

rice grown in South Carolina, available again thanks to the scholars, rice growers, and chefs associated with the Carolina Gold Rice Foundation. I add sautéed onions, because I put sautéed onions in everything. It is traditionally cooked with bacon or fatback but not in Jewish kitchens. Sandra Altman Poliakoff's mother, Annette Sokol Altman Carson, made her Hoppin' John with flanken (short ribs). I don't add bacon or fatback, so I add hot sauce to give the Hoppin' John a little kick! If I am concocting Hoppin' John at the last minute, I open up a can of Glory or Margaret Holmes seasoned black-eyed peas or my favorite seasoned field peas and make five-minute rice. Either way, I prepare Hoppin' John for our New Year's Day celebration. I feel that I am doing my part to bring on health and prosperity for my family for the upcoming year!

LYSSA'S HOPPIN' JOHN

Hoppin' John should be served with collards and can accompany turkey, brisket, or fried chicken. You may want to add bacon, smoked meat, sausage, or flanken. To make this recipe vegetarian, omit the meat and use vegetable broth.

4 cups fresh or frozen black-eyed peas, red peas, or field peas

1½ cups uncooked Carolina Gold Rice

8 cups chicken stock

3 tablespoons olive oil

1 large onion, chopped

Kosher salt, pepper, and garlic powder to taste

Hot sauce to taste

Soak the fresh peas overnight. Drain. Put the peas in a saucepan, give a heavy shake of salt, and cover with 5 cups of chicken broth. Bring to a good boil. Turn the heat down to medium low. Simmer for about 40 minutes (about 20 minutes if using frozen peas). Drain the liquid once it has cooked.

Heat the oil in a medium saucepan and sauté the rice until toasted. Add 3 cups of chicken broth and a heavy shake of salt and bring to a boil. Turn the heat down to medium low. Let simmer for 20 minutes.

Cover the bottom of a large skillet with low sides with olive oil. Add the onions, and cook until caramelized, soft, and brown. Once the onions are cooked, add the rice and peas to the skillet of onions. Add salt, pepper, garlic powder, and a few drops of hot sauce, and stir. Serve warm. Does not freeze well, but leftovers only get better!

MAKES 12 TO 16 SERVINGS

PASSOVER CHOPPED LIVER WARS

JAKE BIALOS AND STEFANIE LEVINSON

———

Native New Yorker, Jake Bialos, recalls his visits to his in-laws' home
for Passover and the chopped liver wars that ensued.

———

MY SOUTHERN PASSOVERS with the Levinson family are a treasured gift that I am proud to share. Arnold and Faye Levinson represented a second helping of joyous Jewish tradition that was an unexpected bonus for this New York city boy. It was my good fortune to marry a southern Jewish girl and become part of her family. The first helpings of childhood seders up north were an occasion for celebration, but also of dread. I had an extended family, and our seders were large affairs conducted in Hebrew by my father. They were very long, prayerful, and dry. My mother's brisket was juicy in contrast.

When I fell in love with Stefanie, Passover with her family was a must every year. I was pleasantly surprised at the difference in the observance and mood of the holiday in Columbia. It meant every year, for over two decades, we flew south for festive seders. Usually, we'd arrive early so Stefanie could join her mother and sisters for the preparations. Springtime in Columbia is always so stunningly beautiful, with blossoming azaleas and dogwood everywhere. The air is fresh and sweet, and the sky is blue and wide.

From the moment we landed, we were caught up in the whirlwind of scheduling visits with relatives and friends. Arnold and Faye took such loving pride in sharing seder. The joy they took in hosting and catering to family and welcoming guests was impressive and genuine. They were focused on the people they loved and knew what made folks relax and feel like family. To contrast my southern seders with my own family's seders, I must say, the Levinsons had more fun. The seders were not solemn affairs by any stretch. The emphasis was on showmanship, laughter, and the deluxe decorations of the table settings. The kids were pushed gently to put on skits, which were scripted, costumed, and hysterical. Needless to say, when you join a Jewish retail clothing family, everyone at seder was fahputzed! We wore suits and ties, and women were chic—part and parcel of the joy of celebration. Even the kids looked smart. There was no tedious

Hebrew davening (praying) at these seders. The food was bountiful and tasty, the singing and reading were done enthusiastically at full volume, and by the end of the meal, as we belted out another rousing round of the favorite Passover song, "Had Gadya," there was a satisfying feeling of accomplishment that filled the house. It established a commitment to joy that lasted the whole year to come.

Passover food at the Levinsons' was plentiful and traditional for South Carolina Jewry. The showcase brisket, nice and gedempte, assumed a place of pride. After the opening course of chopped liver and soup, people served themselves unless someone volunteered to "fix me a plate," which was a level of trust and camaraderie that was not lightly bestowed. Faye was known for her geshmak chicken soup with matzo balls and was no slouch at desserts. The food was almost identical to the food I grew up eating, with one significant exception. Southern haroset is made with pecans versus the walnuts my mother used. It was delicious, oozing with sweet Manischewitz wine, and undeniably better the southern way. Most of the food was lovingly prepared by Faye and frozen in advance, which made the sequence of reheating as precise as the seder service in terms of getting the timing right. It took teamwork. Every year, a few things remained to be done before the big meal. As I graduated from son-in-law to family member, my love of cooking was recognized, and I began to help Faye in the kitchen with things she didn't like doing, like prepping the chicken livers and dicing onions. I remember chopping on the butcher block in the kitchen; one year making homemade matzo; and, with Faye, I grated fresh horseradish root, another eye-watering hit.

Passover was never just about the seder but a whirlwind, three or four days of family activities. Mr. Britton's BBQ at Little Pigs Barbeque was another fun tradition on the first night in Columbia. We'd pack into a couple of cars to enjoy our treyf barbecue and unlimited sweet tea. It was an indulgent sacrilege but also a celebration of being southern and Jewish. We would always run into other Jewish families at the barbecue joint. There were games and activities for the kids, including the annual backyard Easter egg hunt, where more friends and family hung out and caught up.

The one thing that I have taken with me from seders I celebrated in Columbia is that Judaism is a glorious tradition wherever you add generous fellowship and love into it and make it your own.

Chopped Liver Three Ways

As a Yankee looking to fit in down south, I was well aware of the long-standing rivalry between the two. I wasn't as aware of the more friendly North–South divide between the Carolinas until I saw it played out in the chopped liver wars. For the first night seder in Columbia, we had Faye's incredible chopped liver, an oniony, creamier recipe. Second night was often in Charlotte with Aunt Margi Goldstein and family, where we looked forward to her classic eggier blend with a lovely crumblike texture. In between, when on a health kick, someone would throw in mock chopped liver. The chopped liver wars would rage on every Passover. The result? Everyone won!

MOCK CHOPPED LIVER

1 can Le Sueur young peas, drained

1 cup walnuts, finely chopped

2 onions, chopped and sauteed

6 hard-boiled eggs, whites only, chopped

Salt to taste

Blend all the ingredients together. Prepare this dish ahead of time: It is better if it has a day to rest.

MAKES 12 SERVINGS, AS A DIP

FAYE'S CHOPPED LIVER

1 pound of chicken livers (3 to 4 pints)

4 large onions, minced (4 to 5 cups)

3 hard-boiled eggs

Several tablespoons vegetable oil (or chicken schmaltz in earlier years)

Salt and pepper to taste

Clean the livers, cut away the fat, and roast them on a roasting tray or cookie sheet until well done (not pink). Sauté the onions in oil or schmaltz for 20 minutes or more until the onions cook down and are deep brown. Put the onion mixture into a bowl. Combine the chopped liver and eggs and add to the onion mixture. Faye used an old-fashioned chopper for the liver and eggs, not a machine. If the mixture is not moist enough, add a bit of additional oil. The mixture at the end should be finely chopped and creamy.

MAKES 12 SERVINGS, AS A DIP

MARGI'S CHOPPED LIVER

1 pound chicken liver

16 hard-boiled eggs

3 onions, chopped

Safflower oil (makes a lighter mixture, can substitute canola oil)

Salt and pepper to taste

Broil the liver; watch carefully, as overdone liver will get tough and hard to chop. Sauté the onions in the oil until golden brown. Combine the liver, eggs, and onions using a hand chopper. A food processor will make the mixture too much like pâté. The final mixture should have a crumbly texture.

MAKES 12 SERVINGS, AS A DIP

PASSOVER IN ST. MATTHEWS

BRENDA YELMAN LEDERMAN

———

The owner of a favorite chopped liver recipe is revealed many
years later, but the recipe has been lost to time.

———

Gordin and Yelman family Passover, St. Matthews, SC, 1970s.
COURTESY BRENDA YELMAN LEDERMAN.

MY PATERNAL GRANDPARENTS settled in St. Matthews in 1908. They raised five children there, all while running a dry goods store downtown. I remember growing up and feeling very secure in a family with deep roots. My Bubbie and Granddaddy, Hannah and Judah Yelman, were a huge part of my life, and I saw them nearly every day. It's pretty easy to get around in a town of two thousand. Bubbie and Granddaddy kept chickens in the backyard, which provided both eggs and dinner. I do not know if Granddaddy was trained as a shochet, but families from surrounding areas came to get their kosher chickens from him. When he died in 1959, I thought everyone in the town brought food to our family, there were so many callers and so much food! After his death, my Bubbie's heart was broken, and she did not live much longer.

Our annual family seder in St. Matthews is one of my favorite memories. After my grandparents died, seder was at our house. Usually, there were twelve of us at the table—my mom and dad, Helen (nee Insel) and Shep Yelman; my sister, Martha; my brother, Ron; the Gordins from Summerton—Miriam (nee Brotman) and David, their four children: Miriam's mother, Aunt Charlotte Brotman, and me.

The chopped liver stole the show. I think it was assumed by all that my mother, Helen Insel Yelman, made the chopped liver. However, I can now share with the world that she did not. The delicacy was made by Rosa Guinyard, who worked for our family for many years. Rosa's recipe was never written down. Rosa lived in a small wooden house that was within walking distance of us. Rosa took care of my Bubbie during her last years.

Back in the 1950s, we did not have a food processor or any other small electric appliance in the kitchen. We had a handheld chopper that had a wooden handle and two blades. Rosa worked the mixture in a shallow wooden bowl that has a prominent place on my kitchen counter, where it reminds me of those family seders and Rosa.

MY ISRAELI FOOD JOURNEY

RISA STRAUSS

———

After years in Israel, Risa has called Columbia home since 2003. Israeli dishes conjure fond memories of her time living there. She says no matter where she eats Israeli food, it's as if she has come home.

———

Risa Strauss, Israel, 2019.
COURTESY RISA STRAUSS.

I WAS BORN IN NEW YORK CITY, and I am the firstborn child of first-generation parents "trying their hardest" to assimilate during the 1960s and '70s. At best, my family's relationship with food was a perplexing array of dos and don'ts, traditions, and contradictions.

Foodwise, both my parents were products of homes where brisket, chicken soup, chopped liver, pastrami, lox, kugel, corned beef, knishes, gefilte fish, tzimmes, and seltzer in bottles delivered weekly were staples. Fresh vegetables were used as decoration—like a piece of iceberg lettuce under a scoop of chopped liver, or a sliver of onion and a little sliced tomato on a bagel with lox. Cooked vegetables were very boiled, such as carrots in a soup or the tiny carrot slice atop your piece of gefilte fish, but mostly, cooked vegetables were lost in a recognizable sea, such as beet borscht.

If you asked my parents, they said they kept kosher. They had their rules. No milk during dinner, but you could have a cheeseburger. Bacon could be eaten out but not in.

Yes to ham in the Italian deli, but eat it before you get home. Pork chops were a no-no, but Chinese food eaten in front of the TV was fine. My mom loved TV dinners and Tab—so those were okay, too. As kids, we were allowed to mix the Tab with skimmed milk and call it an egg cream—another New York Jewish staple—but you couldn't drink it if we were having cheeseburgers. My lunch box in elementary school regularly consisted of boiled chicken in one baggie and ketchup in the other. During Passover, there was a third bag with matzo.

In 1967 and 1973, when two wars engulfed Israel and its Arab neighbors, New York City and Los Angeles became magnets for many sabras (Jews born in Israel) to escape the pressure of sirens, death, and destruction. In my Jewish-y neighborhood in Queens, life changed dramatically. Sephardic Israelis who kept kosher, but not necessarily through Ashkenazi traditions, moved to the neighborhood and opened many stores—most important for me, kosher pizza and falafel restaurants. Kosher-Middle Eastern, dairy-veggie street food became the hot new commodity. First came Shimon's. My mother would take us there every day after school; I actually think that she was flirting with Shimon, the Israeli owner behind the counter. We got the chickpea fried falafel balls with hummus and tahini with real chopped fresh vegetables served in a newfangled pocket bread called "pita." Whatever you ate, Shimon and his family members would regale you with

ISRAELI HUMMUS

RISA STRAUSS

This is a quick-and-easy, delicious hummus recipe.

3 garlic cloves or more to taste

4 cups of canned chickpeas, drained with up to a cup of liquid reserved

1 cup tahini

4 tablespoons freshly squeezed lemon juice

1 teaspoon salt

Freshly ground pepper to taste

3 tablespoons extra virgin olive oil

3 tablespoons pine nuts

Hot sauce to taste

In a food processor, mince the garlic. Add the drained chickpeas and tahini. Add the lemon juice and salt. Use the reserved liquid from the canned chickpeas to thin the paste to a creamy consistency. Puree until smooth. Season with more salt and pepper to taste.

To serve Israeli style, spread on a plate, drizzle high quality olive oil, and sprinkle with toasted pine nuts. For a South Carolina touch, add hot sauce to taste.

MAKES 9 SERVINGS

stories of his homeland, Israel. After college, in 1985, I made aliyah (when a Jew moves to Israel), and the rest is history.

Columbia, South Carolina, has been my physical home since 2003, and it is in this famously humid southern town that my Israeli food experiences have helped me move forward into the next chapter of my life. Just like many southern households who come together over grits, collards, and fried chicken, many Jewish households come together over challah, hummus, and schug (spicy Israeli chili pepper spread). My friends and I relish eating Israeli foods, because they are a reminder of our experiences in Israel. It transports us to the homeland that keeps us bound together as a people.

Israel is a country that is made up of literally an ingathering of exiles. Its cuisine is reflective of that diversity. Israeli food represents my biblical past, my present, and my future. It binds me with every other Jewish person around the world. Israeli food completes me.

DEBBY HARRISON'S BOREKA

Israeli friend, Debby Harrison, provides many original Israel recipes for the Columbia Jewish community. She produces an amazing boreka—phyllo dough pockets filled with potatoes and cheeses, and even chopped meats—that we serve at many Beth Shalom social functions.

Filling
½ cup feta cheese
⅓ cup ricotta cheese
1 beaten egg
Salt and pepper
(Substitute any kind of mashed potatoes for filling.)

Pastry
1 box puff pastry (has two sheets), defrosted
Sesame seeds
1 egg, beaten

Mix together the filling ingredients.

Stretch out one sheet puff pastry. Cut the sheet into 9 squares. Put 1 tablespoon of filling into the middle of each square. Fold each square along the diagonal, into a triangular shape.

Put parchment paper on a baking sheet. Place the triangles on the sheet. Brush beaten egg onto the triangles and sprinkle with sesame seeds. Bake at 350°F for 25–30 minutes. Borekas should be lightly browned on top.

MAKES 9 PIECES

SHARING CHALLAH

HEIDI KLIGMAN LOVIT

———

With her prize-winning challah, Heidi has become the chief challah baker for her family and friends, and with help from her challah crew, she bakes over one hundred fifty challahs for her synagogue's Jewish food festival each year.

———

CHALLAH, BRAIDED YEAST BREAD, is a traditional staple for weekly Shabbat and High Holiday meals. Many years ago, I took on the responsibility of being the bread maker for my family. I have to admit, I changed recipes several times since my original recipe called for nine eggs. Challah is considered an egg bread, so I thought that was normal until I became conscious of increased cholesterol from that many eggs in one recipe. Several recipes called for more yeast and fewer eggs, and I finally found the perfect combination. I do think that one of the secrets is adding an extra tablespoon of honey to give it a sweet taste, and it also makes the texture slightly moister.

When I was growing up in Columbia, my family would come together every Friday night for Shabbat dinner. At that time, we had challah made from a bakery, because I don't remember my mother baking bread. I learned how to make brisket and meatballs with cabbage and other Jewish foods from my mom, but not bread. My mother's sister, Phyllis Firetag Hyman, shared her recipe with me when I was in high school, and I started baking challahs for the High Holidays. From then on, no more bakery challahs for our family. I would always make sure that we had challah for Shabbats and every holiday. I even made extra round challahs with raisins for Rosh Hashanah to share with family friends. When my children were younger, I got them involved in mixing, kneading, and braiding. When the kids moved away, I always sent them each a fresh challah for the holidays if they could not make it home. My daughter, Morgan, still follows my recipe and bakes challah today. Every time she does, I get a beautiful photo of her fresh baked bread. She loves to share with her friends and coworkers. Sharing recipes with friends is always fun, and I have taught many people how to make challah, but when you share a traditional Jewish recipe with others of different faiths, it helps to teach about

Heidi Kligman Lovit and Lyssa Kligman Harvey, Columbia, SC, 2017.
COURTESY HISTORIC COLUMBIA.

our culture. Sally Patterson, a Presbyterian, and a friend for over forty years, now makes challah for her family.

Beth Shalom Synagogue has a fundraiser every fall called Bubbie's Food Extravaganza. The very first year in 2009, it was Bubbie's Bake-Off, a competition for the best recipes of brisket, kugels, chicken soup, and challah. I entered my challah recipe and won first place. Since then, I had the honor to bake hundreds of challahs in the synagogue kitchen for the annual Bubbie's Food Extravaganza. This has also given me the opportunity to teach dozens of women in our synagogue this beautiful and traditional food art of kneading dough and braiding bread.

HEIDI'S CHALLAH

A sweet challah recipe.

4 cups warm water

4 packages yeast (1 ounce total or 3 tablespoons)

2 cups sugar

2 teaspoons salt

13–14 cups bread flour

3 eggs (save one for brushing loaves)

1 cup oil

2 tablespoons honey

Poppy seeds or sesame seeds

Dissolve the yeast in water and add the sugar and salt. Let the yeast mixture stand until bubbly. Put 7 cups flour into a large bowl. In another bowl, combine the oil and two beaten eggs; then add 2 tablespoons honey to the mixture. Add this mixture to the flour. Slowly mix in the yeast mixture, making sure that all the flour is mixed in. This can be done by hand with a wooden spoon or in an extra-large mixer with a dough hook attachment. Slowly add 5 to 6 more cups flour and mix well until the dough is slightly gooey but easy to manage. Hand kneading is best.

Transfer the ball of dough into a lightly greased bowl and cover it with plastic wrap. Set it in a warm place to rise for 2 hours.

Knead and divide the dough into seven balls to make seven challahs. Take each ball, divide it into three or four strands, and braid, making sure that you pinch and tuck the ends under the loaf. While kneading and braiding, keep flour on the counter surface to keep dough from sticking. Place braided challahs on a pan that is lightly sprayed with non-stick cooking spray. Let the dough rise for another 30 minutes to an hour.

Brush the top with egg wash (one beaten egg should cover all seven challahs). Sprinkle with your choice of poppy seeds, sesame seeds, or both. Bake at 325°F for 30 minutes until golden brown. Let the challahs cool completely before storing them in freezer bags. Challahs freeze well for several months.

MAKES 7 TO 8 LOAVES

OUR MOTHERS AND GRANDMOTHERS 5

MY MOTHER, THE BEST COOK IN THE WORLD 159
Barry and Elaine Krell

Sayde's Mandelbrot
Elaine's Shabbat Potato Kugel

EZELLA'S KOSHER COLLARDS 162
Kim Cliett Long

Ezella's Kosher Collards

JEWISH LIFE AND CAKE 165
Arnold Wengrow

Rachel Pearlstine Wolff's Heirloom Blueberry Cake
Mrs. S. W. Wengrow's Famous Tomato Jam

FROM HER KITCHEN TO YOUR HEART 169
Belle Fields, as told to Robin Waites

Mallo-Fudge Cake with Butter Icing

SHARING LOVE BY THE POUND 172
Nancy Polinsky Johnson

Cream Cheese Pound Cake

JEWISH LIFE IN CHARLESTON IN THE 1950s 176
Sandra Altman Poliakoff

Salmon Mousse

MRS. POLIAKOFF OF ABBEVILLE 178
Edward Poliakoff

Rosa's Farfel Soufflé

MEMORIES OF GRANDMA 180
Gloria From Goldberg

Mrs. From's Cookies

MAMMA LEARNED TO COOK 182
Mickey Kronsberg Rosenblum

Chicken Gumbo

AREN'T CHEESECAKES JEWISH? 185
Cindy Alpert Saad

Eleanor's Cheesecake
Aunt Fannie's Chocolate Roll

STRONG WOMEN, FROM GENERATION TO GENERATION 189
Beth Bernstein

Carol's Chocolate Mousse Cake

WE'LL MAKE YOU FAMOUS 192
Carol Michael

Grandma Tobye's Challah

What a precious find is a woman of valor

Her worth is far beyond rubies. . . .

She is like the merchants' ships, bringing her food from afar.

She rises also while it is yet night and gives food to her household

   and a portion to her maidens.

Extol her for the fruit of her hand

Whenever people gather, her deeds speak her praise.

Proverbs 31:10–31

King Solomon's praise excerpted from Proverbs 31:10-31 is often sung on Friday evenings at the Sabbath meal and recited at the funerals of Jewish women. Praise for the women who came before us, our mothers and grandmothers, resound from the pages that follow. We remember their lives in many ways. Moments around our tables remain some of the most memorable, and their food stories and recipes—whether told to us or handwritten, kept in index files or found in drawers—connect us through aroma, taste, and texture to earlier generations. Many of these stories have similar themes and memories of traditions and rituals in the home. We were taught by our mothers in the kitchen, where we absorbed food culture and family lore. Now that many of our mothers and grandmothers are gone, their dishes have become even more precious, and we strive to never forget what these beloved ancestors shared from their hearts and hands. We crave their soup and mandelbrot. The delicious smell of their cooked brisket lingers in the recesses of our minds. Through the memories of their meals, our mothers became the "best cooks in the world" to us. In Barry and Elaine Krell's story about Barry's mother, Sadye Krell, Barry shares that, "More than even her veal chops and potato latkes and everything else, my mother became known for her mandelbrot."

Our mothers and grandmothers were women of valor. So, too, were the women who worked in their kitchens preparing meals and sometimes learning how to keep a kosher kitchen and prepare kosher dishes. Mostly African American cooks and domestic workers, these women also wrote their own history in the plates that held the ingredients they mixed, cooked, and served. Kim Cliett Long writes about her great-grandmother, Ezella Cliett: "While she was in the Goldstein household, she cooked many southern specialties, attributed to West Africa but without the pork typically used as a seasoning meat. These dishes included black-eyed peas, all types of greens, collards, mustards, turnips, green beans and cabbage, and other vegetables." Beyond the pantry, countertop, and stove, the responsibilities of these women laborers stretched to childcare and care of the home. Contributors to this chapter have powerful memories of the influence and culinary skill of African American women who cooked, cleaned, and helped raise them while caring for families of their own.

Many Jewish women worked outside the home, creating food businesses that further shaped the southern culinary scene. Arnold Wengrow, formerly of Columbia, South Carolina, writes about his grandmother: "[Rachel Pearlstine Wolff] lived one of those stories that are legend for southern Jews in small towns. Widowed in 1914, with three young children, she took over the businesses her husband had started on Main Street in Allendale in 1873. She also kept a kosher boarding house for Jewish salesmen who needed a place to stay during cotton- and watermelon-buying season. She raised chickens and took them in crates tied to the top of the car to Augusta, Georgia, to be killed by the kosher butcher." Indeed, a woman of valor.

Four generations of mothers and daughters, Reznick, Firetag, Kligman, and Harvey, Charleston, SC, 1954.
COURTESY LYSSA KLIGMAN HARVEY.

MY MOTHER, THE BEST COOK IN THE WORLD

BARRY AND ELAINE KRELL

―――――

Sadye Krell from Charleston is remembered by her son, Barry, and his wife, Elaine, for her famous mandelbrot.

―――――

Barry's Memories

My mother, Sadye Krell, was a wonderful cook. She kept a kosher home and cooked all the meals herself. She wouldn't let anyone in the kitchen. We helped clear the table, but that was all she would let us do. Our meals were typical Eastern European–style Jewish food. It was nothing fancy, but we ate very well. Our meat and chicken came from Lash's Kosher Meat Market on King Street. Some of my favorite dishes were veal chops, cabbage soup, flanken, chopped liver with caramelized onions, potato kugel, chopped eggs, and sweet and sour pickled corned beef. As for desserts, I can still taste mother's chocolate pudding and lemon pies made with lady fingers! My mother wouldn't vary the meals—they were always the same and always delicious. She prepared everything by hand using hand graters and meat grinders. When I close my eyes, I can still see the wooden bowl she used for her chopped liver.

Sadye Krell and son, Barry Krell, Charleston, SC, n.d.
COURTESY BARRY KRELL.

Shabbos dinner was just for the family but always special, with a tablecloth, cloth napkins, and veal chops. We were a close-knit family and ate all meals at home. Years later, after Elaine and I were married, we went to my parents' home every Friday night for dinner. When they were old enough to drive, our sons, Kevin and Jonathan, would come to Sadye's for lunch instead of going to a fast-food restaurant, bringing friends along to sit at her small square table in the kitchen nook. They ate pan-fried hamburgers, sloppy joes, or salmon croquettes with ketchup, ending with a Coca-Cola and vanilla ice cream float for dessert. As the kids got older, we ate out on Sundays but often ended up at Mom's. Peppers and eggs on a bagel were one of my personal Sunday favorites.

For years, we went to Colorado to ski with Elaine's brother and family. Mom never came with us, but she sent food. We packed her cabbage soup, the sweet and sour pickled corned beef, the chicken drumettes with fried onions, and a couple potato kugels in a cooler and checked it as baggage. But more than anything, more than even her veal chops and potato latkes and everything else, my mother became known for her mandelbrot.

Elaine Remembers

I used to watch Sadye cook, and I learned so much from her over the years, but she would never let me cook or clean up—ever. While I never asked her to teach me to cook or bake, I gradually began to experiment with some of her recipes. She never measured except when she baked—she cooked by eye and feel, with that culinary sixth sense all good cooks have. Some of my personal favorites were, and still are, her potato kugel (Barry and the boys used to fight over who got the end pieces, the crispiest parts), her chopped eggs, and her mandelbrot.

Sadye's mandelbrot recipe was slightly different. "I don't make it like everyone else," she used to say. Her secret? Half a cup of vegetable oil rather than a whole cup. She made two varieties: one with jelly and one with nuts. Sadye would pack her mandelbrot in cookie tins and send them to Barry's brother, Robert, in Atlanta; to our kids when they were off at college; and to friends. She was asked to make her mandelbrot for all special *simchas* and synagogue bake sales. Sadye is remembered for many things—her kindness, her generosity, her patience, her quiet dignity—and, of course, her mandelbrot.

Sadye's cooking was more than the sum of its parts. Sure, the right ingredients and measurements were important, but there was something else, something less tangible that allowed so many people to be touched by her cooking. This vital ingredient was love. Sadye loved her children and grandchildren unconditionally. Sad to say, our grandchildren never got to meet her, but her namesake lives on through our oldest grandchild, Sadye, her culinary skills through Amelia, and her soft-spoken manner through our grandson, Carlos.

SAYDE'S MANDELBROT

3 eggs

1 cup sugar

½ cup oil

1 teaspoon vanilla extract

3½ cups flour

1½ teaspoons baking powder

Dash of salt

1 cup nuts, broken

In a large bowl, beat the eggs. Add the sugar, oil, and vanilla, mixing well by hand. Add the remaining ingredients, folding in the nuts last. Mix until stiff, but not dry, until dough is formed. Turn out onto a lightly floured board, and shape into five logs about 12 × 2 inches. Place on greased cookie sheets, two logs per sheet. Bake at 350°F for 35–40 minutes until lightly browned. Remove from the oven and cut the logs into 1-inch slices. Lay the slices flat and return them to the oven for 10 minutes, or longer to toast. Cool on a rack and store in an airtight container.

MAKES 24 PIECES

ELAINE'S SHABBAT POTATO KUGEL

2 eggs

5 potatoes, peeled and cut into
   small pieces

1 medium onion

½ teaspoon coarse salt

¼ teaspoon pepper

Garlic powder, to taste

⅛ to ¼ cup oil

In food processor, process the eggs, potatoes, onion, salt, pepper, garlic powder, and oil until fine, or whatever your desired texture. Pour the mixture into a greased loaf pan. Bake at 350°F for 1 hour.

MAKES 6 TO 8 SERVINGS

EZELLA'S KOSHER COLLARDS

KIM CLIETT LONG

———

Great-granddaughter of Ezella Cliett, Kim Cliett Long believes that her great-grandmother's remarkable history reminds us of the power of memory and how it informs culture.

———

THIS IS A STORY ABOUT a great-grandmother, a grandmother, a mother, and her legacy. People often leave their property to their children as an inheritance and in remembrance of them and other ancestors. We also see artifacts reminiscent of the days gone by and other vintage elements that remind us of ancestors in the most vivid ways possible. Such are mesmerizing remnants of the past. This story speaks of such beautiful remnants of family memory, history, and culture—except in this story, they are honored, remembered, and passed on through the sense of taste rather than property or artifacts. It has been said that foodways can take you back in time, helping you remember your past and your roots. I believe this wholeheartedly and soulfully.

Ezella with her first two great grandchildren, Kim Ydette Cliett Long and Kerry DeJuan Butts.
COURTESY KIM CLIETT LONG.

The roots of my ancestry lie in the plantation fields of eighteenth- through mid-nineteenth-century South Carolina. The story of my maternal great-great-grandmother and that of her enslavement began on one of the state's vast rice plantations. Our family knew only a few snippets of information about her. Her name was Peggy. After gaining her freedom, she boarded with, and served as a housekeeper for, an unmarried Jewish schoolteacher, Jewel Jacobs of Aiken. In a time of little to no health services for enslaved or newly emancipated women, Peggy died giving birth to a daughter, Ezella, whom Jewel took under her wing and raised. During Ezella's early childhood, Jewel met a young Jewish storekeeper, Saul Goldstein, of Americus, Georgia. Saul and Jewel later married, and Jewel moved to Americus as they established their new home and life together. Ezella relocated with the Goldsteins, and Jewel taught Ezella how to keep a home.

Although Ezella was quite skilled in sewing, her greatest gift was cooking. She was well known as a great cook throughout Sumter County, Georgia, for which Americus was the county seat at that time. Ezella was always in demand and was called on to cater many special occasions. She was an exceptional baker and excelled in baking and decorating wedding cakes. Tea cakes and fancy wedding and holiday cookies were her favorites to bake. Ezella created a family tradition with her wedding cookies.

Unable to read and write, Ezella did not use recipes; she later taught her own daughters to cook by sight, smell, and taste. She decided that only the oldest girl of each generation should be taught to make the famous wedding and holiday cookies. Because there was no recipe, the methodology required strictly knowing the correct consistency for the dough and taste. Many hours ensured that her oldest daughter, Ida Mae, perfected the cookies and retained the commitment to teach the next generation's oldest daughter: her daughter, Willie Mae. Willie Mae passed on the recipe to me, her eldest daughter.

When Ezella was of marrying age, she was courted by the widowed father of one of her best friends, a man named Ruben Hollomon. Ruben had four children with his first wife. They all coexisted well. Ruben and Ezella went on to have twelve more children; seven of the children reached adulthood. Ruben was a natural businessman, who worked hard, saved his money, and acquired hundreds of acres of land, beginning as a sharecropper and later becoming a landowner. Ruben died, leaving Ezella well provided for as a young, widowed mother with seven children. Once the children reached adulthood, the family moved to Macon, Georgia. This story now has come full circle as Ezella's great-granddaughter came to live in Charleston.

Because Ezella never knew her mother, she poured all her love and affection into her children. She was a nurturing, doting mother who worked and taught her five daughters her gift of cooking and baking. She was also an exceptional seamstress, another skill she passed on to her daughters. After growing up in a Jewish household, there were many dietary customs that Ezella devoutly observed. She did not keep a strictly kosher kitchen, but she did not serve pork or shellfish in her home. She always referred to her cooking as "kosher." While she was in the Goldstein household, she cooked many southern specialties attributed to West Africa, but without the typical pork used to season. These dishes included black-eyed peas, all types of greens, collards, mustards, turnips, green beans and cabbage, and other vegetables. It was an honor to enjoy her meals. Everyone marveled at Ezella's ability to make such delectable well-seasoned dishes without pork. Her recipe for healthy collard greens has been passed down and is shared here.

EZELLA'S KOSHER COLLARDS

2 large bundles of collard greens

1 large sweet onion

2 bunches green onions

2 garlic cloves

1 green bell pepper

Olive oil

Water to cover

One tablespoon hickory smoked salt

One cube chicken or vegetable bouillon

½ teaspoon crushed hot red pepper

½ teaspoon Lawry's seasoned salt or any other brand of choice

Remove the collard leaves from their stems. Wash the collard leaves well in clean water until the water is crystal clear. Stack 5 to 7 leaves, and then roll them like a wrap; cut through the leaves every ½ inch until all the collard leaves are cut. Set them aside.

Chop the following: a large sweet onion, two bunches of green onions (include the green stalks), 2 fresh garlic cloves, and a bell pepper.

In a large stockpot, add enough olive oil or another preferred oil to cover the bottom of the pot. Heat the oil at a temperature just high enough to sauté and add the chopped vegetables. Add water to cover. As the vegetables are simmering, add the following seasonings: one tablespoon of hickory smoked salt, one cube of chicken or vegetable bouillon, ½ teaspoon crushed hot red pepper, and ½ teaspoon of Lawry's seasoned salt or any other brand. Cook on medium heat until tender.

MAKES 12 TO 16 SERVINGS

JEWISH LIFE AND CAKE

ARNOLD WENGROW

————

Arnold Wengrow remembers his independent mother, Sura, as a skilled,
precise homemaker, volunteer, and creative baking entrepreneur
whose decorated cakes tell the history of a community.

————

WHEN I WAS GOING TO Schneider Elementary School in Columbia in the early 1950s, my mother, Sura Wolff Wengrow, instructed me how to identify her when I was asked my parents' occupations. My father, Sam Wengrow, was a dry goods merchant. He owned Wengrow's Department Store in Allendale, where my mother, born in 1908, had grown up. She was to be called a homemaker, never a housewife. "I'm not married to the house," she said.

Indeed, she was never a stay-at-home mom. My mother always was on the go as a volunteer. We moved to Columbia from Allendale in 1950 so my brother could prepare for his bar mitzvah. But just as important, my mother wanted to plunge deeply into the life of the Beth Shalom Congregation, then known as the House of Peace Synagogue. With only four Jewish families in Allendale, my mother had missed being part of a Jewish community for twenty years, and she was determined to make up for lost time. She was president, at least twice, of the women's auxiliary known as the Daughters of Israel, and she ran the shul's gift shop from the time it consisted of a single tall glass cabinet in the downstairs social hall on Marion Street until its expansion into the spacious, built-to-her-specifications, emporium in the education wing at Beth Shalom Synagogue on Trenholm Road.

My mother was an efficient, if not an ardent, cook. She kept a thick loose-leaf notebook stuffed with handwritten recipes gleaned from many sources. In it were year-by-year lists she called her Passover order—how many boxes of matzo were used and what kosher meats to be shipped by Greyhound Bus from Charlotte and picked up at the depot on Blanding Street.

My mother's rule about cooking was that she only prepared one meal a day. That was what she called dinner, a hot meal served in the middle of the day—whether there was

anyone at home to eat it or not. In Allendale, my father always came home at noon for this family meal, and there was a strict rotation of what was served each day. Thursday was meatloaf day, and Friday was salmon croquettes, mixed from Double "Q" canned salmon and matzo meal, formed into beautiful little pyramids, coated with matzo meal, and fried until brown and crispy.

When we moved to Columbia, she made dinner every morning, although my father was there only on Thursdays and Sundays. She left a plate

Sura Wengrow, Columbia, SC, 1962.

RACHEL PEARLSTINE WOLFF'S HEIRLOOM BLUEBERRY CAKE

Sura Wengrow was especially fond of making this recipe from her mother, Rachel P. Wolff, from circa 1930s.

1 quart blueberries

½ cup butter

2 cups sugar

3 large eggs

3 cups sifted flour

2 teaspoons baking powder

1 teaspoon pastry spice (allspice)

¾ teaspoon cinnamon

½ teaspoon ground cloves

2 tablespoons milk

1 teaspoon vanilla extract

Crumb topping

2 tablespoons flour

5 tablespoons sugar

2 tablespoons butter

½ teaspoon cinnamon

Have everything measured and ready before you start. Grease and flour your tube pan. Preheat the oven to 350°F.

Clean the blueberries and drain them in a colander.

Cream the butter and sugar with an electric mixer until light; add the eggs one at a time, beating lightly after each addition.

Sift the flour with the baking powder and spices (I sift 3 times).

Add the vanilla to the milk in a small container.

Add the flour mixture to the creamed butter mixture, about one cup at a time. Then add the milk and vanilla mixture—the dough should be stiff.

RECIPE CONTINUES ▶

for me warming under a big white soup bowl over a simmering pot of water to eat on my own when I came home from school. She was probably off to the shul gift shop. My sister, fourteen years older, was already married in Camden, and my brother, seven years older, was off doing whatever it is big brothers do at Dreher High School. My mother didn't like getting up early in the morning. By the time I was in the fourth grade, I realized that, instead of worrying her that I was going to be late for school, I could make breakfast for myself. For supper, there were always plenty of leftovers in the refrigerator for sandwiches. My mother's greatest kitchen legacy was letting me learn to cook for myself, something I enjoy to this day.

Everyday cooking wasn't enough of a challenge for my mother, but she loved the precision and creativity of baking and home canning. She learned to grow tomatoes in Allendale in a girls' Tomato Club organized by Dora D. "Mother" Walker, the state's first county home demonstration agents. Sometime in the 1940s, my mother came across a recipe for a sweet tomato jam spiced with cinnamon and cloves, and it became one of her specialties. She made mandelbread from a recipe given to her by Ethel Young, the wife of Joe Young, another Allendale Jewish merchant. She was especially fond of a

Lightly flour the berries; you can sift some flour over the berries in the colander. With a 2-pronged kitchen fork, *carefully* mix the berries into the batter, trying not to smash the berries.

Grease and flour a tube cake pan; the loose-bottom one with the "feet" on top is good. Shake out any excess flour. Line the bottom with parchment or wax or other clean paper cut to fit the bottom of the pan. I have used a clean brown paper bag.

Crumb topping:

Add 2 tablespoons flour, 5 tablespoons sugar, about 2 tablespoons butter, and ½ teaspoon cinnamon to what remains of the cake dough in the mixing bowl. Mix together, adding more flour if needed.

Make big crumbs of the crumb topping; make more than called for to make thicker topping.

Cover the top of the batter with the topping.

Place on a rack in the center of the preheated oven.

Bake at 350°F for 45 minutes to 1 hour.

Test (with a toothpick or fork) until the tester comes out clean. Don't let the topping burn!

Before you take the cake out of the oven, put down a paper towel or dish towel under the rack. Some of the topping will fall off when the cake is inverted. If the cake won't come out, try a wet cloth draped over the bottom of the pan for a few seconds. Turn the cake right side up to cool. Use 2 racks.

MAKES 12 SERVINGS

dense and fragrant blueberry cake with a thick streusel topping from a recipe used by her mother, Rachel Pearlstine Wolff.

Mrs. Wolff lived one of those stories that are legend for southern Jews in small towns. Widowed in 1914, with three young children, she took over the businesses her husband had started on Main Street in Allendale in 1873. She also kept a kosher boarding house for Jewish salesmen who needed to stay during cotton- and watermelon-buying seasons. She raised chickens and took them in crates tied to the top of the car to Augusta, Georgia, to be killed by the kosher butcher.

My mother's crowning culinary achievements were her elaborately decorated cakes. They were part of many birthdays and weddings, but she especially enjoyed designing Jewish-themed cakes—torah scrolls, tablets of the Ten Commandments, open prayer books—for bris and bar and bat mitzvahs. One mother froze a portion of her son's bris cake and served it at his bar mitzvah. My mother became a go-to baker-decorator for the Jewish community, and her photograph album of her creations, now in the Jewish Historical Collection at the College of Charleston, is a history in cake of some fifteen or so years of Jewish life in Columbia.

MRS. S. W. WENGROW'S FAMOUS TOMATO JAM

Sura Wolff Wengrow adapted this recipe from one in a Sure-Jell box sometime in the 1940s. Consult canning safety instructions.

2½ pounds (3 cups) prepared tomatoes
1½ teaspoon grated lemon rind
¼ cup lemon juice (from one lemon)
½ teaspoon allspice
½ teaspoon cinnamon
¼ teaspoon ground cloves
1 box Sure-Jell
4½ cups sugar

Use a 6- to 8-quart saucepan.

Scald, peel, and chop the tomatoes, and simmer for 10 minutes. Measure the cooked tomatoes; you should have 3 cups. Add the lemon rind, lemon juice, allspice, cinnamon, cloves, and Sure-Jell. Cook over high heat until the mixture comes to a hard boil. At once, add the sugar, and bring to a full rolling boil, a boil that cannot be stirred down. Boil hard for 1 minute, stirring constantly. Remove the saucepan from the heat and skim off the foam with a metal spoon. Ladle into hot, sterilized jars, leaving a ¼-inch space at the top, and process in a boiling water bath for 15 minutes or follow Sure-Jell instructions. Store in a cool place.

MAKES 3 (8-OUNCE) JARS

FROM HER KITCHEN TO YOUR HEART

BELLE FIELDS, AS TOLD TO ROBIN WAITES

————

Robin Waites, executive director of Historic Columbia, sat down with Belle
Serbin Fields and recorded her oral history for the Columbia Jewish
Heritage Initiative a year before Belle passed away.

————

WHEN LYSSA KLIGMAN HARVEY AND I walked into Belle Serbin Fields's home for our first interview in April 2017, it was as if we took a step back in time; however, this was not the kind of time travel you might expect when entering the home of a woman who is one hundred four years old. What we encountered was a midcentury modern jewel—open floor plan, sunken living room, paneled den, and kitchen with vibrant yellow and orange floral wallpaper. The home design harkened back to 1962, when Belle and her husband, Ed, moved to Columbia so he could pursue property development opportunities in the burgeoning capital city.

As Belle walked us through her Chateau Drive home in Columbia, she explained that the open floor plan was a design concept they brought from Phoenix, Arizona, which enabled her to entertain lots of people in a space "without

Belle Fields, 104 years old, with Robin Waites, Columbia, SC, 2017.
COURTESY LYSSA KLIGMAN HARVEY.

walls." Over the course of two interviews and conversations with her family and community members, I learned that Belle Serbin Fields's home mirrors the way that she approached life and cooking—with warmth, creativity, and unabashed openness.

One of four children, Belle Serbin, was born on December 17, 1912, in Tarentun, Pennsylvania. Her parents died when she was a teenager, and her paternal grandmother, who was Orthodox, raised Belle and her siblings. Although she wasn't the oldest of the siblings, Belle was the first among them to marry. At the time, her grandmother said that she expected Belle to keep a kosher kitchen. According to Belle, when she said "no," her grandmother, the family matriarch, was taken aback.

And she said, "No?" And I said, "Grandma, you have three daughters. You go to their house for dinner, you bring an apple [because they are not kosher enough for you]. . . . I will not have anyone come to my house to bring an apple." She pursed her lips and she said, in Yiddish, "Well, when you go to heaven, and they ask you if you kept kosher,"— that's how important it was to her—"what are you going to say?" "I'm going to say that you taught me what kosher was and how to live a kosher, married life, but that I was not going to keep kosher." She says, "Okay, on your head is the problem. Not on mine. I already did my job."

Although Belle did not keep kosher after her marriage, the kitchen was central to her life. Her cooking was not fancy, nor was it solely focused on Jewish dishes. Instead, she collected recipes from around the world. As her nephew, Stephen Serbin, MD, noted, "She was very wedded to the Eastern European traditions and recipes of her immigrant European grandparents, but she had way too much 'chutzpah' to leave the recipes alone and made some of them à la Belle! The twentieth-century contemporary culinary world interested her, and she experimented with new recipes from the '50s, '60s and '70s."

In my hallway, I had a piece of furniture with drawers, and when I hired a new housekeeper, I would say to her, "Now, I must tell you one thing. If there's a fire in the house, forget everything. Take the three kids, push them out, and then take this drawer." So, she'd open up the drawer, and she'd say, "But Belle! It's just paper, pieces of paper, recipes!" I said, "That's forty years of recipes."

A 1973 article in *The State* newspaper noted Belle's plans to publish a cookbook. Ten years later, her family supported the publication of the book, titled *Gefilte Fish in Lobster Sauce: The Contemporary American Jewish Cook's Book* (1984). According to her son, Fred Fields, "The main assets of this cookbook are that all the recipes have ingredients that most women have in their kitchen. And she goes into detail about how to cook them, so you don't have to be a board-certified chef in order to be able to cook. And a lot of her things not only taste good, they look good!"

My favorite recipe is a rich chocolate cake. When my sons went to military school, every three weeks I would send them something, you know. The first cake came, and the upper echelon of soldiers took it, and then they gave Fred the empty box, and they said, "Your mother is a very good baker."

In 2013, Belle's original cookbook was updated and republished under a new title: *The Melting Pot Cookbook: A Jewish Grandmother's Stories and Good Old Recipes from the Good Old Days.* Belle's son Michael Fields, who was instrumental in the publication and marketing for his mother's cookbooks noted, "Cooking was her way of expressing love." Belle died in February 2018 at the age of one hundred five years old. It seems only appropriate to celebrate her extraordinary life by sharing the chocolate cake recipe that she loved to bake and share.

MALLO-FUDGE CAKE WITH BUTTER ICING

BELLE SERBIN FIELDS

This cake packs and ships beautifully and is a favorite with both my sons. When they were away at school it was their first request—and that of their friends. —Belle S. Fields

3 squares bitter chocolate

¾ cup boiling water

1¾ cups flour

¾ teaspoon salt

1½ cups sugar

½ teaspoon baking power

¾ teaspoon baking soda

½ cup shortening

⅓ cup sour cream

1 teaspoon vanilla extract

2 whole eggs

15–16 large marshmallows, cut up

Butter icing

Place the cut-up bitter chocolate in a large mixing bowl with the boiling water and stir until the chocolate melts. Add the 5 dry ingredients and the shortening and beat for two minutes at low speed.

Add the sour cream, vanilla, and eggs, and beat for another two minutes.

Pour into a greased and floured 9 × 13-inch pan and bake for about 25 minutes at 350°F. Remove from the oven, quickly sprinkle the marshmallows on top, and return to oven to bake for another 5–15 minutes. Test for doneness with a toothpick. Do not overbake, or this wonderful cake becomes dry. Cool and spread thickly with butter icing. Cut into about 48 squares.

MAKES 48 SQUARES

SHARING LOVE BY THE POUND

NANCY POLINSKY JOHNSON

———

*Nancy Polinsky Johnson, formerly of Columbia, lovingly remembers her
mother, Arline Polinsky (1933–2020), and her love of the pound
cake that was waiting for her when she arrived for a visit.*

———

"WHAT DO YOU WANT ME TO MAKE for you when you come home?" was the question
my mother often asked me on the phone. Over the course of forty years, my answer was
always the same: "Your pound cake."

It didn't matter if I was driving back to Columbia from Chapel Hill, North Carolina,
on a college break during the 1970s or flying in from my adopted home of Pittsburgh,
Pennsylvania, with my husband and two sons throughout the 1980s, 1990s, and 2000s.
At the end of the journey, I knew that my favorite cake would be waiting for me.

Frankly, I don't know why Mummy kept asking the question. She knew that every
pleasure center in my brain lit up when I bit into that oh-so-moist cake with its crunchy,
cracked top. Loaded with butter and cream cheese, the finished product—if Mum timed
the baking just right—had a consistency almost bordering on that of a cheesecake. And
it developed a hard, thick crust that would inevitably burst open—with flavor, I would
argue—creating golden cracks and crevices that held the promise of crumbly delicious-
ness. I have always believed that, unlike other pound cakes that might be enhanced by
adding berries and whipped cream, or any other number of toppings, this one tastes best
when it stands alone, and I have never adorned it with anything that would detract from
its pure flavor.

Mummy got the recipe for the cream cheese pound cake shortly after moving to South
Carolina in 1968. She told me years later that it was given to her by a friend named Rose.
I wish I had known Rose to thank her.

I wasn't the only one in the family who loved the cake. So did my father and my sister,
Joanna. After Joanna and I married and had children, our husbands and sons embraced
it too, and Mummy rarely made a trip to Pittsburgh, where I have lived since 1985, without
a freshly baked pound cake wrapped in aluminum foil and tucked inside her luggage.

In a rather surprising turn of events, Mummy and her pound cake became somewhat famous in Pittsburgh. It all began in May 1995, when I invited her to be a guest on *QED Cooks*, a local cooking show I cohosted on the city's public television station, WQED. The station was preparing a special Mother's Day edition of the program, so I asked my mother to make an appearance and demonstrate my favorite of all her recipes.

Mummy, always eager for an excuse to travel north to see her Pittsburgh grandsons, was happy to oblige. Looking beautiful, as always, she stood next to me on the kitchen set and shared her cream cheese pound cake recipe with viewers in a live broadcast. The recipe was an immediate hit. I know this because WQED always produced a cookbook to offer in conjunction with each cooking special, as a way of thanking people for their membership support to the public TV station. When Mummy finished making her cake—and I finished raving about it—I told viewers that the recipe was included in the cookbook being offered as a thank-you gift that day, and the phone banks absolutely lit up. Everyone wanted that pound cake recipe. As was the case with all episodes of *QED Cooks*, that Mother's Day special ran in reruns for many years, and the segment with my mother was included in several "Best of . . ." *QED Cooks* shows that also aired repeatedly.

It wasn't long before Arline Polinsky's cream cheese pound cake became the most requested recipe in the twenty-five-year history of the show, and I couldn't go anywhere in the city without people stopping me to say they had made the cake and their family *loved* it. It became routine to hear strangers sing praises of the cake in the checkout line at the grocery store, during intermission at the theater, or while navigating the crowd at a Steelers game. I also got countless notes and letters from viewers who wanted me to know how much they enjoyed the cake.

One note that I will never forget was from a woman whose husband had indulged in two pieces of the cake one night and, hours later, suffered a heart attack. Thankfully, he survived, and she wanted me to know that the first thing he requested when he returned home from the hospital was a piece of the cake—a cake that she now called "heart attack pound cake," because of the three sticks of butter included in the recipe!

After my mother died of COVID-19 in April 2020, the *Pittsburgh Post-Gazette* devoted an entire page and a half to a feature article about her and her pound cake. That amazed me, considering that my mother never lived in Pittsburgh. However, it speaks to the impact she made when she shared that recipe on the air twenty-five years earlier—and to the absolute yumminess of the cake that Mummy was always happy to prepare for me.

I don't bake. I have neither the time nor the interest in doing so. But my sister inherited my mother's love of baking, and every time I visit Joanna Polinsky Berrens in Florida, she has Mum's cream cheese pound cake waiting. Unlike Mummy, however, she never calls beforehand to ask about making it. She knows some things never change.

CREAM CHEESE POUND CAKE

AS MADE BY—BUT NOT ORIGINATED BY—ARLINE POLINSKY

3 sticks butter

8 ounces cream cheese

3 cups sugar

Dash of salt

1½ teaspoons vanilla extract

6 large eggs

3 cups sifted cake flour

Cream the butter, cream cheese, and sugar until light and fluffy. Add salt and vanilla and beat well. Add the eggs one at a time, beating well after each addition. Stir in the flour. Spoon the mixture into a greased 10-inch tube pan. Bake at 310°F about 1 to 1½ hours.

MAKES 12 TO 16 SERVINGS

JEWISH LIFE IN CHARLESTON IN THE 1950s

SANDRA ALTMAN POLIAKOFF

———

Sandra bridges the Old World foodways of her mother and the new world of contemporary food. She respects the legacy of cooking Jewish food and lovingly does so often for family and friends.

———

I CAN STILL SMELL THE AROMAS as I walked into the house on St. Margaret Street after school on Friday afternoons—freshly fried gribenes (rendered chicken fat) and onions on the stove top, ready to be ground into the liver for chopped liver; homemade challah, with that browned crust and soft chewy interior; chicken fricassee in the soup pot, chicken feet sticking up out of the top; and apple strudel and rugelach, all lovingly made by my mother, Annette Altman Carson, for her family to enjoy on Shabbat.

Sandra Altman (Poliakoff) (left) and Gail Altman (Spahn) (right), Charleston, SC, 1950s.
COURTESY SANDRA POLIAKOFF.

I am a first-generation southern American Jew. My parents, Annette Sokol and Isadore Altman, settled in Charleston after escaping growing religious persecution in Warsaw and Kaluszyn, Poland. They spoke broken English but spoke Yiddish at home when they did not want us to understand what they were talking about. We gradually did. My experience was not much different in the 1950s and '60s than that of many of my friends, whose parents were also recent immigrants just starting out, mostly in retail businesses. For me, everything seemed so easy and safe in the '50s.

We walked to school, played outside all day, walked to friends' houses on our own, rode bicycles in the streets, and came home only for dinner. My sisters and I enjoyed playing hopscotch, board games, and lots of card games. My father worked six days a week in his furniture store, Altman's, in downtown Charleston, which he owned with his two brothers. My mother spent her days playing canasta and mah-jongg. But on Shabbat, we all stopped, sat around the dinner table, and talked, sang songs, and mostly ate. It was all so good and unifying.

As my mother grew more Americanized (even though she stayed within the Jewish community), her cooking became lighter and less European yet still kosher and geshmak (tasty). Mom became known for her salmon mousse, which she always brought to break the fast after Yom Kippur, made in her copper fish mold, unmolded, and garnished with vegetables and horseradish sauce. Delicious!

SALMON MOUSSE

ANNETTE SOKOL ALTMAN

1½ envelopes unflavored gelatin

¼ cup cold water

½ cup boiling water

½ cup mayonnaise

2 tablespoons fresh lemon juice

2 tablespoons finely diced shallots

Dash of Tabasco sauce

1 tablespoon smoked Spanish paprika

2 teaspoons kosher salt

2 tablespoons finely chopped dill

2 cups finely flaked canned salmon, skin and bones removed

1 cup heavy cream

Soften the gelatin in cold water in a large mixing bowl. Stir in the boiling water and whisk until the gelatin dissolves. Whisk in the mayonnaise, lemon juice, diced shallots, Tabasco sauce, smoked paprika, salt, and dill. Stir to blend and refrigerate until the mixture starts to thicken, about 25 minutes. Fold in the salmon. In a separate bowl, whip the cream to thicken, and then fold into the salmon. Transfer the mixture to a 6- to 8-cup mold and refrigerate, covered, for at least 4 hours.

Unmold the salmon mousse by placing the bottom of the mold in hot water for a few seconds and turning the mold over onto a large serving dish to release the mousse. Garnish with vegetables and parsley. Cover with plastic wrap and re-chill until ready to serve.

MAKES 20 SERVINGS

MRS. POLIAKOFF OF ABBEVILLE

EDWARD POLIAKOFF

---

*D. Poliakoff's in Abbeville was a mainstay of the business
community for one hundred years. Edward tells how his mother,
Rosa From Poliakoff, led the family business and the culinary
challenges when hosting family holiday dinners.*

D. Poliakoff Store, Abbeville, SC, 2000.

PHOTOGRAPH © BILL ARON, COURTESY JEWISH HERITAGE COLLECTION, SPECIAL COLLECTIONS,
COLLEGE OF CHARLESTON LIBRARIES.

ROSA FROM POLIAKOFF (1914–99) was one of six Union, South Carolina–born children of Israel and Bertha From, who emigrated from Lithuania. She was a graduate of Agnes Scott College and taught for several years in the Atlanta public school system. In February 1940, at the From residence in Union, Rosa was married to Myer Poliakoff, one of six Abbeville, South Carolina–born children of David and Rachel Poliakoff, who emigrated from Russia. Myer was a graduate of the University of South Carolina and a letterman pitcher on the Gamecock baseball team. Thereafter, Rosa was a lifelong devoted resident of Abbeville, where she and Myer raised their children, Doris (Feinsilber), Elaine (Fenton), and Edward, in an observant Jewish home. Rosa assisted Myer in managing D. Poliakoff's, the dry goods store established in 1900 by Myer's father. After Myer's death in 1985, she took on full-time management of the family business, which closed fifteen years later in August 2000.

ROSA'S FARFEL SOUFFLÉ

ROSA FROM POLIAKOFF

The High Holy Days and Passover seders frequently meant reunions of five Poliakoff brothers and families in Abbeville presenting culinary challenges that Rosa always surpassed. For Passover breakfasts for the extended families, Rosa created farfel soufflé. She would rise very early to make the hot dish, frequently using a large white porcelain basin to make a huge batch of hot farfel—enough for ten or twelve people during the first days of Passover. It was a family favorite in Abbeville and is still a Passover tradition in our families.

2 cups Passover farfel

1 cup hot water

2 tablespoons vegetable oil

2 teaspoons salt

4 eggs, room temperature, separated

Heat oven to 400°F. Prepare an ovenproof pan with cooking spray. Add the farfel to a large bowl and add hot water to soften. Add the oil and salt. Add the beaten egg yolks when the farfel and hot water mix has cooled. Beat the whites to firm, and fold into the farfel–egg yolk mix. Bake for 20 to 25 minutes until the soufflé rises and pulls away from the sides of the pan. A round casserole dish will yield a higher soufflé; a larger pan will have a lower rise and cook faster.

MAKES 10 TO 12 SERVINGS

MEMORIES OF GRANDMA

GLORIA FROM GOLDBERG

———

*Gloria From Goldberg remembers her Grandma Bertha From, mother of
Rosa Poliakoff. She writes about her family being together in Union,
sharing family business stories, cookies, and lots of love.*

———

MY BROTHER, ALLAN, AND I WERE BORN in Union in the early 1950s. Our Dad, Harry From, along with his five siblings, was born there. Our grandparents, Israel and Bertha From, emigrated from Lithuania in the 1890s. My grandfather was a peddler who opened a clothing (schmatta) business in Union. My dad, Harry, had started his own clothing business on Main Street in Union in 1948. My parents met through a traveling salesman. My mother, Edith Small From, was a graduate of New York University and a registered dietician. She paid the bills for the store and did all the bookkeeping.

I was very close to Grandma From and spent most Jewish holidays with her. She lived with us in the family home in Union when I was little. I always heard that when she was younger,

Cookbook cover, Bertha From, Union, SC, 1905.
COURTESY GLORIA FROM GOLDBERG.

she loved to cook big meals for her husband and six children: Ellis, Mary, Sara, Lena, Rosa, and Harry. My mother kept a kosher kitchen, and so did most of her daughters. Most of the children ended up in the clothing business like their father. We had two kitchens in the family home. One kitchen was connected to her room, and that kitchen was kosher. I remember burying dishes in the backyard when a kosher dish was misplaced. Grandma spent her last years in Woodruff, South Carolina, with Aunt Lena Reimer. Grandma From employed Kate Stephens. Kate was born and raised in Spartanburg county and lived there for eighty-two years. Kate was the church clerk at New Bethel Baptist Church in Woodruff for 49 years. She had six children, eighteen grandchildren, and twenty-four great-grandchildren. Grandma taught Kate to make the best chopped liver and other Jewish dishes and how to keep a kosher kitchen. In turn, Kate also helped Grandma From—who never learned to write or read English—by reading to her and acting as her scribe.

MRS. FROM'S COOKIES

Grandma From was famous for her cookies brought to all family occasions. As Grandma From could neither write nor read English, this recipe was written down by her employee, Kate Stephens.

4 eggs

1½ cups sugar

1 cup oil

2 teaspoons vanilla extract

Self-rising flour

Pecans or cinnamon, raisins,
   and coconut

Crack the eggs into large bowl and beat. Add the sugar, oil, and vanilla.

Add enough flour to make a stiff dough. Knead and roll out thin. Sprinkle a little sugar over the dough. Cut into desired shapes. Press a pecan on each cookie. For roll-up cookies, sprinkle coconut, cinnamon, and raisins over dough. Roll up the dough and cut into slices ½ inches thick. Bake in the oven at 400°F until lightly browned, 10–12 minutes.

MAKES 24 COOKIES

MAMMA LEARNED TO COOK

MICKEY KRONSBERG ROSENBLUM

————

*Mickey Kronsberg Rosenblum remembers her accomplished
mother's recipes, which became family favorites.*

————

**Shabbos dinner, Kronsberg
family home. Author Mickey
Kronsberg Rosenblum, front right;
Mary Dunnmeyer in doorway.
Charleston, SC, 1950s.**
COURTESY MICKEY KRONSBERG
ROSENBLUM.

MY MOTHER, FREDERICA (Freddie) Weinberg Kronsberg, never learned to cook until she married my father, Milton Kronsberg. Her German mother and Dutch father raised her in Staunton, Virginia. She met Daddy while she was at Goucher College in Baltimore, Maryland, in 1932. After a nine-year courtship, Freddie and Milton finally married in 1940 and moved to Charleston, where Milton joined his brother, Edward, in the retail business.

Mamma's lack of cooking skills was more complicated, because Daddy had grown up on Tilghman Island, Maryland, where his father owned a general store; his family kept kosher and were the only Jewish people on the island. Almost all their meals consisted of fish, except for a kosher chicken every now and then when it was brought by boat from Baltimore. So, Mamma decided to look to her mother and mother-in-law for their best and most liked recipes. From her mother, she learned to make rich, German-Southern food, and from her mother-in-law, all kinds of fish with some kosher dishes mixed in. She also picked up tips and recipes from friends. Her collection was a gumbo of recipes. Nevertheless, Mamma became a wonderful cook, even surprising my father by deciding to keep a kosher home. (I found recipes jotted down in cookbooks and kitchen drawers, with some written in shorthand and on scraps of paper, but I still managed to record the most popular ones for the family.)

After my parents moved to Charleston, they became active in the Jewish community and the community at large. They had three children: my sister, Gina; my brother, Abe; and me. My parents started a family tradition that all of us were to have the Shabbos meal together on Fridays. Mamma cooked a big meal with dessert, and of course we'd have the Shabbos blessings. When we got married and had our own children, we all still came to our parents' house for Shabbos dinner. Even some of the great grandchildren came for Shabbos dinner. The recipe that follows was one that the children and grandchildren loved the best and we now make ourselves. It is one that my German grandmother sent to my mother by mail some seventy years ago and is not quite as precise as most recipes are today.

CHICKEN GUMBO

FREDDIE KRONSBERG

1 large hen

1 small onion, cut up

4 large tomatoes

2 stalks celery cut up

½ green pepper cut up

2 packages frozen Fordhook lima beans

4 cups water

1 can whole kernel corn

Season the hen. Add all the ingredients, except the corn, in a Dutch oven. Bring to a boil and cook fast for 30 minutes. Then boil on medium heat for 3–4 hours, adding the drained corn for the last ½ hour. Drain off the grease. Slice the chicken off the bone and serve the gumbo on top of the chicken with mashed potatoes.

MAKES 10 TO 12 SERVINGS

AREN'T CHEESECAKES JEWISH?

CINDY ALPERT SAAD

———

Cindy Saad, an artist from Columbia, lovingly remembers her mother,
Eleanor, and maternal family from Sumter, who didn't
talk about being Jewish, but lived it.

———

WHEN ASKED TO CONTRIBUTE to *Kugels & Collards*, my initial thought was that my mother's cooking was not necessarily Jewish. So, what story can I tell? But my mother was known for her cheesecakes, and aren't cheesecakes Jewish?

There were several significant women in my life who were wonderful cooks. First, I'll begin with the woman behind the cheesecake: my mother, Eleanor Jane Calvert Alpert, the daughter of a Jewish mother and Protestant father, who grew up in Columbia, South Carolina, where she attended the Tree of Life Temple and taught Sunday school. A beautiful yet modest young girl, she was

Eleanor Jane Calvert Alpert, Columbia, SC, n.d.
COURTESY CINDY ALPERT SAAD.

an accomplished pianist and a sought-after elocutionist. She was quite serious about her Jewish faith and won a 1932 national scholarship to summer school at the Hebrew Union College in Cincinnati, Ohio. Later, while attending the University of South Carolina, she met the love of her life, Maxie Alpert, at temple. They soon married, made their home in Sumter, reared four children over two decades, and ran the ladies' fine apparel store called Alpert's, founded by my dad's mother, Mary Belin Alpert, who immigrated to the United States from Russia in the early 1900s. My parents enjoyed a very full Jewish life in Sumter. They didn't talk about being Jewish—they lived it. They attended many dinner parties at the homes of friends, the Brodys and the Rubins, unselfishly serving in all capacities.

I never really thought of my mother's cooking as Jewish, but it was. She made potato latkes, matzo ball soup, brisket, and lots and lots of desserts. We also had traditional southern fare, but our meals were never cooked with fatback, and the only cookbook she owned was the *Jewish Settlement Cookbook*, which belonged to her mother, Ginny Pepper Calvert.

It was in Eleanor's later years that she found her passion for baking. Watching Eleanor do her magic in the kitchen while I sat on the kitchen stool sampling her cheesecakes topped with cherries or blueberries is a favorite memory. She was organized and liked to measure out her ingredients the night before and did most of her baking in the early morning when the kitchen was cool. Her sought-after cheesecake was handed down from her mother, but through the years, it became known as Eleanor's cheesecake and she became quite the cheesecake queen, sharing them with many. She kept a freezer full of cakes and brisket, with plenty for me to take away. Eleanor also had a habit of labeling her cheesecakes for cracks or brown spots before freezing. Now I do, too!

Then there was my older sister, Maxine Calvert Alpert Kline, who was my best friend and mentor. She was married to Sol Kline, and they had three beautiful girls. Maxine was a fabulous cook in her own right, and her brisket was to die for. Her brisket is the one that has become my family's mainstay. I always loved her turquoise china, and I'm sure it influenced me to choose a pattern similar in style and color. But when it came to cheesecakes, Maxine relied on Eleanor, buying them from her in an attempt to put her in the business of selling, but to no avail. Sadly, we lost Maxine to cancer way too early in life at the age of forty-five.

I would be remiss not to mention the third significant woman in my life, my Aunt Fannie Alpert Goldstein, my father's sister, who lived in Kingstree and was married to Isadore Goldstein. They had one son, Joseph Goldstein, a 1985 Nobel Prize winner. Aunt Fannie hosted some of the tastiest and most memorable family dinners in her formal dining room with the most exquisite table settings. Her chocolate roll was phenomenal. I can still see it and almost taste it.

It wasn't until after my mother passed away that I taught myself to make her cheesecake, using her mixing bowl and, in the beginning, calling her friend Jackie Brody for guidance as she, too, had mastered it. Every time I bake, I feel her presence and it brings such joy. I hope to impart some of that joy to others by sharing these recipes. Bon *Alpertit*!

ELEANOR'S CHEESECAKE

ELEANOR CALVERT ALPERT

Crust (make ahead)

1½ cups graham cracker crumbs

3 tablespoons sugar

⅔ stick margarine, melted

Filling

3 (8-ounce) packages softened
cream cheese

1 cup granulated sugar

4 large eggs, room temperature,
separated

1 cup half and half

Pinch of salt

To make the crust: Thoroughly blend the crust ingredients. Use a 9-inch springform pan, slightly greased. Press the crust firmly against the bottom and sides of the pan. Eleanor used a medium soup spoon for this, sides first and then bottom. Chill for about an hour.

To make the filling: In a bowl with a mixer at high speed, mix the cream cheese until fluffy. Add the sugar and mix.

Add the half and half to the egg yolks in a separate bowl and mix with a fork. Then gradually add this mixture to the cream cheese and mix at medium speed. Whip the egg whites with a pinch of salt until just beginning to stand in soft peaks. Do not overbeat. Fold the whites gently into the cheese mixture.

Pour into the prepared crust and bake 1 hour at 325°F. Turn the oven off, and leave door slightly ajar. Allow the cake to remain in the oven at least an hour. Remove and cool in the pan on a wire rack.

Refrigerate overnight. Loosen the crust from the rim and remove to serve.

MAKES 12 SERVINGS

AUNT FANNIE'S CHOCOLATE ROLL

FANNIE ALPERT GOLDSTEIN

This chocolate roll is a family favorite. The recipe has been shared with many.

Cake roll

5 egg yolks

3 tablespoons cocoa

1 cup confectioners' sugar

1 teaspoon vanilla extract

4 tablespoons flour

5 egg whites, stiffly beaten

½ teaspoon salt

Chocolate icing

2 cups sugar

2 squares Baker's Chocolate

1 cup water

2 tablespoons light corn syrup

¼ teaspoon salt

2 tablespoons of butter or margarine

1 teaspoon vanilla extract

To make the roll: Beat the egg yolks until thick and lemon colored. Add sifted dry ingredients and beat until well blended. Fold in the vanilla and stiffly beaten egg whites.

Spread thinly in a greased (shallow) 11 × 16-inch pan lined with wax paper. (Aunt Fannie used Crisco to grease the pan and also slightly greased the wax paper.) Bake in a moderately hot oven, at 400°F, for 15–20 minutes. Test with a cake tester until it comes out clean. Turn the cake out on to a damp towel on a cabinet top. Cut off the crisp edges around the cake and pull off the wax paper (some of the bottom of the cake will come off). Roll up in a towel as a jelly roll. Let the roll cool for a few minutes. Spread and fill the center with 2 small cartons of cream whipped and sweetened to taste with confectioners' sugar. Fold the edges of the cake together and refrigerate.

To make the icing: (Aunt Fannie usually did it the next day, but you can make it after the cake is really cold.) Cook the sugar, chocolate, water, syrup, and salt over medium heat, stirring constantly until the chocolate and sugar are dissolved. Cover the sauce for 3 minutes. Cook uncovered to softball stage. It takes about 12 to 15 minutes.

Remove the icing from the heat, add butter, and let it cool to lukewarm. Add the vanilla and beat until the icing is stiff enough to spread on the top and sides of roll. Sprinkle the top with chopped nuts. If the icing becomes too hard or stiff to spread, add a tablespoon of hot water.

MAKES 8 (2-INCH SLICE) SERVINGS

STRONG WOMEN,
FROM GENERATION TO GENERATION

BETH BERNSTEIN

———

*Beth Bernstein, member of the South Carolina House of Representatives,
is a Columbia native. She remembers her mother and Aunt Eleanor
with a story that spans the generations of the
Bernstein Hammer family.*

———

Beth Bernstein (front left) and sisters with parents, Isadore and Carol Bernstein, Sullivan's Island, SC, 2002.
COURTESY BETH BERNSTEIN.

BECAUSE THE JEWISH COMMUNITY in Columbia is small, a significant portion of my Jewish identity was founded on spending the Jewish holidays with my extended family at the home of my father's sister, Eleanor Bernstein Hammer, and her husband, Henry Hammer. My paternal grandparents came to this country from Eastern Europe around 1907, initially settled in Summerville, and, by the end of the 1920s, lived in Columbia by way of Swansea. They kept a kosher home, and Aunt El learned how to cook many traditional Jewish meals from my grandmother, Bessie Bernstein, for whom I am named.

Aunt El felt more like a grandmother to me, as she was fifty years old when my twin sister and I were born. She and Uncle Henry would host Rosh Hashanah dinner and Passover seder annually until her death in October 2014. After that time, I attempted to continue the tradition by hosting holidays at my home. Some of the recipes that our family loved were her chopped liver, homemade gefilte fish, her sought-after mandelbread, and Passover teiglach. Unfortunately, I never perfected most of those dishes, but I do prepare her beloved chopped liver. It's the first thing we eat when we break from services for lunch during Rosh Hashanah, as is custom. We eat it from the same large, green, glass bowl that Aunt El used and serve it with Tam Tam crackers.

Although my mother was not someone whom you thought of as being in the kitchen preparing extravagant Jewish meals, I do have vivid memories from my childhood of her preparing many desserts for bar and bat mitzvahs and oneg shabbats when Beth Shalom used to rotate through its membership for hosting the oneg for Friday night services. The only cookbook I remember her using consistently was *The Stuffed Bagel*, created by the Columbia chapter of Hadassah with many of her favorite recipes highlighted and earmarked. *The Stuffed Bagel* is a staple at my own house today.

Throughout their lives, my mother and aunt always remained passionate in their commitment to family and the Jewish community. My mother was the first female president of Beth Shalom Synagogue, president of Hadassah for many years, and served in many other leadership roles. My aunt was very active in the Sisterhood and served as its president. They both led by example and exuded values of integrity, dignity, humility, justice, open-mindedness, and acceptance, which were instilled in my siblings and me. That legacy is now passed down to our own children. L'dor v'dor.

CAROL'S CHOCOLATE MOUSSE CAKE

This is one of my mother's most popular desserts, served in a trifle dish, which she would prepare for bar and bat mitzvahs.

Crust

3 cups chocolate wafer crumbs

½ cup unsalted butter melted (1 stick)

Filling

1-pound semisweet chocolate chips

2 whole eggs

4 eggs, room temperature, separated

2 cups whipped cream (real whipping cream)

6 tablespoons powdered sugar

Topping

2 cups whipping cream

3 tablespoons sugar

Grated chocolate

To make the crust: Combine the crushed chocolate wafers with melted butter and place in the bottom of a trifle dish to form the crust.

To make the mousse: Soften the chocolate in a microwave. Add whole eggs and mix well. Add the egg yolks and mix until blended. Whip the whipping cream and powdered sugar until soft. Beat the egg whites until they are stiff but not dry. Mix the egg whites and whipping cream together and fold into the chocolate. Pour into the crust and chill at least 6 hours in a trifle dish.

Whip 2 more cups whipping cream with 3 tablespoons sugar until stiff and spread on top of the chocolate. Sprinkle grated chocolate on top and around it. Loosen the edges with a butter knife and serve.

MAKES 12 SERVINGS

WE'LL MAKE YOU FAMOUS

CAROL MICHAEL

———

Carol Michael remembers her grandmother, Charlestonian Tobye Karesh Hollander, and her special "make her famous" challah recipe.

———

Uptown Shoe Store, 545 King Street, Charleston, SC, n.d.
COURTESY JEWISH HERITAGE COLLECTION, SPECIAL COLLECTIONS, COLLEGE OF CHARLESTON LIBRARIES.

GRANDMA TOBYE BAKED CHALLAH every week for Shabbat in her tiny kitchen with the metal cabinets in Stuyvesant Town, New York City. If we visited on Friday, as the elevator rose to the eighth floor, I could smell it baking, amid all the other smells of the apartment building. Her face would appear in the oval window of the steel door as it slid open, and we stepped out. What other treats might there be, since we couldn't eat challah until dinner? Would there be yeast cake?

By the time I was old enough to make challah on my own at our house, I learned that my mother did not have the recipe. "Ask her, Mom!" I demanded. "I have, Carol," she replied. "We'll have to make her famous if you really want it."

Tobye Karesh Hollander grew up in Charleston, above the Uptown Shoe Store at 545 King Street, which my great-grandfather owned and ran. One of nine children in an Orthodox family, she left what she felt was small-town living to move north to New York City when she married my grandfather, Herman Hollander. They met in the mountains of Hendersonville, North Carolina, one summer, both escaping the city heat only to find heat of a different kind; he, a dry goods salesman from the Lower East Side of Manhattan, and she, an intelligent and beautiful southern young woman with aspirations of a bigger life in New York.

Through the hardships of the Depression, they raised my mother and uncles. By the time I came along in the 1950s, on summer weekends they took the Long Island Railroad out to our suburban house on Long Island to escape the summer heat. On early mornings, I used to tiptoe up the stairs and beg to hear the romantic stories of her life growing up in Charleston in the 1890s and early 1900s. They were part of the Jewish merchant class on Upper King Street. On those mornings, we often had grits and a fried egg on top for breakfast, as I longed to be connected to my southern roots.

My mother must have known her mother's long-simmering desire for fame when she wrote a letter to Jean Hewitt, food editor of the *New York Times*, expressing our desire to learn the challah recipe. A wonderful friendship was born, and the recipe and story were published in May 1971. My daughter, Rachel, is now a wonderful cook and food stylist in her own right, and I have tweaked the recipe slightly as we bake it with her two daughters, my granddaughters. L'dor v'dor—from one generation to the next.

In December 2019, I stood in front of 545 King Street. The shoe store is now a wine bar, or was, pre-pandemic. The building had survived Hurricane Hugo, and the tiles in the pavement remain: Uptown Shoe Store. I looked up at the porch and windows that go from front to back and imagined the smells wafting up from the kitchen; the sound of kids' feet; the rustling of long dresses and big hats; and the raising of the staircase to allow the cow to come from the backyard, where the outdoor privy was, to King Street, to be taken to market downtown. I re-read the letters my great uncle wrote to me in his Charlestonian brogue and wondered: What else did they cook in their kosher kitchen? Was there any melding of the richness of the Gullah and African American cooking traditions into their recipes from the old country of Poland and Russia? I can't wait to take my granddaughters to Charleston.

GRANDMA TOBYE'S CHALLAH

ADAPTED BY CAROL MICHAEL

6 cups unsifted unbleached flour

2 packages (4½ teaspoons) active dry yeast

1 ⅓ cups lukewarm water (98–105°F)

1 tablespoon sugar, plus a pinch

¾ tablespoon coarse (kosher) salt

3 tablespoons canola oil

4 large eggs

Honey

Canola oil

Sift the flour into a large mixing bowl. Make a well in the center. Set aside. Crumble the yeast into a cup. Add ⅔ cup warm water and mix well with a fork. Pour the yeast mixture into the flour well. Sprinkle a pinch of sugar on it and cover lightly with flour. Combine the sugar, salt, and oil in a 2-cup Pyrex measuring cup. Add the remaining warm water and mix well. Beat 3 of the eggs, reserving the fourth for later use. Set the measuring cup in a saucepan with warm water and place over a low flame. When the mixture is lukewarm, add 3 beaten eggs. Continue to heat the pan of water while stirring the mixture in the cup until it is smooth and custardlike. Add some honey. Do not allow it to heat above 115°F, or the eggs will scramble.

Add the egg mixture to the flour and yeast and stir to mix. When the mixture forms a soft, cohesive ball, as my Grandma Tobye used to say, "Then comes the revolution. Dig in with both hands and knead away for dear life, up and around, down and outwards. Pat it gently and say a prayer." Moisten the surface of the dough with oil; cover the dough with a towel, and set it in a warm place to rise until doubled in bulk, about 1 hour.

Punch down the dough and knead gently for a few minutes. Divide the dough into 6 parts. Roll each part into a sausage shape, about 10 inches long, and tapered at the ends. Braid 3 rolls together and place them on a cookie sheet that has been oiled and floured or in an oiled 9 × 5 × 3-inch loaf pan that has had its sides dusted lightly with flour. You can also use parchment paper on the sheet pan.

Carol Michael with daughter and grandchildren making challah, Brookline, MA, 2022.

COURTESY CAROL MICHAEL.

Repeat with the other 3 rolls. Cover the pans and set them in a warm place until the loaves have risen to the top of pan or nearly doubled in size.

Preheat the oven to 400°F. Beat the remaining egg. Brush the tops of the loaves with the beaten egg. (You will not use it all.) Bake for 30 to 35 minutes or until browned and done. Remove the loaves from the pans immediately and set them on a rack near an open window to increase the crustiness of the outside.

MAKES 2 LOAVES

THE LEGACY 6

LEGACY 199
Laurie Goldman Smithwick

Mattie Culp's Fried Chicken
Mattie Culp's Biscuits

CREATING A NEW CHAPTER 204
Ali Rosen Gourvitch

Grits and Lox Casserole

MAMANU **PAST AND PRESENT** 208
Emily Levinson

Mimi's Coconut Sour Cream Layer Cake
Tuna Noodle Casserole

IS ONE BRISKET ENOUGH? 213
Gabbi Baker

Matzo Kugel
Aunt Amy's Blintz Casserole

FOOD IS OUR FAMILY'S LOVE LANGUAGE 218
Jordane Harvey Lotts

Holiday or Yontif Chicken and Rice
Kasha Varnishkes
Tzimmes
Passover Matzo Toffee
Lyssa's Jewish Star Poppy Seed Cake

How does one preserve culture? One way is through maintaining the culinary legacies of our Jewish and southern ancestors by including their meals on our tables today. Cherished food stories begin with sensory memories from the kitchen and table, as well as the spoken and handwritten recipes that have been passed down generations. We are guardians of our family traditions. Our Jewish ancestors are looking over our shoulders with words of wisdom and foods of celebration, comfort, and challenge. Our past and the present come together in the foods we prepare and eat.

The essays compiled in this chapter come from young contributors who have similar food memories to those of earlier generations. They are aware of Jewish and southern nuances in their lives and speak of the rich heritage of their families. Family members today do not live near each other as did our immigrant ancestors; however, grandparents as both creators and custodians of memory still influence our feelings and narratives.

This generation remembers meals and memories passed down from elders while reserving the right to invent their own contemporary versions. Jordane Harvey Lotts writes, "When I think back to my grandmother and how hugely important being Jewish was to her, I can't help but think about how inherently southern she was, too. My grandmother, with her southern drawl, loved barbecue ribs, shrimp boils, steamed oysters, and bacon cheeseburgers. It was like being Jewish was of utmost importance, but growing up around these irresistibly delicious foods was too much to withstand, so she gave in—in a big way."

The contributors speak of the past but also about moving forward with their own food traditions. Through their words, we see how gathering around the table and sharing meals is a living link between generations. Each author speaks about her food memories as a love language. Emily Levinson says, "It was ingrained in me by my mom and grandmothers that cooking for your family and friends is a way to show your love. I may not make brisket or meatballs, but I do love to host my friends— both Jewish and non-Jewish—for holidays and Friday night dinners." Each meal, each story, lives on and is shared in the pages of this book—a bound legacy, which we hope years from now is covered in splatters of kugel and collards, evidence of constant use—from their kitchens to yours.

LEGACY

LAURIE GOLDMAN SMITHWICK

Laurie Goldman Smithwick pays tribute to Mattie Culp and her style of encouragement in learning to cook.

Laurie Goldman Smithwick and Mattie Culp, Charlotte, NC, 2001.
COURTESY LAURIE SMITHWICK.

I WOULD LOVE TO SAY that I grew up cooking at my grandmother's knee. That I spent endless hours of my childhood in a steamy, bubbly kitchen dusted with powdery-flecked shafts of light, perched on a stool watching her every move, waiting for those moments when an oversized spoon was touched to my lips for me to learn taste. Well, no. Not quite. I do love to cook, but that story is not my story. All my grandparents died before I was twelve years old. In their place, I had Mattie.

Mattie Culp was born in 1918 in Chester, South Carolina. She had a daughter, three granddaughters, and six great-grandchildren. And she was known to the entire congregation of her African Methodist Episcopal Zion church as "Mother Culp."

Mattie was also the Black woman who worked for my grandparents. She lived in their house, cleaned, cooked, took care of my mother as a child. She also looked after my cousins, my brother, and me, flawlessly filling for us the role of beloved grandmother.

Mattie taught me the kind of cooking that doesn't have a recipe—although she didn't actually teach me. Mostly, she cooked while I watched and asked questions like, "How much flour did you just add to those pan drippings to make gravy?" And her answers sounded like this: "What do you mean how much flour? You look at how much drippings you have, and you add enough flour. If it tastes right, you added enough." She wasn't being mean or rigid, just sensible, as if to say, "Don't worry about measurements—just cook." Like I needed to concentrate and just do it right.

So, I watched, and ate, and watched, and ate. The best fried chicken I have ever put in my mouth. The flakiest, fluffiest biscuits. Sweet potatoes that tasted more like pudding. The most comforting chicken pot pies. And sometime after college I started trying some of her recipes on my own. This usually involved a long phone conversation with Mattie where I took extensive notes that didn't make sense as I wrote them: "Then you add your baking powder. Taste it. If it don't taste right, add some more." Some recipes required two phone calls.

I bumbled through and kept trying to serve people dishes that I called "Mattie's (insert food here)." Now, after years of practice, I can make consistently good buttermilk biscuits having never had a recipe in front of me. I can make fried chicken that mostly comes out right. Sometimes I have good gravy to add to the meal, sometimes not.

In doing this, I have come to understand a life lesson that applies to more than just cooking: If it doesn't taste right before it's cooked, it certainly won't taste right after it's cooked. For me, "right" means that mysterious blend of inexact amounts of salt and spices and secret ingredients that makes it taste exactly like Mattie's.

When Mattie became too ill to cook, it took seven of us to replicate her Thanksgiving meal. Seven people. To put together a dinner usually prepared by one person. Of course, she was there, coaching us every step of the way. But it felt good to cook for Mattie, and it tasted pretty much just like hers. And we were all very proud of ourselves.

Since 2007, we've had to celebrate Thanksgiving without Mattie. Everyone has a job. I make Mattie's cornbread dressing and Mattie's turkey gravy; my mom makes Mattie's sweet potatoes; my brother makes Mattie's turkey. Everything is delicious, everyone is happy, and I'm grateful to have had so many years with Mattie humming her way around my grandmother's and my aunt's and my mom's kitchens.

But I also feel sad. Sad that Mattie's cooking is no longer an activity but a subject. That her gospel purring is no longer something to listen to but to talk about. That her place at our table is no longer a presence but a legacy.

MATTIE CULP'S FRIED CHICKEN

Although Mattie didn't have a written recipe, through trial and error, I have created a recipe as close to Mattie's as possible.

1 quart buttermilk

4 tablespoons kosher salt

8–10 bone-in chicken pieces

2½ cups flour

2 tablespoons table salt

2 teaspoons paprika

1 teaspoon black pepper, freshly
ground

1 quart oil (peanut or canola)

Pour the buttermilk and kosher salt into a bowl or large Tupperware container. Stir to dissolve the salt. Place the chicken in the bowl and cover/coat with buttermilk. If you have enough time, cover the bowl and set it in the refrigerator for a few hours. If you're making the chicken right now, let it sit on the counter while you get everything else ready.

Pour the oil into a Dutch oven with a lid and heat just below medium until the oil is about 360°F.

While the oil is heating, mix the flour, table salt, paprika, and black pepper in a large bowl until fully blended. Taste a tiny bit of the mixture. You should be able to taste all the ingredients. If not, add more of whichever ones you can't detect.

Working with one piece at a time, dredge the chicken in the flour mixture until well coated. Shake off the excess flour mixture and place the chicken on a wire rack.

Carefully add the chicken to the hot oil (4–6 pieces per batch), skin side down. Cover the Dutch oven and cook for 7 minutes. After 7 minutes, remove the lid (be careful not to let any condensation drip into the pot). Turn the pieces over and cook for 7 more minutes. Turn the pieces again and cook for up to 4 more minutes. Legs and thighs should be 165°F, and breasts should be 150°F. You can tell when the legs are ready when the skin is shrinking up onto the bone.

Remove the chicken and place on a wire rack set in a rimmed baking sheet. You may keep it warm in a low oven or at room temperature. Repeat with additional batches.

MAKES 8 TO 10 PIECES

MATTIE CULP'S BISCUITS

2 cups all-purpose flour (300 g)
1 tablespoon baking powder
1 teaspoon salt
⅓ cup shortening (60 g)
1 cup buttermilk

Preheat the oven to 450°F.

Whisk the flour, baking powder, and salt together in a large bowl. Cut the shortening into the flour mixture with a pastry blender until the mixture resembles coarse crumbs (you can also do this with a fork or with two knives—one in each hand, slicing away from each other). Once you have the sandy crumb texture, stir with your hand, squeezing bits of flour between your fingers into little coins.

With your hand again, make a well in the flour mixture and slowly pour the milk into the well. Gently stir with a fork just until the dough holds together (there shouldn't be any dry flour left in the bowl). Do not overmix.

Turn the dough out onto a floured work surface. Dust the top of the dough with flour, and rub some flour on your hands. Gently gather the dough into a rough ball, and then pat into a "rectangle" about 1 inch thick. Fold it once and then pat it down again. Repeat this once more, and finish with a rectangle about ½ inch thick. Don't overhandle the dough—it should remain rough and slightly shaggy.

Cut out the biscuits by lightly jiggling a metal biscuit cutter into the dough. Do not twist, because this seals the sides and keeps them from rising as much. (If you don't have a biscuit cutter, you can use a glass, but choose one with the thinnest glass you can find.) Place the cut biscuits on a cookie sheet. They can be very close together.

After cutting your first batch, gently gather the leftover dough together, form into a new rectangle, and repeat cutting. Repeat until all the dough is used up.

Bake for 10–12 minutes or until golden brown on top.

MAKES ABOUT 12 BISCUITS

CREATING A NEW CHAPTER

ALI ROSEN GOURVITCH

———

Ali Rosen Gourvitch writes about her families' embrace of America.

———

Jewish wedding, Charleston, SC, 2012.
PHOTOGRAPH BY PAIGE
WINN, COURTESY ALI
ROSEN GOURVITCH.

I KNEW THAT MY FAMILY wasn't the typical Jewish family: My Jewish father and Christian mother raised us to learn about both faiths, but that just made me feel like I knew more, not less. It never seemed odd to me to be the only Jewish kid in a classroom. It never struck me as strange that my extremely common Jewish last name was mispronounced *Rah*-zen, instead of *Roe*-zen. I didn't know that most synagogues don't have organs like mine, the oldest Reform synagogue in America, Charleston's Kahal Kadosh Beth Elohim.

Every member of my family in Charleston was Jewish, and it never occurred to me that there was any other way to be Jewish. My dad's grandparents emigrated through Ellis Island from Russia and Austria in the typical story of so many American Jews, but they made their way south rather than staying in larger communities up north. That risk reaped rewards. My great-grandparents ran a grocery store in Charleston, and within a single generation, my grandfather became Charleston's first Jewish city attorney. As a result, however, I always saw my Jewish family as Charlestonians first. They were American, they loved Charleston, and they were also Jewish. They socialized and lived among the other Jews in the city, but it wasn't their leading identity. We made latkes on Hanukkah, ran around with all the other kids looking for the afikomen on Passover, and ate matzo ball soup on Rosh Hashanah, but at my bat mitzvah, there was as much southern food as Jewish. I never gave it a thought.

I didn't really appreciate the specificity of my southern Jewish heritage, and its impact on my culinary identity, until I moved to New York and had an Israeli mother-in-law. She was the kind of cook who made gefilte fish from scratch and had multiple courses at every holiday meal. She was incredible. She gave me a whole new dimension to my Jewish identity. We had common ground being Jews who had grown up with traditions different from those of the vast majority of Jews residing in New York City. But with us, it was usually more about the food than the religion.

Weddings always have a way of showing us so much about ourselves, and this joining of two people—a southern great-granddaughter of shtetl-born immigrants and a New York City–bred child of Israelis—certainly laid bare the cultural differences that exist even within one religion. It started at our engagement party, hosted by my in-laws. My mother-in-law made every morsel of food and beamed with pride. My ninety-one-year-old grandfather had flown up to New York, and I saw him chatting in a corner with one of my husband's family friends of a similar age. She had grown up in Poland and survived Auschwitz to become a loyal New Yorker. The bulk of their conversation centered on her surprise that he didn't speak any of his parents' mother tongues—no Russian, no Yiddish, and no Hebrew. It had never struck me as odd that the ultimate Charlestonian had only spoken to his parents in a language they didn't learn until they were adults.

However, the real reckoning came, as it always does, over food. My in-laws ate everything and certainly never kept kosher. But with something as religiously significant as a wedding, the context was apparently different. On a trip to Charleston to do some wedding planning, we started to discuss options for the rehearsal dinner. I suggested a pig roast, without a single hint of irony or self-awareness. My mother-in-law, respectful and kind to her very core, tried her best to gingerly explain to me why a large slab of pork in the middle of a Jewish wedding celebration might be a bit tone-deaf. Here we were, two Jews with exactly the same dietary habits in everyday life but with a totally opposite sense of what a wedding looked like.

I give her credit for allowing the unkosher shrimp and grits that I requested for the rehearsal dinner and for also not saying a single word about the post-wedding oyster roast my dad's family hosted in our honor. It was the first time in my life I had been struck by the interwoven texture of what it means to be a Jew in the South.

The truth is, there was very little Jewish culinary identity for most of my family before they left Europe due to difficult times that often included hunger and bare larders—a critical part of *why* so many Jews came to the United States. In an interview my father recorded with his grandfather, he mentions subsisting on mostly potatoes, herring, and cabbage in his Russian childhood. He reminisced about an aunt in Moscow who once sent the family half a watermelon, a highlight of his young life. If a piece of cutlery touched meat and then dairy accidentally, they stuck it in the ground to "make it kosher again." We like to romanticize our pasts, but poverty and pain are also a part of our histories.

I think about what it must have been like for my great-grandparents. They raised their children in a Jewish community but discarded most of their language and food for a culture that, for them, lived up to the ideal of the American dream that propelled them to leave their homeland for a strange new world. My father grew up eating collards and grits along with his grandmother's matzo ball soup. Charleston allowed them to keep their Jewish identity while growing interwoven roots into the society that had embraced them.

Generations later, in front of the Ashley River, beneath centuries-old oak trees on a warm October day, two Jews were married. Their Jewish families both left Russia and Eastern Europe for a better life—but one family found Israel and the other, the American South. We have come together in the end, but the culinary traditions we are creating together are writing a new chapter in our Jewish lives.

GRITS AND LOX CASSEROLE

This grits recipe feels quintessentially southern, and the lox is the perfect nod to my Jewish life in New York. It also feels like family, because it's the kind of no-nonsense dish you bring to a family brunch.

5 cups water

2 cups whole milk

1 stick salted butter, cut into 1-inch pieces, divided

2 cups stone-ground grits

1 teaspoon salt

2 cups sharp cheddar cheese, grated

16 ounces lox, cut into small pieces

3 large eggs, beaten

Preheat the oven to 350°F.

Bring the water, milk, and half of the butter to a boil in a heavy pot on medium-high heat. Add the grits and stir continuously until the mixture returns to a boil. Reduce the heat, cover, and stir frequently for 10 to 15 minutes, until the grits have thickened but are still a bit al dente to taste (your brand of grits really could make a difference here, so always keep tasting as you cook, in case it takes less time).

When the grits are done, remove the pot from the heat. Add the remaining butter, salt, and 1½ cups of the cheese to the mixture until incorporated. Add the lox and eggs and stir quickly and vigorously so the eggs don't cook before being incorporated. Pour the mixture into a 9 × 13-inch or 8-inch baking dish, and sprinkle the remaining cheese over the top. Bake in the oven for 45 minutes to 1 hour, or until the top is golden.

MAKES 6 TO 8 SERVINGS

MAMANU PAST AND PRESENT

EMILY LEVINSON

———

Grandmothers left a lasting imprint on
Emily Levinson's culinary journey.

———

"*MAMANU, MAMANU!*"— I can still hear my Mimi, Faye Lomansky Levinson, saying in her Southern drawl, an accent she developed growing up in Camden. When we would ask what *mamanu* meant, Mimi would always reply, "from your lips to God's ears." She said it was an old Yiddish saying, but in all my searches, I could never verify this.

The matriarchs of my family were all wonderful cooks. Whenever I visited my Nana, Miriam Brotman Gordin, in her kosher-style home in Summerton, we would always have barbecue chicken, rice, and broccoli for dinner, and I would help her bake meringue "kisses" for dessert—which would only turn out edible if the weather was just right. My Mimi would host our family holidays and was famous for her baked goods (most notably, brownies, chocolate pound cake, coconut cake, and mandelbread) and hearty family feasts, which always included matzo ball soup, brisket, and roasted potatoes. My aunts would set extravagant tablescapes, and we would spend the day cutting flowers and foliage from Mimi's yard and making floral arrangements for the table. My mom, Rachel Gordin Barnett, drew from her small-town Summerton and Jewish roots serving fresh squash casserole, succotash, and corn pudding alongside her brisket and smoked turkey every Christmas. We weren't a kosher household—often noshing on steamed oysters before the Christmas brisket—l'chaim!

When I left South Carolina for college at Auburn University, I began my own cooking journey—usually microwaving frozen chicken nuggets and Easy Mac in my dorm room or eating Panda Express on our meal plan. I quickly realized how lucky I was growing up with a delicious home-cooked meal every night for dinner. When I went home, my mom always packed a casserole to take back to the dorm and share with friends. As my kitchen situation improved, I attempted to cook real meals. For years, I thought tuna noodle casserole was my specialty, but every time I cooked it, I managed to leave out an ingredient. Over time, my meals became more palatable—I finally mastered the tuna noodle casserole—

and now I love to bake. When I started graduate school, I used baking as a stress reliever. My go-to cookie recipe was an oatmeal butterscotch that I made for my friends. They kept telling me, "You could sell these!" Staring at my empty graduate student bank account, I thought, maybe I *should* really sell these. I learned about Alabama's Cottage Food Law, took a course and test, and was ready to create my business. When branding my little baked goods business, it only made sense to honor the best baker I knew, my Mimi. Thus, *Mamanu Baked Goods* was born. Beyond my oatmeal butterscotch cookies, I learned to make mandelbread, rugelach, and Mimi's famous brownies. I sold them at a local coffee shop and introduced many Alabamians to the joys of Jewish baked goods.

One summer in graduate school, I had the opportunity to study abroad in Italy with the Auburn Department of Nutrition, where I learned about the Mediterranean diet and the Slow Food movement. As you can imagine, the trip was an incredible month of cooking classes, farm tours, wineries, and olive oil manufacturers. Before the trip, I had already drastically reduced my meat intake—because of a nutrition course I had taken and because I just never really liked meat. My study-abroad trip was the final push I needed to go fully pescatarian. (Giving up meat was easy for me, but giving up fish and seafood was another—I'm a Southerner!)

Since moving to Atlanta and starting a full-time job, *Mamanu Baked Goods* has been retired. Occasionally on a nice, chilly Sunday afternoon, I still love to bake, but my love of cooking and my skills have drastically increased. It was ingrained in me by my mom and grandmothers that cooking for your family and friends is a way to show your love. I may not make brisket or meatballs, but I do love to host my friends—both Jewish and non-Jewish—for holidays and Friday night dinners with the help of OneTable, a nonprofit dedicated to encouraging Shabbat dinners. I'm creative in my get-togethers, often setting an extravagant table. I've hosted a Passover seder with veggie matzo ball soup and an egg hunt, as well as an Italian Shabbat dinner with eggplant parmesan and wine tasting.

I've adapted some of my family's traditional Jewish recipes to make them pescatarian or vegetarian friendly and a little more contemporary. Some have turned out delicious— some not so much. If you're looking to create your own spin on an old classic, my recipe for tuna noodle casserole won't steer you wrong. You can trust me—after all, *mamanu*— from my lips to God's ears!

Left to right: Miriam Gordin, Emily Levinson, Faye Levinson, Auburn, AL, 2014.

COURTESY RACHEL BARNETT.

MIMI'S COCONUT SOUR CREAM LAYER CAKE

Faye Levinson's coconut cake was THE cake for family birthdays and special celebrations and was cherished by all.

1 (18½-ounce) butter-flavored
   cake mix
Eggs, oil, and water as listed on
   the cake mix package
2 cups sugar
1 (16-ounce) sour cream
1 (12-ounce) package frozen
   coconut, thawed
1½ cups frozen whipped
   topping, thawed

Prepare the cake mix according to the package directions. Make two 8-inch layers. Bake according to the package directions. When the cake is completely cooled, split both layers into two, creating four layers.

Combine the sugar, sour cream, and coconut. Blend well and chill. Reserve 1 cup of the sour cream mixture for frosting. Place the layers on top of one another, with the filling between each layer.

To prepare the frosting: Combine the reserved 1 cup of sour cream mixture with the whipped topping, blending until smooth. Spread on the top and sides of the cake. Seal in an airtight container and refrigerate it at least three days before serving.

Tip: If you can't get the mixture to firm up enough, you can add 1 dry package of coconut cream instant pudding to the mix.

TUNA NOODLE CASSEROLE

My mom made this 1970s iconic dish when we were kids and passed it down to me. I have revised her recipe for twenty-first-century tastes.

1 tablespoon extra-virgin olive oil

4 tablespoons butter

1 onion, chopped

1½ cups roughly chopped Baby Bella mushrooms

Salt to taste

Pepper to taste

Thyme (dry or fresh) to taste

1 (12-ounce) package egg noodles

English peas (frozen or fresh)

5 tablespoons flour

1¼ cups milk

1 cup grated cheese

1 (5-ounce) can good tuna (albacore in water preferred)

Breadcrumbs

Heat 1 tablespoon oil and 1 tablespoon butter in a pan on medium heat. Add the chopped onion and cook until translucent. Add the mushrooms to the onion and cook down. Sprinkle salt, pepper, and thyme into the mixture.

Meanwhile, boil the egg noodles in salted water. Cook according to the package instructions. Drain when ready and set aside.

Microwave the English peas; add to the mushroom mixture.

Make a roux by melting 3 tablespoons of butter in a small pot; once melted, add 5 tablespoons of flour and whisk together until smooth and bubbly. Whisk in 1¼ cup milk and ½ cup cheese.

Drain the tuna and flake into the cheese mixture. Add salt and pepper to taste.

Transfer the vegetable mixture, noodles, and cheese sauce with tuna into a bowl and mix together. Once mixed, transfer to a 9 × 13-inch baking dish. Top with the remaining cheese and breadcrumbs.

Bake at 350°F until browned on top and bubbly around edges. Once baked, you can broil to get a crunchy top. Keep an eye on this as it will brown quickly.

MAKES 12 TO 14 SERVINGS

IS ONE BRISKET ENOUGH?

GABBI BAKER

———

*Sunday night dinners or holiday meals—it's always a celebration
for this family who enjoys gathering together.*

———

"DO YOU THINK WE HAVE ENOUGH FOOD?" The question is asked with a hint of sarcasm, as we look at the kitchen counter overflowing with brisket, roast potatoes, salmon, Hoppin' John, various kugels, marinated cucumber salad, fruit, and more—all for only ten of us to eat for dinner.

The occasion? There often isn't one. In our family, gathering to eat good food isn't reserved for major holidays or life events. Growing up, we'd have weekly Sunday night dinners with my mom's (Marcie Stern Baker) side of the family. We'd go to my Aunt B's (Beryle Stern Jaffe) or host everyone at our house, and, as I got older, my cousin Erin Jaffe Gardner also hosted. On the day of the gathering, there was discussion and

debate as to where we'd eat and who would bring what, but often those conversations culminated in Aunt B spending the day cooking while we all showed up to enjoy the bounty.

My mom and my cousin Erin are "clean as you go" cooks; their kitchens are in pristine condition when everyone arrives. Aunt B, on the other hand, is notorious for showing up with a new dish she wants us to try that invariably requires a large frying pan and lots of oil. Spending these meals together every Sunday became part of our family ritual, and I always looked forward to this special time.

When it came to the Jewish holidays, we'd go all out. My mom and aunt spent a few years on the bar and bat mitzvah planning

Gabbi Baker and her mother, Marcie Stern Baker, Columbia, SC, 2021.
COURTESY MARCIE STERN BAKER.

circuit—printing invitations, decorating ballrooms, and making flower arrangements—so organizing a get-together for a few dozen family members was something they could do in their sleep, or at least they made it look easy!

For the first day of Rosh Hashanah, Aunt B hosted forty to fifty family members and friends. She joked that she could never stop having the luncheon, because people would show up anyway. My mom made the brisket and roast potatoes, and Erin made her apples sautéed in butter and brown sugar. While waiting for the main meal to be served, we caught up with everyone, shared well wishes for a sweet new year, and noshed on Aunt B's mouth-watering chopped liver.

Our turn was at Passover, when we'd have a dozen or so family members at our home. My mom would call Aunt B several days before the seder to reclaim the round tables and little black folding chairs that we'd used the holiday before. Furniture was rearranged, and the round tables were set with crisply ironed table linens, beautiful china plates, and sterling flatware wrapped in vintage monogrammed napkin rings. Our seder was short and to the point, but we got the message and enjoyed laughs along the way. Although the gefilte fish came out of a jar and the lamb shank was often printed on a piece of paper, the matzo ball soup, matzo kugel, and charoset were homemade and beyond compare.

For Hanukkah, we'd celebrate multiple nights together, lighting candles, frying latkes, and eating Krispy Kreme donuts. I can picture my late Papa (Henry Stern) standing next to the stove, waiting to eat the first latkes as they came out of the frying pan piping

Passover at Baker home, Columbia, SC, n.d.
COURTESY GABBI BAKER.

hot. They only went on the platter once he approved them. (I don't think Papa ever met a latke he didn't like.) After the company left, we'd have multiple meals of leftovers with just our family. We changed into comfortable clothes, ate with plasticware, and didn't bother to reheat some of the dishes that *we* think are just as delicious cold. (I'm thinking in particular of Aunt Amy Berger's blintz souffle.) And sometimes adding even *more* food. Remember: "Do you think we have enough food?" We firmly believe that a baked macaroni and cheese is a welcome addition to almost any meal.

As impactful as these holiday memories from my childhood are, I've come to realize that a large part of the sheer joy that I have from them is not strictly religious—it comes from sharing these moments with the people I love. Rabbi Abraham Joshua Heschel expressed the belief that Judaism is a religion of time rather than space. And while he was referring to Shabbat, his bigger message is that that time is holy and sacred. As time goes on, and we've sadly lost loved ones, we are forced to introduce new rituals and traditions. We no longer can enjoy the beautiful challahs that my cousin, Samuel Kramer, made each Rosh Hashanah or his horseradish at Passover seder, but we remember him as we celebrate each holiday. These days, it's become more important than ever to take every chance we have to come together with family around food—whether we're celebrating a holiday or just a Sunday dinner.

MATZO KUGEL

This is one of my favorite Passover dishes from my Aunt B—who is an incredible cook but never follows a recipe. So, I decided to give her a call and record exactly how she describes making her kugel.

Crush up pieces of matzo, not quite as small as matzo meal. Put in some water to dampen it. Add orange juice to keep it moist. Add cinnamon and sugar to taste. I put in raisins. And pecans. And apples. And then, I put some melted butter in. There's just not a real recipe. Every time I do it is a little different. I put 6–7 tablespoons of oil on it. I use a box and a half of matzo.

I bake it—oh, I put a couple of eggs in and mix it around. I take a little oil in a Pyrex, and I put it in the oven, so that when I put the kugel in, the bottom gets crispy. Then I bake it for about 45 minutes in an oven at 300°F to 350°F. I honestly don't know. It's never the same way twice.

Oh, you have to add a little salt to taste.

AUNT AMY'S BLINTZ CASSEROLE

A favorite for holidays, brunches for brides, or family get-togethers.

Filling

2 (8-ounce) packages cream cheese, room temperature

3 (24-ounce) packages small-curd cottage cheese (not Sealtest)

2 eggs, beaten

2 large lemons, juiced

¾ cup sugar

Pinch of salt

Batter

4 sticks butter, very soft

1 cup sugar

4 eggs, beaten

2 cups flour

6 teaspoons baking powder

Pinch of salt

½ cup milk

2 teaspoons vanilla extract

To make the filling: Mix the softened cream cheese with the cottage cheese. Add the beaten eggs, sugar, lemon juice, and a pinch of salt.

To make the batter: Put the softened butter, sugar, beaten eggs, flour, baking powder, salt, milk, and vanilla extract into a mixing bowl. Blend together using an electric mixer.

Assembly: Spread the bottom of a large 9 × 13-inch (or larger) glass baking dish with some of the batter (enough to coat the bottom of the dish). Leave enough batter for the top of the casserole. Pour the filling on top of the batter, leaving a little room to spread the remaining batter to cover the filling.

Bake in an oven, preheated at 350°F, for 1 hour, 15 minutes until the top is browned. Let the casserole cool for at least 30 minutes before serving with a large spoon.

MAKES 14 TO 16 SERVINGS

FOOD IS OUR FAMILY'S LOVE LANGUAGE

JORDANE HARVEY LOTTS

———

*A southern grandmother's passion for preserving Jewish tradition
through food is passed down to her granddaughter, Jordane.
The recipes shared are Jewish holiday family favorites.*

———

WHEN I REMINISCE about Jewish foods, I feel nostalgia for my grandmother—a beautiful, proud Jewish woman with a passion for delicious food. Because Jewish food and celebrations were so important to my grandmother, Helene Kligman—"Ema" to her grandchildren—I feel emotionally and spiritually connected to her through food. I think of her soft hands, her wrist and its bracelets, and the rings on her fingers, as she rolled up rugelach with layers of nuts, sugar, and spices. Food also reminds me of the love of my grandfather, Melton Kligman, affectionately known as "Poppy" to his thirteen grandchildren.

Jordane Harvey Lotts and grandmother, Helene Firetag Kligman, Columbia, SC, 1997. COURTESY LYSSA KLIGMAN HARVEY.

I think of my grandparent's home, cozy with holiday smells, the dinner table beautifully set with fine china, crystal glassware, lacy tablecloths, and silver place settings used exclusively for the High Holy Jewish holidays. There was the anticipation and comfort of being surrounded by people whom I love and who love me, all of us gathered together, dressed up—no jeans—sitting around the table, giggling with cousins, and hoping to get on with the prayers so that we could eat.

Each season and holiday, I look forward to particular foods with excitement. Autumn brings the Jewish New Year and the Rosh Hashanah meal. I think of my grandmother's tender brisket, dripping in its rich juices with whole sweet apricots. In case there was not enough, she also made apricot chicken and rice, along with sweet and sour stuffed meatballs. My mom and maternal aunts made kasha varnikes, tzimmes, and challah.

Apples were traditionally dipped in honey, and honey cake was served for dessert. At Yom Kippur, the Day of Atonement, we repent for our sins, trying not to think about food but longing for the break-the-fast meal, with its warm bagels, cream cheese, tomatoes, onions, and heaping piles of lox. In winter at Hanukkah, I think of kosher hot dogs and potato latkes to symbolize the oil that miraculously lasted for eight nights. In spring comes Passover and the celebration of the journey from slavery to freedom, with memorable symbolic foods, including boiled eggs, parsley dipped in saltwater, matzo ball soup, gefilte fish, and matzo with bitter herbs and charoset. This holiday also has excellent desserts. The long seder is worth the wait for the pairing of red wine and semi-sweet chocolate, toffee crumbles, chopped toasted pecans melted over buttery matzo, and a velvety flourless chocolate torte.

My grandparents' religion and culture were passed down through their love and devotion. They are my legacy and those of my siblings. My brother, Kyle, recalls the role Ema and Poppy played in shaping us: The Rosh Hashanah luncheon of Ema's brisket and my mom's chopped liver meant a day out of school, the start of the all-important college football season—even better when the High Holiday fell on a Saturday and the Gamecocks were playing—and a whole day with cousins, aunts, uncles, and good family friends. We sat at our grandparents' big table, eating foods from another era and listening to Poppy recite Hebrew prayers. This will always be a lasting impression for me—and maybe also for the University of South Carolina students or young soldiers from Fort Jackson who often were guests at our holiday table. These events undoubtedly shape the fond recollections of my sister, Eden, whose love of family and tradition draws more from a spiritual and relational place than from a plate laden with traditional Jewish foods. Her contribution is the favorite Passover dessert, matzo toffee.

On Saturday mornings after services, and especially after bar and bat mitzvahs, the congregation and guests are invited to a kiddush luncheon. There is tuna salad, egg salad, herring in cream sauce, whole smoked whitefish or whitefish salad, bagels, cream cheese, and lox. There are similar spreads for wedding brunches and after a funeral. My mother, Lyssa Kligman Harvey's Star of David poppyseed cake shows up at all Jewish events, happy or sad. This cake has become a family and Columbia Jewish community favorite.

When I think back to my grandmother and how hugely important being Jewish was to her, I can't help but think about how inherently southern she was, too. She was born and raised in Charleston, and she experienced daily firsthand Lowcountry cuisine. My grandmother, with her southern drawl, loved barbecue ribs, shrimp boils, steamed oysters, and bacon cheeseburgers. It was like being Jewish was of utmost importance, but growing up around these irresistibly delicious foods was too much to withstand, so she gave in—in a big way. She definitely lived to indulge in some of the most delicious foods the South had to offer. I feel connected to her through Jewish and southern food cultures.

Ema was the perfect role model and created the feeling of warmth and love that comes from sharing a special meal together. Her love, warmth, comfort, and strength reinforced our Jewish culture, traditions, and food heritage. My mother continues to make her mother's traditional dishes and has gathered and shared those recipes. I love to cook and hope that these traditions will continue for generations to come through recipes new and old, passed down through our family's love language of food.

HOLIDAY OR YONTIF CHICKEN AND RICE

LYSSA KLIGMAN HARVEY

A sweet and savory family recipe to celebrate the sweet New Year.

2 chickens, cut up (do not use the backs; if the breasts are large, cut in half)

2 cups instant brown rice or wild rice

4 cups chicken broth

1 onion, chopped up

2 cloves garlic, pressed

1 jar of apricot preserves

½ cup dried apricots

½ cup dried pitted prunes

½ cup lemon slices

Fresh oregano

Olive oil

Kosher salt

Pepper

Salt and pepper the chicken. Brown the chicken in olive oil in a Dutch oven or large saucepan and set it aside.

Brown the onions and garlic in the chicken juice and olive oil that is left in the pan.

Oil the bottom of a large baking pan, Pyrex dish, or aluminum pan. Put the 2 cups of wild rice or brown rice in the pan. Place the chicken on top of the rice. Pour in the 4 cups of chicken broth. Put the onions, garlic, and oregano on top of the chicken. Spread the apricot preserves on top of the chicken. Sprinkle the apricots, prunes, and lemon slices on top of chicken. Bake the chicken, covered, for 1½ hours at 350°F.

Serve with the apricots and prunes and lemon slices on top of the chicken.

MAKES 12 SERVINGS

KASHA VARNISHKES

LYSSA KLIGMAN HARVEY

A modernized Ashkenazic dish. Serve with brisket, chicken, or sweet and sour meatballs and cabbage. The kasha varnishkes are a good base for juicy meat dishes.

1 box small bowtie noodles

1 large onion, chopped small

A dollop of chicken fat (schmaltz) or butter

1 box of kasha (buckwheat groats)

4 cups chicken broth

Salt and pepper to taste

Cook the noodles and drain. Fry the chopped onions in the chicken fat or butter until they are caramelized. Put the kasha on a cookie sheet covered with aluminum foil and sprayed with Pam nonstick cooking spray. Toast the kasha grain, being careful not to let it burn. Bring the 4 cups of chicken broth to boil and put in the kasha grain. Cook on medium heat until all the liquid is absorbed, about 25–30 minutes. Mix the cooked kasha, onions, and boiled noodles together in a large baking dish and bake at 350°F for about 30 minutes. It will be dry. If it is too dry, add more chicken broth.

MAKES 16 TO 18 SERVINGS

TZIMMES

MINDY KLIGMAN ODLE

My aunt's traditional root vegetable dish has a different twist with the addition of beef.

1 onion, chopped

A small piece (one pound) of chuck roast or brisket, cut into large pieces

1 bag of carrots, chopped into large pieces

3 sweet potatoes, peeled and chopped into large pieces

½ box pitted prunes

¼ cup brown sugar

1 can cut pineapple

Butter

In a Dutch oven or a stew pot, brown the cut onions. Add the cut meat and cover with water. Cook the meat slowly until it softens, and the water is absorbed. Parboil the carrots and sweet potatoes. Drain and add to the meat. Add the prunes, brown sugar, and pineapple. Put this mixture into a buttered Pyrex dish. The traditional way is to mash the vegetables; the more modern way is to leave it in large pieces tossed together and cooked. Bake in a 9 × 13-inch pan for 30–40 minutes at 350°F.

MAKES 12 TO 16 SERVINGS

PASSOVER MATZO TOFFEE

EDEN HARVEY HENDRICK

Easy and popular Passover treat.

1 box thin matzos or 4 regular
matzos
2 sticks butter
1 cup brown sugar
½ cup chopped nuts
1 cup chocolate chips

Grease a cookie sheet. Lay the matzos flat on the cookie sheet. Combine the butter and sugar. Bring to a boil for 5 minutes, stirring constantly. Pour the nuts into the mixture. Pour the mixture over the matzos. Bake at 350°F for 10 minutes. Do not let it burn. Take out of the oven and sprinkle with chocolate chips. Let it cool and break into big pieces.

LYSSA'S JEWISH STAR POPPY SEED CAKE

LYSSA KLIGMAN HARVEY

A Star of David Nordic Ware pan makes this delicious moist cake look very special for Jewish events.

1 box yellow butter cake mix
1 box instant vanilla pudding
1 cup yogurt
1¼ cups canola oil
4 eggs
1 teaspoon vanilla extract
A couple splashes of brown
liquor or brandy
2 ounces poppy seeds
Powdered sugar

Preheat the oven to 350°F. Spray a Bundt pan with Pam baking spray. Add all the ingredients, except the powdered sugar, together and mix. Pour the cake mixture into a pan, and bake for about 55 minutes. Check with a toothpick if done in the middle. Let the cake cool. Sprinkle the top and sides with powdered sugar before serving. Freezes well.

MAKES 12 SERVINGS

AFTERWORD

THE IMPETUS BEHIND chronicling this culinary legacy was born in 2017, as an outgrowth of the Columbia Jewish Heritage Initiative, an expression of Historic Columbia's larger Connecting Communities through History Initiative. Interest in incorporating the stories of Jewish citizens into the larger narrative of the capital city's (and county's) past bore abundant fruit—oral histories, historic markers, web-based and guided tours of Jewish sites in Columbia, and dynamic public programs. The *Kugels & Collards* blog, established by Rachel Gordin Barnett and Lyssa Kligman Harvey to document one core aspect of Columbia's Jewish community, ranks among the partnership's most popular and savory products.

Appreciating the memory-making power of food—how sights, smells, and tastes can help us tell stories—Rachel and Lyssa sought to share their community's heritage by making generational connections through recipes and recording stories about cooking. Not surprisingly, the *Kugels & Collards* blog became an extraordinary repository and one that generated interest far beyond the bounds of Columbia and its environs.

Excitement over the blog's recipes and irreplaceable stories, prompted a greater setting for a larger table—one that could host meals from Jewish household across the Palmetto State. Just like the individual dishes passed among family members, friends, employers, and employees, we hope that *Kugels & Collards*—in book form—is bound for kitchens where the daily, seasonal, and celebratory meals documented here will be recreated and enjoyed.

As is only possible when you have women as inspired and energetic as Rachel and Lyssa, *Kugels & Collards* gets to the core of what it means to be southern and Jewish. This book captures the nuances of both cultures and reveals the humanity and the heart found within the union of the two.

ROBIN WAITES

EXECUTIVE DIRECTOR, HISTORIC COLUMBIA

Rivkin Grocery, Columbia, SC, 1936.
COURTESY JEWISH HERITAGE COLLECTION, SPECIAL
COLLECTIONS, COLLEGE OF CHARLESTON LIBRARIES.

Mildred Bernstein (fourth from left) and Minnie Weinberger (third from left) with B'nai B'rith Women, Charleston, SC, 1940s.

ACKNOWLEDGMENTS

THE KUGELS & COLLARDS BLOG has been a wonderful journey the past six years. This book, an expansion of the Historic Columbia *Kugels & Collards* blog initiative, has been a project of love for us. People happily shared their food stories and family recipes when we all felt the need for human interaction during the 2020–22 worldwide pandemic.

Kugels & Collards belongs to two organizations that hold a special place for us: Historic Columbia and the Jewish Historical Society of South Carolina. Appreciation goes to the leaders of the two nonprofits who have supported our work. Without their encouragement and resources, *Kugels & Collards* would not be possible.

We would like to acknowledge the following for their inspiration and support.

Our deepest gratitude goes to our touchstones—Marcie Cohen Ferris and Dale Rosengarten. Marcie's deep knowledge of southern food, particularly southern Jewish food is renown. Dale has spent twenty-nine years documenting and collecting South Carolina's Jewish history and creating the Jewish Heritage Collection at the College of Charleston. They encouraged us to go forward with the project. They gave us the impetus from the very beginning to write a proposal. They encouraged excellence and genuineness in our writing. Their edits made this a better book. We feel incredibly fortunate to have these mentors guiding us along the way.

Many thanks to John Sherrer, who has been our stalwart editor, working diligently by our side for the past three years. He is a talented, sharp writer and wordsmith and made the editing process enjoyable with his constant playful puns. His knowledge of southern history has been expanded now to include South Carolina Jewish history. He has been an eager student of all things Jewish, from learning Yiddish words to eating kugel.

Without Robin Waites, executive director, Historic Columbia, *Kugels & Collards* wouldn't exist. Her support of our vision was instrumental in giving a place for southern Jewish food stories to be told. We are grateful for her leadership and for the talented team over the years she assembled for *Kugels & Collards*: Katharine Allen, Catherine Beltran, Renee Chow, Eric Friendly, Brian Harmon, John Sherrer, Emily Brown, and Chandler Yonkers. A very special thanks to Katharine Allen for being our conscience guide and editor.

Our beloved mothers, Miriam Brotman Gordin and Helene Firetag Kligman, who created Jewish homes that fostered our respect for our religion and food.

Our grandmothers, whom we remember with love and gratitude—Charlotte Salz Brotman, Sarah Levin Gordin, Ida Lomansky Kligman, and Mildred Reznick Firetag.

Our sweet husbands, Henry Barnett and Jonathan Harvey, for their patience and enthusiasm for the book and for being longtime fans of our cooking.

Annie Gailliard and Ethel Mae Glover, whose intellect, resilience, labor, and culinary expertise reflect the power of the African American foundations of the southern table.

Kim Cliett Long, for her friendship, gifts, and insight and knowledge of the African American experience.

Martin Perlmutter, o.b.m., retired executive director, Jewish Historical Society of South Carolina, and Lilly Filler, past president of the Jewish Historical Society of South Carolina, who steered financial resources to the project.

Aurora Bell, Pat Callahan, Cathy Esposito, and Kerri Tolan at University of South Carolina Press, for their expertise in supporting the vision of *Kugels & Collards*.

Forrest Clonts, for his photographic talents and expertise.

Terri Wolff Kaufman and Vernon Dunning, for their talents and assistance in restoring historical images.

To our media and public speaking guru, Sally McKay, many thanks for your friendship and sharing your expertise.

Tonya Dotson, Sara Moncada, Stephanie Copple, Alyssa Neely, and Margaret Dunlap for their support in providing images.

To our cooks and bakers who assisted with the photo shoot: Ellen Marcus Smith, Amy Rones Berger, and Cindy Alpert Saad—thank you for sharing your culinary talents!

A special thank-you to the contributors for their essays, recipes, and photos. *Kugels & Collards* is made possible because of your willingness to open your hearts and minds.

Generous support for the book has been provided by The Norman J. and Gerry Sue Arnold Foundation, the Jewish Historical Society of South Carolina, and Historic Columbia.

Ashkenazi (Hebrew, native of Germany; pl. Ashkenazim)—Jews from central and eastern Europe

Ashkenazic (Hebrew)—referring to Jews of Eastern European descent

Blintzes (Yiddish) —cheese-filled thin pancakes similar to crepes

B'nai B'rith—international Jewish service organization

Brit milah (Hebrew, "covenant of circumcision")—ceremony of circumcision

Bris (Yiddish, bris-mile)—circumcision of Jewish baby boy at eight days

Borscht (Yiddish)—beet soup

Borscht Belt—colloquial name for the Catskill Mountains

Bubbe (Yiddish)—grandmother

Bubbe meises (Yiddish, pl.)—untrue fable or old wives' tales

Challah (Hebrew)—egg bread

Chanukah (Hanukah, Hebrew)—Jewish holiday, Festival of Lights

Cholent—(Yiddish) traditional stew simmered overnight and served for Shabbat dinner

Erev (Hebrew, evening)—the evening before a Jewish holiday or Shabbat

Fapitzed (Yiddish)—all dolled up

Farfel (Yiddish)—small matzo for Passover

Farfalle (Italian)—small pasta shaped like bowties

Flanken (Yiddish, pl.)—beef short ribs that are boiled

Fleishig (German)—made of or prepared with meat

Gefilte fish (Yiddish, stuffed fish)—chopped whitefish formed into patties or loaf

Gedempte (Yiddish)—cooked until it falls apart

Geshmak (Yiddish)—delicious

Gullah Geechee—African American culture from Wilmington, North Carolina, down to Jacksonville, Florida

Haggadah (Hebrew)—text that sets forth the order of the Passover story

Hamotzi (Hebrew)—blessing over bread

Kasha varnishkes (Yiddish)—dish of pasta bowties with buckwheat groats

Kasher (Hebrew)—to make meat or utensils kosher for use according to Jewish law

Kashrut (Hebrew)—kosher laws

Kibbitz (Yiddish)—to talk

Kibbutz (Hebrew)—communal farm usually found in Israel

Kiddush (Hebrew, holiness)—blessing over wine

Kishka (Yiddish)—stuffed derma

Kneidlah (Yiddish)—matzo balls

Knish (Yiddish)—dumpling filled with mashed potatoes, kasha, or cheese that is baked or fried

Kol Nidre (Hebrew)—prayer at beginning of Yom Kippur (Day of Atonement)

229

Kreplach (Yiddish)—dumplings filled with ground meat, mashed potatoes, or another filling, usually boiled and served in chicken soup, although they may also be fried

Kugel (Yiddish)—noodle or potato pudding, sweet or savory

Kushkie (Yiddish)—duck

Latkes (Yiddish)—potato pancakes

L'dor v'dor (Hebrew)—from generation to generation

L'shana tova (Hebrew)—Happy New Year

Lukshen kugel (Yiddish)—sweet noodle pudding

Mandelbrot (Yiddish)—almond bread

Manischewitz—food company specializing in kosher products

Mashgiach (Hebrew)—supervisor authorized to ensure kosher standards

Matzo balls—similar to dumplings, made of matzo meal and served in chicken soup

Nosh (Yiddish)—to nibble

OBM—of blessed memory

Oneg shabbat (Hebrew, Joy of Sabbath)— reception following Shabbat services

Parve (Yiddish)—foods that may be eaten with meat or milk dishes

Pesach (Sephardic Hebrew) or Passover— holiday, recounting the story of Exodus

Pickled tongue—usually cow tongue, considered a delicatessen delicacy

Purim (Hebrew)—early spring holiday recounting the story of Esther and Haman

Rebbetzin (Yiddish)—rabbi's wife

Rosh Hashanah (Hebrew)—Jewish New Year, beginning of High Holidays, which end with Yom Kippur

Rugelach (Yiddish)—rolled pastry with various fillings

Sabbath, **Shabbos**, or **Shabbat**—Judaism's Day of Rest on the seventh day of the week (i.e., Saturday)

Schmaltz (Yiddish)—chicken fat

Schmata (Yiddish)—clothing; rags

Seder (Hebrew)—ritual meal that commences the festival of Passover

Sephardic—Jews of Spanish or Portuguese descent; any Jew from the Middle East or North Africa

Shavuot or **Shavuos** (Hebrew)—Jewish holiday, known as the Feast of Weeks, marking the wheat harvest in Israel and commemorating the revelation of the Torah to Moses

Shochet (Hebrew)—kosher butcher

Shtetl (Yiddish)—small towns with sizable Jewish populations, usually in Eastern Europe

Shul (Yiddish)—synagogue

Simcha (Hebrew)—gladness or joy; any festive occasion

Tikkun olam (Hebrew)—to repair the world

Tzedakah (Hebrew)—meaning righteous or charity

Tzedakah box (Hebrew)—box for donations to be placed, usually in a home

Tzimmes (Yiddish)—stewed vegetables dish that includes sweet potatoes, prunes, and carrots

V'aad HaKashrus (Hebrew)—governing board that decides what is Kosher

Yeshiva (Hebrew)—school for the study of the Torah

Yiddish kop (Yiddish)—good head for business

Yom Kippur (Hebrew)—Day of Atonement, solemn holiday

Yontif (Yiddish)—for holiday

Zayde (Yiddish)—grandfather

SOURCE: MERRIAM-WEBSTER.COM

CONTRIBUTORS

Larissa Gershkorich Aginskaya,
Columbia, South Carolina

Katharine Allen,
Columbia, South Carolina

Marilyn Schaeffer Arsham,
Mahopac, New York

Gabbi Baker,
New York City, New York

Henry Barnett,
Columbia, South Carolina

Beth Bernstein,
Columbia, South Carolina

Jake Bialos,
Hillsborough, North Carolina

Rita Miller Blank,
Tallahassee, Florida

Harold J. Brody,
Atlanta, Georgia

Olivia Brown,
Charlottesville, Virginia

Michele Schaeffer Cline,
Baltimore, Maryland

Lisa Collis Cohen,
Atlanta, Georgia

Debbie Bogatin Cohn,
Columbia, South Carolina

Sheila Brody Cooke,
Columbia, South Carolina

Sandy Bernstein D'Antonio,
Charleston, South Carolina

Jacquelyn Dickman,
Columbia, South Carolina

Janis Dickman,
Atlanta, Georgia

Jerry Emanuel,
Columbia, South Carolina

Lilly Stern Filler,
Columbia, South Carolina

Gloria From Goldberg,
Columbia, South Carolina

Judy Kurtz Goldman,
Charlotte, North Carolina

Ali Rosen Gourvitch,
New York City, New York

Esther Goldberg Greenberg,
Columbia, South Carolina

Aaron Hyman,
Charleston, South Carolina

Eli Hyman,
Charleston, South Carolina

Nancy Polinsky Johnson,
Pittsburgh, Pennsylvania

Sharon Kahn,
Charleston, South Carolina

Carol Aronson Kelly,
Charleston, South Carolina

Barry Krell,
Charleston, South Carolina

Elaine Krell,
Charleston, South Carolina

Shelley Spivak Kriegshaber,

Columbia, South Carolina

Barry Lash,

Charleston, South Carolina

Ira Lash,

Charleston, South Carolina

Teri Bernstein Lash,

Charleston, South Carolina

Brenda Yelman Lederman,

Charleston, South Carolina

Emily Levinson,

Atlanta, Georgia

Stefanie Levinson,

Hillsborough, North Carolina

Kim Cliett Long,

Charleston, South Carolina

Jordane Harvey Lotts,

Charleston, South Carolina

Susan Reiner Lourie,

Columbia, South Carolina

Heidi Kligman Lovit,

Columbia, South Carolina

Casey Manning,

Columbia, South Carolina

Ernie Marcus,

Washington, DC

Rhetta Aronson Mendelsohn,

Charleston, South Carolina

Carol Michael,

Brookline, Massachusetts

Bruce Miller,

Columbia, South Carolina

Faye Goldberg Miller,

Charleston, South Carolina

Minda Lieberman Miller,

Columbia, South Carolina

Laura Moses,

Charleston, South Carolina

Natalie Moses,

Sedgwick, Maine

Robert Moses,

Sumter, South Carolina

Edward Poliakoff,

Columbia, South Carolina

Sandra Altman Poliakoff,

Columbia, South Carolina

Ronald Port,

Columbia, South Carolina

Anita Moïse Rosefield Rosenberg,

Charleston, South Carolina

Mickey Kronsberg Rosenblum,

Charleston, South Carolina

Cindy Alpert Saad,

Columbia, South Carolina

Lori Lash Samuels,

Charleston, South Carolina

Jack Schaeffer,

Charleston, South Carolina

John Schumacher,

Charleston, South Carolina

Donald Sloan,

Myrtle Beach, South Carolina

Ellen Marcus Smith,

Columbia, South Carolina

Laurie Goldman Smithwick,

Charlotte, North Carolina

Risa Strauss,

Columbia, South Carolina

Michael Tonquor,

Washington, DC

Joe Wachter,

Myrtle Beach, South Carolina

Robin Waites,

Columbia, South Carolina

Laurie Baker Walden,

Columbia, South Carolina

Arnold Wengrow,

Asheville, North Carolina

Artichoke pickles, 59

Baked stuffed squab, 87
Bing cherry mold, 137
Biscuits, 59, 203
Blintz casserole, 216
Blintzes, 91
Blueberry cake, 166
Boreka, 150
Brandied peaches, 67
Brisket, 110, 133

Brownies, 133
Butterflies, 121

Cabbage rolls, 116
Cake
    blueberry, 166
    coconut, 210
    cream cheese pound, 175
    hot milk, 73
    chocolate mallo, 171
    chocolate mousse, 191
    Passover sponge, 30
    pecan nut, 60
    poppyseed, 222
    rum, 16
Challah, 128, 153, 194
Cheesecake, 187

Chicken
    barbeque, 17
    dressing, 74
    fried, 61, 202
    gumbo, 183
    liver, 70, 145
    savory chicken and rice casserole, 19
    soup, 27
    white chicken stew, 15
    Yontif, 220
Chocolate roll, 188
Chopped herring salad, 118
Chopped liver, 145
Collards, 10, 164
Cookies
    butterflies, 121
    Mrs. From's, 181
Cornbread dressing with optional
    oysters, 138

Dressing, 74, 138
Duck (kushkie), 22

Farfel souffle, 179
Fig preserves, 65
Fried green tomatoes, 97

Gefilte fish, 32
Grits and lox casserole, 207
Grouper (fish), 15

Herring, chopped salad, 118

Hoppin' John, 141

Hummus, 149

Kasha varnishkes, 221

Kishka (stuffed derma), 23

Kneidlach (matzo balls), 27, 51

Kreplach, 26

Kugel

    lokshen, 11

    matzo, 215

    noodle, 52

    potato, 161

Kushkie (duck), 22

Lemon meringue pie, 136

Mandelbrot, 161

Matzo balls, 27, 51

Matzo toffee, 222

Meatloaf, 106

Okra gumbo, 56

Peaches, brandied, 67

Peach cobbler, 87

Pickles, deli style, 101

Pickling spices for corned beef
    and tongue, 37

Potato latkes, 36

Rugulah, schnecken, 42

Salmon and grits, 98

Salmon mousse, 177

Savoure cheese spread, 103

Scones, 60

Soup

    chicken, 27

    flanken barley, 113

    mushroom barley, 34

Squash casserole, 76

Stuffed derma (Kishka), 23

Stuffed cabbage rolls, 116

Tomatoes, fried green, 97

Tomato jam, 168

Tuna noodle casserole, 212

Tzimmes, 221

Watermelon preserves, 67

Wine jelly, 62

ABOUT THE AUTHORS

Rachel Gordin Barnett and **Lyssa Kligman Harvey** are passionate about all things southern, Jewish, and historical. Native South Carolinians, Rachel hails from small-town Summerton and Lyssa from Columbia. Both now live in Columbia, South Carolina.

Rachel and Lyssa have been instrumental in preserving Jewish history across the state. Founding members of the Historic Columbia Jewish Heritage Initiative, they created the *Kugels & Collards* blog to preserve and share Columbia's Jewish history by collecting food stories, recipes, and photographs in a digital venue. Rachel is executive director and a past president of the Jewish Historical Society of South Carolina (JHSSC). Lyssa is a past chair of JHSSC's Jewish Cultural Arts committee and chair of the Columbia Jewish Community Center's Cultural Arts.

Rachel and Lyssa's families are longtime South Carolinians. Their mothers were born and raised in Charleston and passed down recipes from their Jewish heritage to their daughters. Exploring southern and Jewish foodways enables Rachel and Lyssa to honor their own family histories and preserve those stories for future generations of South Carolinians.

John M. Sherrer III is director of preservation for Historic Columbia and author of *Remembering Columbia*. He lives in Columbia, South Carolina.